Jessie] [Maclaren, Author of Until the shadows flee away

Drifted and sifted

a domestic chronicle of the seventeenth century

Jessie] [Maclaren, Author of Until the shadows flee away

Drifted and sifted
a domestic chronicle of the seventeenth century

ISBN/EAN: 9783337414160

Printed in Europe, USA, Canada, Australia, Japan

Cover: Foto ©ninafisch / pixelio.de

More available books at **www.hansebooks.com**

A DOMESTIC CHRONICLE OF THE SEVENTEENTH CENTURY

BY THE AUTHOR OF

'UNTIL THE SHADOWS FLEE AWAY.'

WILLIAM P. NIMMO:
LONDON: 14 KING WILLIAM STREET, STRAND;
AND EDINBURGH.
1876.

PREFACE.

IT is the hap of some people not to carry chronology at their fingers' ends. For behoof of individuals so circumstanced, and who purpose reading the subjoined narration, it may be well to jot down those historical facts which form, as it were, the woof and warp thereof.

Be it therefore borne in mind, that, at the Reformation in 1560, Scotland adopted Presbytery as her national mode of worship, its formula being modelled after that recently introduced in Geneva by Calvin. In this scheme no supreme ecclesiastical *ex-officio* magnate was recognised, the administration of church-affairs being devolved on Presbyteries, Synods, and General Assemblies, each and all composed of lay elders and clergymen. In the very nature of things, such a form of church government behoved to be somewhat democratic, and tended to foster political sentiments rather too liberalized to suit the ideas of the then Crown and *noblesse*.

By-and-by the latter began to fancy that their personal interests would probably suffer quite as much at the hands of this severely simple Presbyterianism, as they had already done under the greedy domination of Rome. So they cast envious eyes upon Episcopacy (as established in England), considering it decidedly less republican in its leanings than the *imperium in imperio* church of their native country. Bickerings which, sooth to say, were nearly as much political as religious, resulted from this state of matters; but after a time these said squabbles were suspended by those political convulsions in England which followed the rebellion against Charles the First.

At this period, while Presbytery remained unopposed by Episcopacy, the famous 'Solemn League and Covenant' was signed at Edinburgh, by delegates from both sister-kingdoms. Among other items in this document, the subscribers vowed to 'extirpate popery and prelacy, and to preserve the Reformed religion, as established in Scotland.' In process of time, however, the restoration of the Stuarts to the throne came to pass, speedily followed, on the part of the Scotch Government, by the abrogation of that same League and Covenant, formerly so solemnly sworn to. The bickerings recommenced with ever-growing rancour, and at length His Majesty climaxed the feud by imposing Episcopacy as the national religion. The Presbyterian ecclesiastical courts were abolished, the clergy dispossessed, and bishops, curates, etc., set in their room.

Now the majority of the people (especially the peasantry of the southern and western districts) were ardently attached to the Presbyterian form of worship, and voted Episcopacy neither more nor less than rank heresy. *They* therefore resolved to oppose it with might and main, and not only refused to attend the ministry of the clergy appointed by the Crown, but in some cases used violence.

Government waxed fearful of the political and religious consequences of tolerating such proceedings, and straightway set about supporting Episcopacy by force of arms.

The Presbyterian party, in order to worship according to conscience, betook themselves to secluded places, there to enjoy the precarious comfort of some 'outed' minister's preaching. Ere long an Act was passed prohibiting these assemblies, and rendering the attenders thereat liable to severe punishment. Large bodies of English cavalry, backed up by hordes of half-savage Celts, were let loose on the unfortunate dissenters. To this ruthless soldiery unlimited power was given, and, as might be expected, hideous cruelties were the result. Shooting, hanging, and torture became the order of the day; pillage and ruin things of course.

Foremost among the brave spirits in the Covenanters' camp was James Renwick, the subject of the following chronicle. After the lapse of nearly 200 years, a monument has recently been erected to his memory in Ayrshire, once the scene of his fervent apostleship; and a few years since a white marble statue of the youthful divine was raised in the new cemetery of ancient Stirling.

THE DARIEN SCHEME.

In the reign of King William the Third a company was formed for trading between Scotland, Africa, and the Indies, and establishing a settlement on the Isthmus of Darien. The scheme created a perfect *furore* of enthusiasm throughout the country, it being universally supposed that the *locale* of the proposed colony would secure to Scotland the entire trade both of the Atlantic and South Seas, and bring to her enormous wealth. Accordingly all classes, from richest to poorest, embarked in the speculation, even till one-half of the whole national Scottish capital was invested. At first everything seemed to favour the enterprise, and many traders, English as well as Dutch, were ready to support it with their influence, and subscribe great sums. Some large ships, built at Hamburg, were fitted out for the expedition, laden with an immense traffic-cargo, besides artillery and military stores. In these vessels over 2000 persons sailed from Leith for Darien, intending forthwith to plant cities, etc., as empowered by a recent Act of Parliament, dated 1695. But the colony of New Caledonia was overwhelmed by disaster at its very start, for King William (partly at the instigation of some leading English merchants, who feared the success of the scheme might transfer the world's carrying-trade into the hands of the

Scotch; partly through the menaces of Spain, jealous for her own American dependencies, and perhaps partly out of overdone regard for the interests of his Dutch compatriots) suddenly resolved to crush the infant colony. He accordingly disowned the Act of Parliament and Letters Patent which he had granted to the Company, and caused his Resident at Hamburg to present to the senate of that city a memorial threatening the Dutch subjects with his resentment if they joined the Scots in their undertaking. He sent orders to the governors of Jamaica and other English settlements abroad, commanding them to issue proclamations forbidding (under the severest penalties) 'any of his Majesty's subjects from holding communication with the Scottish colonists, or assisting them with ammunition or provisions.'

The issue is well known, famine and the attacks of Spanish settlers soon made of New Caledonia 'a memorie onlie.'

CHAPTER I.

'Praise the Lord from the earth.'—Ps. CXLVIII. 7.

TALLA LINN is a pretty little waterfall in one of the small glens of Tweedsmuir, in Peeblesshire, and Tweedsmuir may be defined as a nine-miles-square monotony of treeless hills, well stocked with sheep.

Even in this 'poke-your-nose-into-every-corner' nineteenth century, the district is scantily peopled, but was, a couple of hundred years ago, almost a solitude.

This normal condition of unfrequentedness was probably the chief reason why, one fine autumn morning in 1683, Talla Glen became the trysting-place of divers persons belonging to the then persecuted sect called 'Society People,' or Cameronians.

At daybreak, ay, and before it, men, matrons, and maidens came stepping, by twos and threes, across the dewy hills from various directions, but all bound for one spot.

Grave, earnest, yet cheerful of aspect, were most of those

travellers, and, albeit comfortably clothed, none of them wore the showy gauds whereby the fashion of the time indicated holiday attire for attendance at fair or 'weapon-show.'

The hours ran on, and still from north, south, east, and west wayfarers continued hieing to Talla.

Morning mists rolled up the hill-sides, up to the top, and away into space.

The sun shone out bravely, shimmering the grass with a sheen of liquid diamonds that seemed laughing a bright good-morrow to the blue sky, and still the assembly beside Talla Linn kept increasing.

But by-and-by the arrivals became fewer, and many of those persons already present slipped away to sequestered nooks, there, by prayer, to prepare for partaking of that solemn ordinance about to be celebrated, to wit, 'The Lord's Supper.'

Other individuals (and these, I must confess, were chiefly young maidens) surreptitiously smoothed their braided hair with the palm of the hand, or slyly tugged and shook plaid and cloak into the most becoming 'set' attainable in the circumstances.

High and higher mounted the sun in the 'lift o' blue,' till the rocks, standing sentry at the right side of the narrow valley, commenced flinging shadow-bridges across to the opposite verge.

Noting this, some half-dozen serious-looking men, grouped close beside the Linn, evidently grew anxious, and forthwith despatched the most agile of their number to a higher standpoint, whence, perchance, he might 'sight' the absentees.

Curiously enough, a series of 'minniken' contingencies co-occurring in two different places had detained the expected parties, but both were now close at hand.

Coming from the Moffatdale direction, four persons might be descried walking rapidly, and in couples.

The pair in front were Mistress Elspet Ker and her orphan nephew, Walter, a boy of twelve years old.

The lady seemed rather on the shady side of fifty, but albeit black-a-vised, and somewhat bony and big in build, had a gentler heart than beats under some handsome outsides.

The two young persons in rear were alike remarkable for good looks and an air of more restful happiness than is common in this moiling world.

But small wonder if so it was with James Renwick and Marjorie Ker that Sabbath morning, for twenty-four hours had not come and gone since they plighted their mutual troth. Plighted it, come weal come woe! Plighted it, though the times were very troublous, and the church they both loved was in deep waters, yea, in hourly increasing peril; when that goodly fair-haired youth (the maiden's 'beautiful and brave') was being hunted like a partridge upon the mountains, and martyrdom seemed his probable doom; when to harbour him, even for an hour, exposed those who did so to risk of heavy fines, if not loss of life itself.

Yet, ah me! with all this full in view, how restfully did Marjorie Ker and James Renwick rejoice in their mutual affection, as a heaven-bestowed pleasant gourd, albeit not a tabernacle—a God's gift, sent in due season, not to slacken the receiver's pace glory-wards, but that they might from the terrestrial mercy expiscate a new link to things celestial.

Their engagement had taken place without premeditation, just, as it were, on the 'spell of an impassioned moment.' But although, at three o'clock of Saturday afternoon, neither of these young persons had any expectation of being troth-plighted ere night, their love was no such fitful 'flash' as sometimes passes current now-a-days. On no supposable emergency of mere 'excited emotion' would Marjorie have accepted the 'to and from my love' which hung around her neck. Still less would she, with her own hands, have threaded the corresponding half of the said 'parted siller token' on a cord of true blue silk, and adorned Renwick therewith. No! no! the pure, warm love had, for many a day, been burning clear and steadily, although it was only by chance that the curtain which hid its rays had been blown aside. Three years previously, James Renwick was studying in Edinburgh, and used then to eke out his scanty means by private tuition. Among his few pupils was Walter Ker, Marjorie's only brother, the self-same youth now squiring 'Aunt Elspet' across the hill. At that time the boy's mother was alive, and reputed a lady of rather uppish notions on some points, albeit godly in the main. The family, although not wealthy, was distantly related to some of the best blood in Scotland; and on this plea it was that Mistress Ker held her head a trifle higher than some 'unca guid folk' thought consistent with her great religious profession. (Mayhap they were right; but it is no easy matter to put one's feet in another person's shoes, and, at any rate, we know who has commanded that 'honour be given unto whom honour is due.') According to Mistress Ker's way of thinking, her son's dominie (albeit quite a gentleman in manner) was no fit associate for Marjorie, so at first he used just to fulfil his paid service and then depart.

But it chanced one day that the young lady was sent by her mother with a message to Aunt Elspet, who at that time abode in Covenant Close. Just as she (Marjorie that is) reached the close-mouth, a vagrant swine, belonging to Lady Lawson, ran out of the cruive under her ladyship's entrance-door, and rushed furiously at the terrified girl. At that moment her brother Wattie's young tutor chanced to come past, and rescued her, not only from her original assailant, but from some half-dozen of his congeners that had gathered around, with their snouts in the air. But besides saving Marjorie from being trodden in the mud, James Renwick took her affections into permanent possession. It proved a veritable case of 'love at sight.' Somewhat boy and girlish at the start, it is true, but deepening with the speeding years, and growing solemn and holy in proportion as the life-views of both intensified. Since their first meeting many changes had come into the lot of each, and now, at length, here were the pair, once more re-united, walking hand in hand to Tala, where the youthful divine was that day to do ministerial work.

Whilst they proceed on their way a horseman is advancing from the Lanarkshire end of 'the muir,' and Marjorie, albeit he sees her not, occupies a large share of his thoughts. He is Antony Baigrie of Halket, and among his co-religionists goes by the cognomen of the 'young elder,' because of having, before his thirty-third year, attained to the honour of being an office-bearer in the church. For above four hundred years the Baigries had possessed Halket, and albeit in these latter times the estate was wofully curtailed, Antony owned the remaining acres thereof, and resided in the ancient fortalice of his ancestors. Ever since the Reformation the family had been out-and-out Protestant,—not, perhaps, as a race, gifted with startling powers of ratiocination, but many of them, nevertheless, good men and true; endued, moreover, with an aptitude for kicking against certain pricks of Church and State, which tendency had subjected them to penalties and fines that had sorely clipped their erst well-feathered wings.

Two hundred years ago, custom did not favour very close domestic intercourse between parent and child. But Antony's mother having died shortly after his birth, the widowed laird was thus moved to take more than common interest in the boy she left him. Hence it was that divers peculiar dogmas were betimes impressed upon the lad; and, to tell the truth, these one-sided opinions were, so to speak, mental heirlooms, having been regularly and unquestioned handed down from sire to son of the house of Halket.

At the period whereof this chronicle treats, Groningen, in Holland, was the great *alma mater* of persecuted Presbytery, and thither was Antony duly sent to complete his education. However, before he had been there six months, his father died of apoplexy, and of course the young man behoved to return and enter on possession of the estate. There, accordingly, he had 'vegetated' ever since, walking in the steps of his forebears, in so far as that meant holding on by tooth and nail to the family idiosyncracies, civil and ecclesiastical.

Observe him this Sabbath morning as he approaches the rendezvous. A personable-enough individual at first sight; that is, supposing the *coup d'œil* of his six feet two inches to be taken in front. Viewed in profile, a sort of imbecility in the knees of his long legs gives him, even when standing 'at attention,' the appearance of partly sitting down. As he canters along the demi-defined bridle-path that twines out and in among the hills, his thoughts (to judge by his countenance) are so vivacious as to require a frequent 'pull-in.' The application of this mental curb is indicated by the tighter pursing-up of a mouth that at all times seems in the act of pronouncing the word 'prunes.' The anti-Sabbatical escapades which, according to Antony's theory, require such retributive mental castigation, are ruminations concerning that very Marjorie Ker who comes tripping across the sward scarcely half a mile distant as the crow flies. With that sweet, pure damsel the young elder was what *he* considered over head and ears in love! But, unfortunately, his conception of the tender passion savoured so much of earth, that it was small wonder if the very affection for pretty Marjorie which uplifted James Renwick's heart Godward in gratitude, should, in Antony Baigrie's estimate, rank as a snare, yea (when experienced on the Sabbath), as a sin! To the young elder (more was the pity) the glory of the terrestrial and the glory of the celestial appeared not only different, but actually antagonistic.

CHAPTER II.

'Shall leap up in God's sunning.'

IN the eighth place, O friends! I would pose you with this question—Whether there be not in some of you disputings anent God's way of conveying you to heaven, and much straitening and repining at your cross dispensations? Believe me, the day is coming when ye will justify the Lord, and write this upon the gates of the New Jerusalem, "He hath done all things well!"'

I wonder if ever the Sabbath sun shone on a fairer scene than Talla Glen presented when James Renwick spoke these words. 'Our young Josiah,' as the elder folks delighted to call him, was standing there bareheaded, beautiful in youthful grace and holy zeal, engaged in what was termed 'fencing the tables'—albeit, in point of fact, no actual communion table was spread before him.

The intending celebrants of Jesus' dying love were seated orderly upon the grass, in two long rows facing each other, and from his place at the end nearest the waterfall, the handsome, fair, boyish-looking minister addressed them, with outstretched hand and thrilling accents. Grouped around him stood twelve elders, some listening with rapt attention, others unable to leave off gazing at that young, spiritual hero, so fearless and so calm amid the perils that environed him. Even to those unpoetically rigid men, there was something pathetic in the idea of such a mere lad having from force of principle launched out bravely on the mighty waves that threatened to engulf their Zion. Not a sound divided, with the preacher's voice, the noontide stillness, save the trickling and dropping of the water in the linn, which just then happened to be rather low.

Whilst Renwick was discoursing, tears that did not fall rose now and again in the eyes of a young girl, seated among the intending communicants. Sweetly and inspiringly fell the preacher's accents on Marjorie's ear, albeit the 'soul-dews' in her eyes blurred his face into indistinctness.

'Welcome trial,' said he, 'yea, welcome death itself, if so be our precious Redeemer knoweth that for us these are the fittest path to glory.'

Poor Marjorie! She had not (so uncertain were the times) reckoned very confidently upon the bliss of actually being married to her betrothed. But now (just for one brief second) the fact that his ministry to God's persecuted people was a terribly imminent danger to himself, became as it were bristled all over with terrors. Every pain and penalty inflictable by tyranny did her quickened imagination pile upon him, till she almost fancied she saw his head on the block. If, instead of casting her eyes downwards, the girl had chanced at that moment to look up, it is probable the expression of Antony Baigrie's face would have startled, as well as astonished her. Standing at his post, among the twelve office-bearers, there was he, glaring alternately at the minister and herself. (O Jealousy! most evil of alchemists, rapidly art thou transmuting into slate-stones the poor supply of golden coin which Antony Baigrie purposes this day to offer, by way of quit-rent, unto him who is Lord of all.) Coercing his memory into random quotations from sacred metre was of no use just then. Heretofore, in the various passionless experiences of his life, he had tried that talisman, confident that thereby he could, at will, cut off obtrusive terrestrials from impinging on things celestial. But alas! in the present onslaught of temptation, the very pithiest texts he could call to mind rushed forceless through his brain.

The sacred elements are being dispensed. In solemn silence the elders move slowly along the seated lines of celebrants, carrying, as behoves their office, the bread and wine. It is Antony's part to hand unto Marjorie the sacred memorial-cup. He glances from the girl to where Renwick stands, with clasped hands and adoring upturned face. The 'young elder's' hand trembles as he presents the pewter vessel. He lets it fall, spilling the wine over Marjorie. Intense was the horror of those who remarked the accident, because very deep was their superstition,—so deep, indeed, that even the most enlightened among them forgot the possibility of those unfortunates buried under the tower of Siloam being neither murderers nor thieves.

It had been arranged by the 'managers' of the 'Society-folk' that when James Renwick came to officiate at this conventicle in Talla, he should on the Saturday abide with Mistress Ker at Greendykes, and on Sabbath night be accommodated under the 'young elder's' roof. This agreement was duly carried into effect, and after the day's solemn duties were concluded the two men rode to Halket, arriving there, right tired, about ten o'clock. The domestic staff of the 'young elder' was limited, for albeit he adhered to the fine-paying tenets of his ancestors, he was none the less of a gear-gathering disposition, and stingy in regard to many things. His establishment, therefore, numbered only three persons, to wit, an aged housekeeper named Madge, her girl-fag (*scogie*, in the vernacular), and an old man called Jamie Murray, who acted as groom, gardener, and, in short, general 'doer.'

The ancient fortalice of Halket, although considerably in need of repair, was an imposing structure. Originally, it had merely been a three-storied 'peel-tower,' with immensely thick whinstone walls, and a cork-screw stair twisting up its centre. But succeeding Baigries had from time to time added thereto a variety of architectural 'whimsies,' till the general effect resembled a gigantic hen surrounded by a brood of cowering chickens. In latter days, however, fines had been heavy and repairs few, so, on the whole, the 'young elder's' abode, when seen by daylight, looked slightly 'out at the elbows.'

But on this Sabbath evening, as Renwick and his temporary host draw near, 'time's bites' do not show obtrusively in the demi-darkness, and the glow of a rousing fire, which Madge has kindled in the cavernous chimney of the hall, projects itself through various window-slits in ambient forklets, making the place look so comfortable that the outlawed minister, poor lad, delicate of constitution, and worn out with fatigue, inwardly thanks God for the gourd under whose shade he hopes to abide for a few hours.

'Eh! Maister!' exclaimed old Jamie Murray, as, after peeping through the shot-hole, he opened the heavy iron-hasped door, 'there's ane comed for ee; I kenna wha he bees, but ony gate, he's no ane o' the sons o' Baliol, for he's busy readin' the Word o' Life in the muckle chammer.'

Renwick and Antony started. Judases were rife, and might, for aught anybody could tell, assume the guise of Bible-perusing Covenanters.

Leaving the outlawed minister in the dark entrance, Baigrie at once proceeded to the hall. A huge mass of glowing peats was heaped on its ample hearth, near which, asleep, sat a slight fair-haired man.

Who could this stranger be? He was slumbering calmly,

too placidly, Antony thought, to be either a 'time-serving Erastian,' or a bloodthirsty betrayer of 'the elect.'

Baigrie stepped nearer, and gently lifted an ill-coloured, home-made tallow-candle from the iron sconce whence it dispensed its feeble rays. The grease guttered athwart his fingers as he held it, slanting, close to the sleeper's face.

'Antony Baigrie! you recollect me, don't you?' cried the fair-haired man, opening his eyes, and jumping to his feet. 'I'm certain I should have recognised *you* anywhere. Why, you are not altered in the least. Ah! I see you are still at fault. Is it that you have quite forgotten Angus Gordon, who was in the same logic-class with you under old Professor Puffendorf of Groningen? Well! I must be more changed in appearance than I imagined—that's all.'

At length, however, Antony *does* contrive to recognise his umquhile fellow-student, and the two men shake hands across an interval of fifteen years.

James Renwick was then bidden enter, and on learning who he was, Mr. Gordon expressed deep regret that, owing to his horse having met with a mishap, he had not got forward time enough to share in the day's commemorative feast. A remarkably pleasant, frank person this Mr. Gordon appeared, and within a few minutes after their introduction had placed both his companions *au fait* of his personal history, past, present, and prospective.

'I was a merchant in Leyden,' said he, 'realized a good

deal of money, retired from business, and have now, with my wife and little girl, come to settle in old Scotland for the rest of my days, I hope. My wife is Dutch. Poor thing! she suffered so much from sea-sickness during our rough passage, that I was obliged to leave her and the infant in Glasgow, in order that they might recruit a bit, whilst I execute a secret mission to one of our " United Society " friends near Dumfries. I should have liked to be present with you in to-day's services, but, as I said, "Bergen-op-Zoom'' chose to stick his hoof into a hole. No doubt, however, it was so ordered by Providence. But for this slight accident, friend Tony, I should not have now been within your gates, but gone straight on my journey. At any rate I 'm right glad it has been the cause of our meeting once more. And by the way, sir,' added he, turning to Renwick, 'can you guess under whose roof I have left my wife ?'

'Our young Josiah' shook his head, and smiled.

'They 're with your worthy mother, sir. If I had only supposed I should have the chance to meet *you*, I might have brought some message or token. I can tell you, however, that she is very well; so is her niece Katherine, who, of course, is your cousin. For your sake and the young lady's, I'm sure I wish I were a carrier-pigeon. Yes, a remarkably clever, pretty girl is Mistress Katherine, to my way of thinking at least.'

Renwick laid aside his plaid and leathern cap, while Antony did the same by his cloak and sword, and then supper was brought in by Madge and her aide, 'wee' Ailie. A sharp little damsel was Ailie, albeit dwarfish of stature, and squinting right and left with a pair of eyes as black as sloes. She and the housekeeper speedily placed creature-comforts on one end of an unpolished oaken table, that was nearly thrice as large as a modern billiard-board. Tablecloth there was none, such articles being unknown save in very high places of the land; but the mutton-ham reposed on a shiny pewter dish, and the thick pease-bannocks lay in a huge wooden receptacle shaped somewhat like a trough. A big 'whanger' and three cherry-wood platters stood at the landlord's right hand, flanked by a tall flagon of unimpeachable claret wine. Such was the meal, neither knives nor forks being provided, as it was customary for gentlefolks to carry, each man, his own carving implements in a small case, while the commonalty made fingers serve *their* turn.

When everything was ready, Ailie stirred the peats on the hearth into seven-fold heat, and then was retiring with Madge, when Renwick (who during some five or six minutes had been sitting upon a settle beside the fire, shaded from observation by one of the large projecting jambs) fell forward helplessly. ('The bit spirit o' him's as strong as steel, tho' the bodily frame is but weakly,' used his worthy mother often to say of her son in those days of his childhood that now seemed to him so very far away in the past.) In point of fact, it was so still with the outlawed preacher. During the bygone week he had slept four nights in the open air;—perhaps it would be more correct to say, that when utterly exhausted with wandering (for the Government orders were, 'Seize him, alive or dead!') he had lain down to rest where and when he could.

'Oh, the bonnie godly bit laddie!' exclaimed Madge, helping to raise him from the floor. 'The pitifu'-like, curly-headed bairnie, puir thing! Ay, it's only a faint; I was mortal feared it was death.'

When Renwick was restored to consciousness, they set him on one of the huge elbow-chairs, whereof the apartment contained four-and-twenty, and then Madge made him swallow some mulled claret which she had heated in a porringer among the peat-ashes. The motherly-hearted old body forthwith hurried away to prepare the 'Prophet's chammer' for her patient's reception. And a very quaint, 'illogically-architectured' closet it was, which for many a year had in Halket gone by this name of 'Prophet's chamber.' Not an elegant apartment by any means, but concealed in an out-of-the-way corner, unlikely to attract notice, as sundry proscribed 'Testifyers' could avouch, having therein lain hidden from 'rampaging Philistines' who sought their life.

'Surely I was doited when I fancied Marjorie Ker could care a bodle for such an insignificant youth as this Renwick!' cogitated Antony, as he was bidding his guest good-night at the door of the 'Prophet's chamber.'

It is half-past three in the morning. Cold, clammy fog

wraps the hills, and a change in the atmosphere betokens coming rain. Did angels, then gazing from the upper world upon the wilds of Tweedsmuir, turn toward the ineffable glory within the emerald arch, and unto Him in its midst (who once sojourned on earth) did they exclaim, 'How long, O Lord? Doth it not repent thee concerning thy suffering servants down yonder?'

Hark! there are sounds in the muir, though the dense mist hinders them from floating far. Not continuous sounds; an occasional coarse guffaw, or the tramp of horses' hoofs when, quitting the soft earthy turf for a few paces, they come across some bit of rocky road. It is a party of fourteen dragoons in search, *they* would say, of that 'rebellious, heretical firebrand, James Renwick,' and their commission is to slay him should he attempt resistance. Lieutenant Ker, their commanding officer, likes not the expedition; for, in spite of her 'covenanting tendencies,' his cousin Marjorie remains, in his esteem, a perfect chrysolite among women, and scarcely three-quarters of an hour have elapsed since she favoured him with rather a pithy commentary on the word *duty*.

All is dark and quiet around Halket. The lieutenant, who is in for a heavy cold, has shivery, creeping sensations through his back and limbs, and, being a young man of elastic theology, would just then prefer a warm bed to hunting traitorous preachers. In his inmost soul, not a stiver did he care whether mitres or Geneva bands gained the day. What *he* desiderated was to rest his aching head and watery eyes upon a pillow.

The road along which the troopers were riding did not run close past Halket, but, at eighty or ninety yards from the house door, turned sharply to the west. At this bend a high green knoll intervened betwixt the path and the fortalice, passing which rising ground Lieutenant Ker urged his horse to a gallop, and stared steadily right before him. I should mention, by-the-bye, that as a native he thoroughly knew the geography of Tweedsmuir, whilst his men, being English, were totally ignorant of the locality. Nearing Halket, the lieutenant, for reasons of his own, kept a particularly keen look-out; whereas the soldiers were jesting and singing catches of roughly-worded ditties, by way of passing the time. The clinging damp fog well-nigh blots out the house. The small cavalry party is nearly past, and all but round the knoll indeed. Ah me! wherefore did not Antony Baigrie remain quietly asleep, instead of quitting his bed at that untimeous hour to light his 'cruizie,' with intent, by aid of its illumination, to march to and fro his apartment, and think about Marjorie Ker? Oh! if that thick-walled little dormitory of his had only been situated on the reverse side of the building. If in it there had but been fewer window-slits with the gleam of the cruizie shining out through them like slender stripes of congealed sunset! One of the soldiers chanced to turn half round in his saddle, in order to make some foolish remark to his rear-man, and thus espied a glimmer of light. It came from a flint which at the moment Antony was striking, to set the cruizie-wick ablaze withal.

'Hallo! what's that?' cried the trooper. 'By jingo, captain, we had nearly lost a chance of drink-money. I'm blessed if we don't need all we can get in this confounded climate.'

Woe's me, for the unhappy subaltern thus brevetted by his sergeant! Marjorie or no Marjorie, he behoved to do his 'duty' when actually thrust in his face. So with a violent sneeze he issued the order to halt. In less than three minutes the horses were picketed, and their riders kicking the massive old castle door, as if they purposed dragging it off its hinges.

Presently Jamie Murray, arrayed in the undyed woollen garments which he wore day and night, peered through the shot-hole, and tried to take stock of the assailants.

'Twa, four, aught; gude guide us!'

Evidently it was useless to attempt resistance. He therefore threw open the door, and assuming an air of crass stupidity, asked what was wanted.

'You've got a stranger in the house, my man, have you not?' queried the lieutenant.

'What's ye're wull?' responded Jamie, who had more than once been in a similar predicament, and knew his cue perfectly. 'What's ye're wull, sir?'

'Come, come, we've got no time for delay. I know, for a fact, that the traitor James Renwick arrived here to-night. So no lies, if you want to keep a whole skin. Where is the bloody rebel? Lead us to him without more ado. Idiot as you seem, you've surely sense enough to understand that I must be obeyed, and instantly too. Come—look sharp!'

'I'm sure it's an unco thing that a body canna get sleepit in peace. There's naebody wantin' tae hide frae ye wha's in the hoose, or to tell ye lees either. A gentleman *did* come here this nicht, riding on a brown naig, and I suppered the beast wi' my ain hands afore I gaed to my bed. I daresay the gentleman's sound sleepin' up the stair at this very minute. A fair-headed young gentleman ye mean, sir?'

Just as Jamie finished speaking, his master, wrapped in a not too tidy *robe-de-chambre*, appeared at his back, while Angus Gordon brought up the rear.

All this time Renwick remained sound asleep in the 'safety-chamber.' Verily his danger was imminent, but over yonder at Greendykes, Marjorie was even then on her knees praying the Almighty on his behalf. Moved by a strange dream, the girl had risen from her couch thus to pass the night-watches.

Angus Gordon, being naturally quick-witted, saw at a glance the possibility (for a brief space at least) of passing himself off as the young preacher, who thereby might gain a chance of giving his foes the slip.

Therefore, while answering *verbatim* the lieutenant's queries concerning his own who, whence, and whither? he apparently suffered these replies to be, as it were, dragged so unwillingly from him that the dragoons took for granted he was telling lies. By-and-by, however, he changed his tactics, and gradually led Lieutenant Ker to imagine he had, after all, been making game of him by playing on his credulity, therefore with a very bad grace the irate officer gave the order to mount and go. Away accordingly rode the troop, uttering oaths sufficiently pungent, one might fancy, to heat even the chilly mist that was blowing down the cursers' throats.

'O the blessed, godly, yallow-haired laddie, puir chield!' sobbed Madge, falling on her venerable knees, beside her pallet, in a far-away corner of the vaulted stone-floored kitchen. 'The precious young Josiah! O God o' Jacob, thanks be to Thee for a' thy preservin' mercies throughout this nicht! O Lord, confoond Thou thae bluidy Ishmaleets! Break Thou their spears in sunder, O God, and let another take their bishopreek! And the innocent bit bairnie sleepin' as sound as a tap a' the time tae,' she added, with a burst of hysteric tears, by way of postscript.

The enemy had departed from Halket, but the night's mishaps were not ended.

Madge had set the porringer, wherein the claret-wine for Renwick was boiled, upon a small stone projection in the passage, intending at her leisure to carry it hence. But in

Antony's hurried, darkling descent, he, while groping his way, sword in hand, hit the little vessel off the perch, and broke it into sherds.

Thus it came to pass that after the fracas at the outer door was over, Angus Gordon, remounting bare-footed to his chamber, trod upon one of these sharp-edged fragments and cut his instep very severely.

Before cock-crow Renwick was once more away on his weary pilgrimage, but his late fellow-guest remained at Halket, bed-fast and suffering. The wound in his foot was jagged and inflamed, its ugly appearance being probably aggravated by some feverishness in his system, the result, no doubt, of his recent bad voyage, and subsequent travelling.

In those days country surgeons were, as a rule, so unskilful that literal 'auld wives' frequently proved safer practitioners than their male congeners.

Madge's celebrity as a 'leech' was current even beyond the scanty muir population, so it was with the proud certainty of being quite able to effect a cure that she prescribed for Angus Gordon's injured member. And right carefully, as well as tenderly, did the kind old 'bodie' perform her ministry. From a gallipot, whose cover was a linen rag, pierced full of holes, she fished up the solitary household leech, and applied it to the hard, purply environs of the hurt. She culled *this* herb and *that* weed for poultice, drink, and lotion, but when Tuesday morning arrived the patient was worse instead of better. Still nobody dreamt of danger; Madge 'the renowned' was surely able to manage a common wound.

Nature had bestowed upon Angus Gordon one of those hopeful, elastic temperaments that even pain can scarcely daunt, and now he made so light of his personal discomfort that Antony (who was anxious to put *himself* out of disquietude concerning Marjorie) thought it no breach of hospitality to go a-wooing without more loss of time. He therefore apologized to the invalid, by stating that he behoved to absent himself for five or six hours on urgent business, and then gaily mounting his horse, hied to Greendykes, the abode of his lady-love. The details of this visit fall to be given in a subsequent chapter, but for sake of continuity it will be best at present to go on describing matters as they occurred at Halket. On Thursday, Angus Gordon felt so much worse that he penned a note to his wife, having hitherto delayed doing so till he could say he was well. And then, the steed being stolen, an Esculapius from Peebles was entreated to come and shut the stable door. But alas! before his arrival mortification had seized the patient's foot, and not all the drugs in the pharmacy could stay it. Death was in the cup thus unexpectedly held to Angus Gordon's lips, but at the drinking thereof he neither shuddered nor murmured. Yet, albeit resigned to God's will, being a right leal and loving husband, you can easily understand that to 'go hence' without taking leave of his dear wife was a very sore trial indeed.

In our day, I suppose, there is no part of the kingdom

whence, on any emergency, one could not obtain some means of speedy conveyance. But it was very different when poor Angus Gordon lay a-dying, and yearning (oh! how fondly) for the wife and 'bairnie' he was never more to embrace. To a bird flying through the air, the distance betwixt Halket and Glasgow was perhaps no great stretch, but it seemed a formidable journey to be undertaken by a delicate foreign woman, seeing there was neither any made road, nor mode of transit save a horse's back. Aware of this, and being a God-fearing man, Angus Gordon humbly bowed to Providence, said, 'It is well,' and solemnly set about preparing to cross the 'Jordan,' assured of a safe landing in Canaan that is above. But first he will arrange for the comfortable maintenance of the dear ones he must leave behind, believing it the duty of a Christian to faithfully exercise the earthly stewardship committed to his trust. Considering, therefore, that Antony Baigrie, albeit of late years a stranger to him, was an 'elder of the kirk,' and a brother in the faith, he felt it advisable to constitute him trustee of his wealth for behoof of the wife and child with whom he had hoped to enjoy it. This transaction being settled, he expressed a kindly farewell to Madge, 'Wee' Ailie, and Jamie Murray, then turned his face to the wall, and rendered back his soul unto the great Giver thereof. The King of Terrors, though he came thus suddenly, took not this young man at disadvantage. For, at the eleventh hour of life's day, his Redeemer was not to seek, having since his servant's early youth been unto him a friend and guide.

CHAPTER III.

'Evil is wrought by want of thought
As well as want of heart.'

WHO of us can fathom the passions lying dormant in his own breast, and only awaiting the touch of some suitable temptation to spring into vitality?

Till his thirty-fourth year, Antony Baigrie had, by a mechanical impetus, so to speak, journeyed along the same path which divers of his ancestors had trodden, because of their conscientious conviction that it was the only *right* way. Some minds are of an exploratory cast, as it were; others remain in the rut where the Fates place them, and perchance even make a merit of not straying far a-field. Ah me! just as if always wearing a bandage over one's eyes were the same thing as turning them away from viewing vanity! For such a man as Antony Baigrie, it would have required more pluck deliberately to quit the beaten family track than to follow it. Hence, with no little self-approbation, he had from time to time given house-room to reverend outlaws, and paid a few swinging fines in consequence. But his experiences had not lain among the more demonstrative passions; not at least till at a field-preaching he became enamoured of pretty Marjorie Ker. This occurred some six or eight months before the Conventicle in Talla Glen, but opportunities of meeting between country folks, who in our day would rank as neighbours, were so rare, that in the interval he had only seen her thrice. Each time, however, with an increasing determination to wed her, albeit convinced there was no hurry about bringing the affair to an immediate issue. Mistress Elspet Ker lived in so secluded a manner that he considered the risk of a rival claimant for her niece's hand was small indeed. 'I daresay,' thought he, 'she'll be very thankful to get a seriously-disposed husband, and one, too, who comes of as good a stock as herself, although I'm not *quite* so well-off as my forebears were. That's neither here nor there, however, for I gathered from her aunt's conversation that Marjorie will have a tolerable "tocher" of her own. She is a remarkably comely maiden, and no doubt will jump at my offer when I make it. In these sifting times, it is a great matter for a young unprotected female to obtain a help-mate who is of "Israel," and not a "worldling." Now I think of it, I'm almost certain Mistress Elspet intended me to take a hint that day she began lamenting over the lonely state in which her own demise would leave her niece.' Underneath all this mental bravado, however, there crouched a vague fear that he was special-pleading his own case; albeit he persistently ignored the fact that it requires two persons to clench a bargain. So in the meantime he took no overt step, but opiated himself with his 'home-made' love-philtre, dreaming that by-and-by Marjorie should be his bride. At present was she not at Greendykes, blushing unseen by marriageable man, and busy, as beseemed a well-brought-up young lady, with her spinning, and her white-stitch, and her pickling, and what not?

In this comfortable frame of mind, the 'young elder' went to the Conventicle at Talla, and, as we saw, waxed jealous of James Renwick. Not having observed the young minister and Marjorie even exchange words, it would have puzzled Antony to give a tangible reason for his annoyance. Ah! but that glance of the maiden's, which he had seen as it flashed toward Renwick! He dimly felt that *it* betokened a higher, holier kind of love than he could quite comprehend. However, it begot a suspicion that the prize he imagined so securely his own was slipping from his grasp, which enhanced its value tenfold, and of course his eagerness to clutch it. Ah! that glance! Such a *fiasco* it made of the Sabbath-keeping frame of spirit he had gotten up to the requisite pitch with so much labour! Why, had not the very *idea* been an impropriety, I fear he would then and there have cursed Renwick in vocables as well as in heart. Being a man of little real feeling for others, Baigrie was a determined believer in himself. When, therefore, on the Monday morning after the soldier's visitation, Renwick departed on his hazardous journey,

Antony's hopes once more mounted above his fears, and he voted himself a fool for ever doubting that the course of his wooing would run smoothly. Nevertheless, the well-concocted programme of his loverizing operations was slightly altered in consequence of his recent fright. He therefore resolved that instead of delaying till spring the announcement of his matrimonial intentions, the affair should be cut and dry before next Sabbath, in order that no terrestrial burden should clog the transcendentalism of his prayers to Him who has declared that He numbers the very hairs of our heads. So, although his inmate, Angus Gordon, was in great pain, he made himself as sedately smart as possible, and hied to the feet of his purposed bride.

'Gude guide us!' cried Madge, 'whaur can the laird be goin' the day, wi' 's cocket-hat on, and his best blue coat too? He is nane o' ye're licht-minded gentry that cares for women-folk, else I would expect that he's awa' to the courting.'

'I'll tell you what, Madge,' answered old Jamie Murray, 'men's kittle cattle to understand. He's putten on a clean shirt. Did ye no' notice? He's setting out to seek a wife, as sure as my name is James Murray. Ye'll see.'

'Weel-a-weel, Jamie, man; I'm the laird's servant, that keepit him in my arms afore he were a span long, and noo he's an elder o' God's kirk; but be his leddy wha she may, tak' my word for't, she'll no need to travel far to find her sorrows, if so be she's a feeling-hearted kind o' person. No' that he would use ony body what ye might call ill, but it's no' in him to feel the bit kindly, warm love for ony living cratur.'

'Be he bound for where he may, Madge, woman, and be his errand what it will, I'm no' thinking it concerns the asking o' a helpmate. That business is no' sae extraordinary pressin' as to cause him to quit the castle, when the stranger gentleman is lying so ill wi' his sore foot up the stair.'

'Eh, wow! Jamie, man, but "he's" a rale fine man, sae humble and sae cheery, in spite o' the pain he's in, puir lad. The evil nat'ral heart o' me canna help cleaving till him. Yet I ken that he's no serious nor solid-minded, like our ain laird. I wonder if, puir lad, he's after all but a son o' Belial? It's sore to be lamentit that he's no exactly one of "oursels" for his soul's sake. Ay, ay, it's a pity, dear young man.'

'Gae 'wa, woman, wi' yer daft-like clavers! Solid and serious, quo' she. Losh! Div ye think that laughin' folk canna get to heaven? Did ye no' see godly Maister James Renwick, woman, or hear the prayers he offered up afore he gaed awa' at dawn o' day, tae wander and better wander, puir fellow, wi' nae provision either for a meal o' meat or a pillow to lay his head on gin night comes on? In spite o' a' his hardships, yon's a cheery, happy lad, or I never was sairer cheatit in my life.'

Whilst the two old domestics were thus chatting (Madge being at the same time employed in 'knocking' barley for the household dinner), their master was making the best of his way to the residence of Mistress Elspet and her niece. It took twice as long to ride to Greendykes as it would have done to go thither a-foot across the hills. But Antony was at no time a first-rate pedestrian; and, moreover, when one goes to seek a wife, one naturally takes advantage of all reasonable modes of adding prestige to one's personal appearance on the scene of action.

Like Halket, Greendykes possessed an ancient peel-tower, and had been nearly four hundred years in the Ker family. Its present proprietor was young Walter, Marjorie Ker's only brother. At the time of his mother's demise the boy was in delicate health, and the first act of Aunt Elspet's guardianship was to remove both him and his sister away from the evil odours of 'Auld Reekie' to the fresh native air of their patrimonial lands. 'Let the little chap run wild and drink plenty of milk,' said the physician, 'otherwise he'll not live six months.'

But do not, I pray you, imagine, because of this one bit of auntly arrangement, that decision of character was Mistress Elspet's peculiarity. The very reverse was the case. Nature, which actually seems to relish an occasional freak, had, in one of her whims, fitted up the interior of the spinster's ungainly, big, human frame, with a set of feelings as sentimentally sugar-and-waterish as it was possible for feelings to be. The inner history of her girlhood, if duly chronicled, would read thus:

—First, a craving for love that never, never came. Second, a series of unrevealed, unreciprocated attachments. Third, an unwilling but inborn conviction that she was personally —'a mistake.' Being constitutionally good-tempered, she did not, on arriving at this conclusion, turn Turk against the world, but subsided into a state of chronic deprecation. Her sentimentality being engrained, did not, so to speak, get washed out, even by the bitter experience of its uselessness. No, but to change the metaphor, it ran to seed. We are all, more or less, creatures of circumstance, and it sometimes happens that the self-same qualities which, exercised by a wife or mother, are termed 'sweetly-amiable,' rank, when belonging to some lonely old maid, as mawkishly eccentric. In default of the coveted affection she had missed, she gradually became (though not exactly in St. Paul's acceptation), all things to all men. Always feeling as if she were on sufferance, she acquired such a habit of seconding everybody's opinions upon every subject, that her neighbours in Covenant Close used to crack many a sly joke at her expense.

Nevertheless, in spite of these little frailties, the kind old body was well liked, and the very persons who laughed loudest at her 'universal amen' were, in case of any emergency, the first to receive her 'good offices,' as a matter of course. 'Poor Madame Eppé, droll she is, but not evil at all,' was the oft-expressed opinion of Madame Rougemont, an aged Papist lady, whose abode in Covenant Close was directly opposite the spinster's, and (thanks to the narrowness of the street) in such proximity thereto that the two women would sit day after day in their respective windows chatting by the hour, not forgetting an occasional little sparring-match by way of variety.

The late widow Ker, with her blue-blood theories and angular affections, had always rather scared her timid sister-in-law; but Marjorie, from the time she was three years old, took as it were the whip-hand of Aunt Eppie, exercising her power with a loving force that almost drew the hungry-hearted old maid out of her imagined inferiority to women who were 'cared for.' So when widow Ker died, and Aunt Elspet, as nearest relative of the two orphans, became their legal guardian, the yoke she laid on them was easy indeed. I am far from certain that she would have stuck so persistently to the 'Outed' Kirk party had not Marjorie kept her steady in her allegiance.

'There's a hantle gude, my dear bairn, in some folk o' the Episcopal persuasion,' would Mistress Elspet occasionally suggest. 'I'm told that whiles divers among them have followed the Saviour, whilk, after all, is the main thing; and there was my former neighbour in Covenant Close; weel, I *could* fancy her a God-fearing woman, albeit unfortunately a Papist.'

'Hush, auntie dear, ne'er mind them; what you and I have got to do is to stick firm to our persecuted Kirk.'

'Weel-a-weel, my bairn, of course that's but right.'

The mansion of Greendykes was modern, having been built by the late laird at a considerable distance from the ancient tower, which then was converted into a byre.

The new house was roomy, square, and unadorned, having three rows of very small windows (eight to the row), and an entrance-door, fabricated on the most severe model of simplicity. To tell the whole truth, Laird Ker's ambition had been a 'grand residence,' but what he began with an eye thereto he was not able to finish conformably, because of the strictures concerning his vain-gloriousness which beset him; ay, even in the solemn congregation. Therefore, honest man, being somewhat like his sister Elspet in the matter of allowing himself to be over-ridden, he compounded for the foolishness of erecting wide walls by making them as plain and ugly as possible. During the three years' incumbency of Mistress Elspet and her young charges, a step had been made towards the 'pretty,' if not even the 'beautiful' itself. Need I say that this was Marjorie's doing? Go where she might, that girl had it in her, ever to be, as it were, finding out the gold that was in the dross. This seemed her natural bent. Her soul joined affinity with the 'exquisite' in its numberless manifestations. To judge by her taste in colours, one might have supposed her of eastern origin rather than a native of the ungorgeous north. The glowing purples and crimsons she affected in dress! The gay roses and scarlet rowans wherewith she covered the bare house-walls seemed to give breathing-room to the human side of her soul, whilst it vainly tried to image the palpable splendours of the 'golden city,' whose gates are pearls. Does this sound profane? *She* did not feel it so. Even in this matter-of-fact world there ' are ' individuals who

> ' Lie in Abraham's bosom all the year,
> And worship at the temple's inner shrine,
> God being with them, when *we* knew it not.'

Therefore, clambering all over the dark whinstone housefront were flowers of the most brilliant hues procurable then and in Tweedsmuir: a very uncommon style of ornamentation at that period, being in point of fact a worked-out idea of the girl's own. But the 'hymns' these 'dumb creations' used to sing to Marjorie, who shall tell?

'What are you looking sae dull about, my dear?' said Aunt Elspet one day on finding the girl, then about fourteen, gazing thoughtfully at a wild rose-bush. 'What are ye looking sae dull about, my dear?'

'I was just wishing, auntie, that the flowers could speak to me.'

But to return from this descriptive digression, let me say that it was nigh noon when Antony Baigrie came ambling up the avenue that led to his beloved's abode, with its many windows and parti-tinted florages.

'Wha, in the name of wonder, Marjorie, can this be, riding up here?' exclaimed Mistress Elspet, catching sight of Antony and his steed from the parlour-window, where she, and her niece were busy discussing a letter which had come by express that morning.

'I declare, it's—it's the queer-like laird of Halket,' answered the girl, turning as white as a sheet. 'What, what can he be wanting here? Can any evil have befallen James?'

Poor Marjorie! where the treasure is, the heart follows. Her first thought was about Renwick, of whose safety she had, as yet, no certainty. Was it possible her cousin and his men had after all seized him on Sabbath night, or had he escaped?

'Oh, auntie dear! cried she in dreadful anxiety, what *can* Laird Baigrie be come here for, do you think?'

'Dearie me, my lamb! dinna look sae like a ghost. Never fear but what your joe is safe and weel. Just sit down a minute till you compose yoursel', an' I'll step away to the laird and ask what's wrang. Maybe, after all, there's naething amiss.'

To the 'young elder's' disappointment, the vision that met his eyes when the withdrawing-room door opened, was not that of a queenly damsel, but a tall, dark, bony, old woman clad in sage green 'Say,'[1] with a somewhat slovenly linen toy on her head, and a sprinkling of snuff on her upper lip.

'Ye're welcome to Greendykes, laird,' said she. 'Is there onything wrang wi' our precious young Josiah? He's no taken, is he? If it be so, Marjorie will lose her senses. It's an unco thing that love, sir. Her that looks like a queen, and might wed wi' ony duke, cleaves might and main unto that

---

[1] A sort of worsted fabric, softer and smoother than serge.

bit fair-haired laddie. For her sake, laird, I trust James Renwick's safe. I'm sure I hope so, for my dear bairn's sake as weel as for the Kirk's.'

Thus gabbled Mistress Elspet, being quite elated by even playing second fiddle in a real love affair. True, she was not the actual Rose, but growing in close proximity thereto felt as if impregnated with its exquisite aroma.

'Ye canna conceive, laird, how terrible fond she's o' Maister James. He is doubtless a true sanct o' God; but it's no' what ye may call onything o' a guid match for her, especially when I have gotten sic a fortune that'll be all hers some day. What's your opinion about it, laird?'

Antony stared in mute astonishment, half inclined to think the old lady had taken her 'bitters' rather strong that morning.

'A fortune, said ye?' he presently blurted out.

'Troth ay, laird, what else can ye call it? It's the visible hand o' Providence. To think o' my auld neighbour, Madame Rougemont the Papist, leaving me all her gear! I even yet can hardly believe it's true, tho' me an' Marjorie were readin' the lawyer's letter about it for the third time, when ye arrived here. It came no' three hours since. Me and the bairns are going to Edinburgh. The man-of-business says in his letter that we behove to do that. Poor madam, altho' a rank Papist, she was a nice body. It seems it's stated in her 'will' that I maun occupy her dwelling in Covenant Close, and likewise maintain the dead-chamber, whilk is painted black. I've aften been in it. Being a Papist she was particular about keeping it up. Her forebears came ower from France lang syne wi' auld Mary o' Guise. They were all Papists. But puir madam hersel' wasna an ill body; and it's a grand fortune she has left me. Ye ken, laird, it'll be Marjorie's some day. It's maybe a sin in me to say sic a thing, but I am kind o' sorry that she's troth-plighted to Master Renwick, godly though he be. Wi' sic a tocher as she'll noo have she *might* perhaps have gotten some lord or duke in Edinburgh. Siller is greatly thought o' there.'

O foolish Mistress Elspet! Compelled during so many dreary years to view earth's delights through the wrong end of the telescope, her present prospect well-nigh drove her crazy. At all events it rendered her unobservant of the effect her communications had on Antony, who paled and reddened alternately, and primmed his mouth into the smallest possible disc.

His feelings it would be difficult to describe: self-gratulation that he had not actually opened out his matrimonial projects,—annoyance at having missed his aim, and envious rage against 'godly Maister James.' These kept chasing one another through his head and heart in a way that, had anybody else been their subject, would have caused him to arraign that unfortunate as worse than a heathen.

To Mistress Elspet's astonishment, the 'young elder' rose to go at the end of her outpouring. 'Nonsense, laird,' she cried, 'ye're never thinking o' ganging already after coming sae far to visit *me*. I'm sure I take it uncommon friendly o' ye tae ride all this road.'

Like the fabled traveller, who in the storm drew his heavy cloak around him, but cast it aside when the first blink of sunshine glittered on his head, so now, under the stimulus of her wonderful good luck, did the spinster's long-worn garb of self-depreciation begin, as it were, to slip off. Nay more, like the very tyro she was in the science of 'being somebody,' she even went a little too far.

'I'm sure,' she repeated, 'it was really extraordinary kind o' ye, laird, to come all this gate just to see *me*. But stop, not a step shall ye budge till yer beast is rested, and ye yoursel' have gotten some refreshment. Excuse me for one minute till I tell Marjorie to step down and see ye. Dear lambie, she'll be main glad to learn that Master Renwick got away frae Halket in safety. He's a remarkable youth, I grant, but somehow, sin though it may be, I canna help grudging him my niece, now that Providence has gi'en me sic a windfall o' gude luck.'

So saying, away went the old lady, intent on hospitality, and presently Marjorie entered all smiles and affability.

Many months before, when first introduced to the 'young elder,' she had taken toward him one of those unreasoning dislikes for which there is no accounting. Being, however dissatisfied with herself, because of this uncharitable spirit, she tried very hard to overcome her feelings of repulsion, and had just, as she fancied, succeeded in so doing, when the accident at Talla Communion once more inspired her with actual horror of Antony. Good, clever girl though Marjorie was, she possessed her full share of the national superstition, and at that period Scotch people in general made almost a religion of belief in omens. Therefore, when by mistake the 'young elder' spilt the sacramental wine over her shoulders, she knew for certain that he would either cause her own death or that of some one very dear to her. This morning, however, the tidings of Renwick's escape lifted off her spirit such a load of anxiety that, womanlike, she rebounded into immense assiduity towards that very news-bearer whom hitherto she had so pointedly eschewed. Being normally on excellent terms with himself, Antony quite misinterpreted Mistress Elspet's jerky communications, as well as her niece's newborn civility.

'Doubtless,' thought he, 'now that they've gotten this siller, they are provoked at having allowed themselves to be taken in by that Renwick creature. As matters have turned out, it would hardly suit for me to propose marriage this morning, as I intended; but some day next week, before they remove to Edinburgh, I'll come back here and ask her to be my wife. By that time I'll surely hae gotten rid o' Angus Gordon, and be at liberty to choose my own hours. She's even bonnier than I fancied. I wonder what may be the exact amount o' this siller the auld woman has fallen heir to? Ay! ay! Marjorie is uncommonly handsome. Somewhat like my conception of Vashti or Judith; no, I mean Ruth. I never used to suppose tho', that she would make hersel' so humble and pleasant-mannered, as she is to-day.'

He was right in regard to the queenly style of Marjorie's beauty, to which, however, her natural dignity of deportment gave a tone which people, who did not know her, were apt to mistake for haughtiness. On this occasion of the laird's visit her dress happened to be one that became her remarkably well. It consisted of a white linen gown, made with tight sleeves reaching to the elbow, and the body wrapped across the bust, but left partially open in order to show her rich French silk napkin of a deep crimson hue. The conjunction of colour was pictorially perfect, the pure white linen, the rich crimson silk, the clear pale complexion, dark eyes, and rosy lips. In any assembly of people Marjorie's tall, lithe figure and swan-like neck would have attracted admiring notice. What wonder then that, backed by her present winsome kindness, they half turned Laird Baigrie's head? When, after a substantial luncheon, he at length rode away from Greendykes, he was nearer being seriously in love with the prospective heiress than ever before, although that is not perhaps saying much for the intensity of his affection.

In olden times, as well as in our day, it held to reason 'that out of nothing, nothing could come;' and, as old Madge remarked, 'It wasna *in* the laird to feel the bit warm love for ony living creature.'

CHAPTER IV.

' Dead friends' faces, so weirdly, thronging,
    Flit through my sleepless brain ;
Still in my ears goes singing, songing,
    Ever the same sad strain.

' Can it be, that at last I 'm lying
    On Death's cold twilight shore ?
Sometimes I fancy that I 've been dying
    These three long years and more.

' Darker, darker the room is growing,
    Dim eyes can barely see ;
What of that, to a spirit going
    Where Heaven's own light shall be !'

S was stated in the preceding chapter, Antony's visit to Greendykes took place on a Tuesday, and one of his reasons for going a-wooing thus early in the week was that he might have no carthly care wherewith to 'trouble' God when Sabbath should arrive.

Laird Baigrie's 'declared creed' was orthodox, but little did he guess that his purposed offering of worship was rather strongly impregnated with 'Pharisee odour.' However, his anticipations proved futile, for before the week ended, so did Angus Gordon's life; and on Sabbath, instead of having a helpmate bespoke, and a mind so transcendentalized as scarcely to require the Holy Spirit's aid to help its infirmities, Antony found himself charged with the burial of a dead man, and the care of his widow, child, and fortune. In this so sudden onset of hitherto undreamt-of possibilities, the 'young elder's' thoughts became unmanageable, ever and anon bolting aside, as it were, from the extremely narrow path wherein he professed to exercise them on the first day of the week.

These little escapades were doubtless to be deplored; yet, even while pulling a tightish rein on them, and inwardly praying Heaven to note his strenuous adherence to the letter of the law, he yet consciously rolled the impending contingencies as a luscious morsel under his tongue. Did this hidden comfit sully the simplicity of his, in one sense, perfectly orthodox petition? God knoweth. At any rate, he behoved, without delay, to arrange about the funeral, loudly lamenting the while that the present routine-rupturing dispensation had not befallen on a week-day. In that case he perhaps could have ridden or walked off certain *pros* and *cons* which now hindered his approach to the divine footstool; whereas, as things were, his brain almost reeled under a continuous mental catechism concerning worldly matters. What with the perfunctory fight against this, and what with the sensation of sin which sprang up in his breast every time he desisted therefrom, that Sabbath-day was literally a weariness unto Antony's soul; albeit, by way of speeding the lagging hours, he thrice assembled his little household for devotional exercises. Really, each minute seemed as long as ten, and the way in which conjectures concerning the as yet unconscious, young, wealthy widow's charms, and recollections of Marjorie's alabaster neck and crimson napkin, and marvellings as to the extent of Mistress Elspet's windfall—kept zig-zagging through his imagination. Why, it was perfectly dreadful!

However, it is a long lane that has no turning. The day of rest limped past somehow, and welcome Monday at length dawned a permit for Laird Baigrie's spirit to rove unshackled among terrestrials; to roam, as it were, 'free among the dead.' Does this appear an improbable state of mind for a man who had made considerable pecuniary sacrifices on behalf of the church whereof he was a member? Woe is me! who of us has not occasionally felt more buoyant among clay idols than in the recognised presence of heavenly purity?

On Monday morning Antony wrote to poor Angus Gordon's widow a formal, consolatory epistle, bestudded with labyrinthine texts concerning 'election,' stating also in the postscript that, after assisting at the obsequies of the deceased, he should wait upon her at Glasgow.

Madge, who besides being learned in simple leech-craft, considered herself an authority anent mortuary details, determined to hold a lyke-wake in honour of the dead man, and likewise in consideration of various small gratuities he had bestowed on her during his short illness. Very much scandalized would the 'young elder' have been had he known of the preparations for the death-watch which were being made by his housekeeper. And she, honest woman! when solemnly placing on the breast of the corpse a dish full of salt, and setting at its head and feet a couple of lighted candles, had not the slightest idea she was fingering some 'rags' of that very Popery her soul abhorred. However, on the night before poor Gordon's burial, the laird avoided the death-chamber, so Madge and her cronie, the shepherd's wife (who by express invitation shared her watch), had it all their own way.

In grim state, accordingly, sat the two old women throughout the night hours, snuffing the candles with finger and thumb, praying alternately and singing lugubrious canticles in solemn, albeit rather 'timber-tuned,' concert.

The grave was dug in a spot not likely to be disturbed, and there Laird Baigrie, his two shepherds, and Jamie Murray laid the remains of Angus Gordon.[1]

[1] More than one hundred and thirty-two years afterwards, when the Baigrie family was extinct, and the times so altered for the better that all men might, without let or hindrance, worship as they listed, an English gentleman purchased Halket. In digging a foundation for the cottage ornée he proposed to raise, the masons came upon the disjuncted skeleton of Angus Gordon, and thereupon a report went abroad that the remains of a martyr, killed by a dragoon in the terrible 'killing-time,' had been discovered.

When, next morning, Antony set out to Glasgow, his sensations were positively ecstatic, and he had no little difficulty in keeping his facial muscles fixed at the precise contortional angle which in presence of his domestics he considered necessary under existing circumstances. Not being constitutionally courageous, and aware that the roads just then were unsafe for solitary travellers, Laird Baigrie felt half-inclined to take Jamie Murray with him by way of body-guard. Why he hesitated about doing this, he could not very well explain to himself. Was he dimly conscious that out yonder, in the busy world, he might possibly (should strong temptation supervene) do things which it were best ignorant folks, like Jamie, should not witness? Directly he got beyond sight of Halket, he felt as frisky as a boy just escaped from school, and urged his steed to execute a series of gambolling progressive movements which must have a good deal amazed that steady-going animal. After a couple of days' ride, the 'young elder' arrived in Glasgow. He found poor Gordon's youthful widow in a timber-fronted, two-storied house in the Gorbals, the tenant whereof was one Betsy Renwick, relict of a weaver from Minniehive, and mother of that famous young preacher whom the leaders of the Cameronian sect had recently recalled from his college-studies in Holland to be their minister. A wholesome, sedate, motherly body was Mistress Renwick, with a broad, low forehead, calm hazel eyes, and a much more refined expression of countenance than was usual in the social class to which she belonged. And her lodger, what of her? Rarely, I trow, could there be seen a gentler, sweeter, paler, human lily-flower. Ever since her debarkation from Holland, she had remained bedfast, and now, albeit confined to her couch, and suffering great feebleness of body, she at once admitted Antony to the interview he desired. Mistress Gordon's frame, being naturally tender, had been severely taxed by her rough passage to Scotland, and the restoration of strength, hoped for by her husband when he left her in Glasgow, had not been vouchsafed. After his departure she had had several attacks of vomiting, which resulted in the rupture of a blood-vessel. For two days prior to Antony's arrival, she had been peacefully and trustfully awaiting the dismissal of her soul from the fragile casket that held it. Lying thus, the young creature (she was barely twenty years old) had only two regrets that slightly marred the entirety of her peace. One of these was sorrow at leaving her baby motherless; the other (ah! how much deeper a grief!) was yearning pity for Angus, when he should learn that their mutual love was as a tale that is told, in so far at least as related to this world. Fully was she certified that the moment her soul quitted its clay covering, it would be present with the Saviour, and right willing was she to answer, 'Here, Lord!' whenever His call should be heard. But she was a very fond wife, and therefore the *ourcome* of her whispered petitions was ever, 'Blessed Jesus, support and comfort my husband when he hears that his poor little Dorettle is no more.' The Lord, who, however, tries none of us above what we are able to bear, was pleased speedily to disperse the cloud which damped His young handmaiden's comfort by sending Antony Baigrie to advertise her of her widowhood.

'I thank Thee, O God!' This was her response to the sad tale her visitor now told. 'I thank Thee, O God!'

Antony was horrified, and as indignant at the young widow's apparent lack of feeling as if he himself possessed the most sensitive of hearts. Unaware how closely she was nearing the unseen world (for albeit very pale, Mistress Gordon was not emaciated), he debited her with 'disgraceful stony-heartedness.' Yet! yet! truly she was beautiful; and that her wealth would be ample he had good reason to know. To quote the rapidity of thought is trite; but it is worth while to note the many incoherent projects that within the next two minutes skitted across Laird Baigrie's imagination.

Ex gr., Why not marry her himself, and thus keep hold of the money he now held in trust for her; and—ah! her child —he had forgotten it; but anyhow years must come and go before it could lay claim to its portion of the fortune. Were the money his to spend, he should buy a great estate, and live *en grand seigneur*. Riches and all the glory of them. Ah me! such a bewitching bewilderment of delights kept undulating before his mind's eye, while, with solemn visage and pinched-in lips, he stood staring at the pretty widow. Riches and all the glory of them, if—oh, but surely the old-world suggestion which that 'if' implied could not apply to the 'young elder's' circumstances. Surely he who in daily life so skilfully thrust, as it were, his 'earthlies' and his 'heavenlies' into separate pouches, could manage to keep the latter clean, even while turning over the former with world-soiled fingers. He *might* occasionally carry clipped coins in his week-day purse, but the pocket wherein were held his Sabbath-money—his church collections—his 'many things' done willingly, why, he should take care *it* was kept intact. No, no! he would do nothing *positively* to forfeit his religious reputation. Woe's me! he forgot that for men of a certain temperament it is a risky thing even to *look* at the wine when it is red in the cup, and moves itself aright in sparkling ruby bubbles. Angus Gordon had left a large fortune; where could be the harm of stepping into the dead man's shoes? Riches, and all the glory of them! why not enjoy terrestrial things and things celestial apart from each other. Marjorie Ker, with her regal gait, her neck of snow, and crimson taffetas napkin. Mistress Elspet's 'windfall,' that might render her niece a wealthy heiress. Angus Gordon's fortune, lying in the shape of golden pieces within these heavy coffers. Ah! how should his hungry soul give up any or all of them? For an instant his own spirit passed (so to speak) before his face, and caused him to shudder. But 'riches, and all the glory of them!'

Presently the pale pretty widow spoke, and in girlish,

almost childish, fashion explained her reason for uttering that thanksgiving which had given such umbrage to the 'young elder.'

'Angus and I,' said she, 'could neither of us have borne the other's death, and now we shall soon be together again, never to part any more. When the doctor told me I must die, I was so doubtful of God's mercy as nearly to break my heart with thinking of the sorrow my husband would feel when he came to know that I was gone away for ever. And now, after all, our separation is not worth naming. Perhaps I may even see him again this very night. O God, I *do* heartily thank Thee!'

But the end was not so near; she lingered on through eleven days and nights. Weakening gradually and painlessly, yet looking all the while so sweetly cheerful, that, but for the doctor's verdict, her attendants could scarcely have believed her to be in danger. For you must understand, that although every tinge of pink had faded out of her cheeks, her lips remained coral-red, and illness had not lasted long enough to emaciate the girlish features. She spoke frankly to Antony concerning her child's future, and her own past. 'Oh, sir, I am *so* thankful you are here to take charge of my poor little Letty! You will find all Angus's money in those two coffers beside the window-seat. Katherine will explain everything. Before you arrived, fearing I might die suddenly, I told as much as I could about our affairs to her and good Mistress

Renwick. They promised to keep poor baby and the coffers safe till Angus should return here. But it is far better that you are come—far, far better. Oh, sir, do be kind to my bab—' Here her voice quivered into a sob just as the Katherine of whom she spake entered the small bed-chamber with baby-Letty asleep in her arms.

Short, slender, fair of skin, and 'peachy'-cheeked was this Katherine Renwick, seeming, moreover, in virtue of her small proportions, full eight years younger than her actual five-and-twenty. Yet, despite juvenile features and delicate tints, there was a hard expression in the steel-grey eyes that betokened indomitable strong-will. And in very truth, unknown to herself, 'I say it, therefore it shall be done' had, for many a year, been the motive-power of her life.

Her late father (a step-brother of worthy widow Renwick's deceased partner) had made a good deal of money in the sea-faring line. But for the last ten years he and his spouse had been gathered to their fathers, and their heiress resident with her aunt.

The girl was by nature of such a reticent disposition that Mistress Renwick, honest woman, not being much given to anatomizing character, had no conception of the wild passions that leaped and raged under her niece's babyish exterior. One of her intensest aspirations was to climb *out* of her own humble sphere *into* real fine ladyhood. With this in view she acquired the accomplishments of reading and writing, arts, be it remembered, by no means indispensable at that period even in much more elevated society than she was likely to mix in. She likewise contrived to learn dancing, unknown to Mistress Renwick, albeit that discreet matron ranked saltatory exercises in the same category as Cartes, Robin-Hood plays, and similar carnalities. As the years ran on, another of Katherine's self-contained urgencies kept growing into a passion that ignored alike God's decrees and providential obstacles. This passion was a furious affection for her cousin, James Renwick; to term it 'love' would be a misnomer. Although the youth's birth was no better than her own, his graceful person, accomplishments, and learning constituted him Katherine's *beau-idéal* of a gentleman.

Simple Mistress Renwick and her neighbours unwittingly added fuel to the flame by speaking, partly in joke partly in earnest, as if she were the destined bride of her handsome cousin.

And alas! all the while he looked upon her as a sister; nothing more. Being near himself in age, too, he had made her the confidante of various day-dreams, youth's day-dreams, in which he could scarcely expect his widowed mother's sympathy. In process of time James went to study in Edinburgh, and there acted also as pedagogue to one or two youths of noble family. Divers of these scholars were hardly younger than himself, and, attracted by his innate kindliness and genteel manners, made him quite a companion, and had him received as an equal at their respective homes.

During this portion of his life his visits to the wooden-fronted house in Glasgow were of necessity few, his funds being scanty and the journey expensive. However, when he *did* go home, he used, by way of amusing the two women there, to detail minutely the sights and company he had seen in that wonderful metropolis neither of them expected ever to visit personally.

Widow Renwick being, as I mentioned, rather a superior sort of person for her rank in life, was intelligently pleased with and proud of her boy's success, but Katherine's blood boiled with jealousy. Not clearly defined, specific jealousy of any fair one in particular, but of everybody and all things in Edinburgh, which to her fancy seemed a very Hesperides. She felt indignant at her cousin for the increased polish of his demeanour, because, as it were, it opened a gulf betwixt his conventional elegance and her own plainer breeding. She detested the very names of the beautiful, highly-trained ladies he incidentally mentioned, with their soft sheeny raiment and grand surroundings. In short, she now and again worked herself into an 'infernal' fever of which her nearest and dearest had not the slightest idea. But wherever Katherine took hold she never let go, and having fixed what represented her love on James Renwick, woe betide the damsel, however noble, who should attempt to balk her desire!

When James's college course at Edinburgh was almost completed, an event took place which, in the hand of Providence, proved the turning-point of the young man's life. This was the public execution of an aged minister, named Cargill, who suffered death rather than defect from the purity of God's worship. For what afterwards was remembered as 'The Killing-Time' had commenced in Scotland, and Christ's folk behoved to preach and pray with sword on thigh, ready for the fight.

Until that morning, when young Renwick saw saintly Cargill's benignant countenance, and heard his touching farewell to earth, he had not quite made up his mind about the choice of a profession. But, strange to say, the very scene that (it might be expected) would scare a bright youth, had the effect of causing him, then and there, to dedicate himself to the service which the grey-haired martyr had that minute laid down. Thenceforth Renwick, although ever religiously disposed, became more deeply serious, but of this the two women in the wooden-fronted house at Glasgow had not much opportunity to judge, as, within six weeks, he went to complete his studies at Groningen University.

When, however, at the end of seven months, the 'United Societies' invited him to take his life in his hand, return to Scotland, and lift up his voice on behalf of Christ's crown and covenant, there was no mistaking the intense depth of his fervent zeal. Katherine observed this, and as absence had rather increased her 'furious affection' than otherwise, she determined to leave no stone unturned that might help her to the fulfilment of her wishes. So she got up a considerable show of religiousness which does not always mean religion. I do not imagine she dreamt of acting deceitfully, but none the less did she follow Christ for sake of what to her represented 'loaves and fishes.' Yes, she was fully resolved that her fate *should* turn out as she intended; albeit, for the present, Renwick's wandering life and the unsettled state of church affairs put marriage out of the question.

'Katherine can explain all about baby and the trunks to you, sir,' said the gentle, feeble little widow to Laird Baigrie. 'You were a friend of Angus, so I'm sure you will be kind to my child.'

Not a single doubt of anybody's trustworthiness ever seemed to cross the pure mind of the girl-relict. The heavenly atmosphere that surrounds infancy enveloped her still, after twenty years' experience of this world. It was this very simplicity of hers which had first attracted Angus to the penniless orphan-daughter of an old Dutch professor of mathematics. And *she* had well-nigh adored her Scotch husband, and with good reason; for a kind spouse had he ever proved to her, taking the while good care to keep intact, as far as possible, her ignorance of the evil that is in the world.

As the mother of 'renowned James,' Mistress Renwick was

had in excellent reputation among 'the brethren.' Therefore it was with an easy mind that Angus Gordon had left his wife and infant under her roof. And now, here lay poor Dorettle a-dying, telling Laird Baigrie, with a gentle smile, that Katherine would repeat to him the information previously given to herself about baby and the coffers full of gold, standing beside the window-seat. As she feebly uttered the words, Antony glanced at the female indicated, then at the child in her arms. 'Riches and all the glory of them!' Not above twenty minutes since the young elder's wrath had waxed hot at the widow's calm reception of his sad tidings; but in that brief space of time his whole inner life seemed altered—its horizon indefinitely widened. 'Riches and all the glory of them!'

The abode of James Renwick's mother, although as clean and trig as hands could make it, was neither roomy nor handsome, being only half of an upper storey of a 'land,' entered from the street by an outside door. But when poor Angus Gordon left his young foreign wife under the good woman's care, he thought more about the motherly kindness she was likely to receive than of tapestry hangings or Venice looking-glasses.

Mistress Gordon's bed-chamber, albeit the largest room in the house, measured but fifteen feet by twelve, and the ceiling was so low that it barely cleared Antony Baigrie's head. The walls boasted neither leathern nor silken draperies, but were lined with boards of the same dark brown wood as the floor. Within a recess with doors stood a stump-bed, and on the opposite side of the room were a couple of extremely small windows, latticed like those of a modern prison. Not a gay interior, certainly; but, when one is sick unto death, willing hands are more admirable than inlaid tables, and warm hearts decidedly preferable to costly cabinets.

Dorettle Gordon would have been quite satisfied with her surroundings, even if unrelieved by the presence of various foreign articles of her own, which imparted a picturesque air to the plainly-furnished apartment. Upon the clumsy, stumpy-legged oaken table lay a hand-bell of elegantly-chased silver, and an elaborately-carved case filled with crystal spirit-bottles, patterned in gilt starlets. Poor Dorettle's best saque, made of canary-and-blue striped damask, had been hurriedly unpacked and pinned up by way of curtain, to keep air-draughts off the bed, and her pink taffetas petticoat, converted into a temporary blind, for one of the minniken windows.

Dr. Fairlie, the surgeon in attendance, although a man nearing the end of his threescore and ten, was sometimes on entering so struck with the quaint aspect of the room and the beauty of his patient as to almost forget to ask how she felt.

Woe's me! Too soon that question became at best a mere matter of form. Nearer and nearer drew Dorettle to the 'land o' the leal.' Day by day, as the days glided on, *she* glided on and could not stay! And how sweetly childlike she was, even in her lovingness! Her life had, so to speak, been a continuous psalm of trust, and now, at its close, she confidingly leant her weakness upon the Redeemer's strength. 'God was Love itself. Everybody was very kind. She was going to Angus, and by-and-by Jesus would bring baby-Letty to heaven also.'

The process of dissolution, which sometimes horrifies sterner minds, she involuntarily overleaped, turning to the coming joy as naturally as a sunflower seeks the light and eschews gloom.

Mistress Renwick and Katherine were unremitting in service, but Antony was at a loss what to do with himself and his leisure. On his deathbed, Angus Gordon had stated what were the contents of those two strong coffers standing beside one of the window-seats, but neither the young widow nor Katherine had offered him the keys.

The laird's present situation was really most awkward, for he felt like a fish out of water, yet to quit the Gorbals and leave the coffers and trunks at the mercy of Katherine was not to be thought of. No, however wearisome the post, he must continue at it till Dorettle's demise should give him, as the infant's trustee, full possession of her goods and gear. In the adjoining half-flat Mistress Renwick had secured a bed for him, but tiresome as his present existence was he could not sleep both day and night. Besides, the widow's end might come at any moment, and he behoved to be on the alert in order that the instant death claimed her, he himself might hold 'her estate' for behoof of the little girl whose squalling in the meantime nearly drove him frantic. Oh, if he could only, beforehand, get hold of the keys, and, like the king in the nursery rhyme, amuse his vacuity by counting over his— No! baby-Letty's money.

Mistress Gordon was so unsuspicious and frank that he once or twice thought of asking her to tell him where the keys were, if only he could see her without witnesses. But the two other women never gave him the chance; and indeed the dying girl's state required some one to sit by her continually. So his next resource was to sound Katherine, and to that end his energies were directed. Success attended his efforts in so far that the girl left off nurse-tending in the sickroom and took to promenading the dark little passage with the child in her arms, and its state of unrest, consequent on teething, as an apology. Not that Katherine swerved from her firm determination to wed her cousin by-and-by. But in the interim the opportunity of flirting with a 'real gentleman' fitted so nicely into the folds of her ambitious disposition that she was tempted to enjoy it to the full. Why, to be on hand-and-glove terms with one of the aristocracy (for in point of fact there was no middle-class in Scotland at that period) appeared almost next thing to being noble herself. But as the game became most interesting, she discovered that making a quarter-deck of the little dark passage rather impeded the flow of conversation. So thereupon baby-Letty was consigned to Mistress Renwick's box-bed in the kitchen, where also stood that good woman's spinning-wheel, with its rock full of flax, that from one cause or another had remained unused for nearly half a year. Katherine, not being practised in high-bred idleness, felt at a loss where to bestow her hands whilst her tongue and Antony's were busy. So from sheer nervousness she was seized with a sudden fit of industry, and set to work at her aunt's cumbrous machine, as if for very life. The paddling of her foot on the treddle, and the whir of the fly-wheel whizzing round and round, excited her as the sounds of trumpet and drum inspirit a soldier on the battle-field.

Although not one whit in love with her companion, she was nevertheless so carried away by his 'genteelity' and the situation altogether as to be perfectly willing to answer his queries either concerning Dorettle's affairs or those of anybody else. But, after all, her budget when opened contained little information on the subject just then most interesting to her auditor.

'Ay, sir!' said she, 'puir Mistress Gordon thought she was dying the day before ye came here, and she was feared that the guidman wadna get back to Glasco' till she was dead and gane. So she bade my auntie and me be guid to the bit bairnie, an' keep the kists an' other things safe, till her guidman could come an' get them. Forbye that, sir, she made auntie promise to take the gowd weddin'-ring aff her finger after she was dead, and when the guidman came hame, bid him keep it for the bairn for a remembrance o' her mither. Na, na, sir! Mistress Gordon ne'er gied *us* ony keys. But I'm thinkin' she was intendin' to do 't, if you hadna come.'

This comprised the gist of Katherine's information, and it considerably allayed the laird's anxiety, albeit, for fear of contingencies, he remained at his post of observation. Thus, while in the darkened front-chamber the 'old Scythesman' was sheering thinner and thinner the veil which hung between Dorettle and the Unseen, Laird Baigrie lolled on the settle in the kitchen, and sought to wile away his weariness by discursive talk with Katherine.

Now, when a couple of not brilliant conversationists sit for days together idly speaking, to kill time, the chances are they severally babble something or another for which, later, they will feel ready to bite out their too fluent tongues: nay, more thanks to luck than good guiding, if out of some foolish remark the Fates do not twist a cord round the babbler's neck strong enough to drag him (in some life-crisis) whither he would not.

From the mutual confidences of Antony and Katherine two facts emerged, sharp and clearly defined, viz:—that *she* was ferociously enamoured of her cousin, and that *he* intended to wed Marjorie Ker, Mistress Elspet's presumptive heiress.

The condition of Katherine's affections gave Antony good hopes that the obstacle to his own successful loverizing might eventually be removed, and not being a very sensitive man he spake thus to his *vis-à-vis*—

'There's no doubt, Katherine, that Mistress Marjorie has just been making a fool of your cousin James, so keep up your heart. He's not what a body might call plain-looking, but he's weakly, and no' in Marjorie's station, ye ken. Indeed,' he ran on, waxing irate and dignified as he remembered that 'love-lit-naphtha glance' he had, at Talla Conventicle, caught *en route* from his lady-love toward the elegant young preacher, 'indeed her kinswoman, Mistress Elspet Ker, told me she was convinced their betrothal wud end in smoke, especially now, when she hersel' has gotten ever so much siller added to what she had, and might reasonably look higher than before for a husband to her niece. It's no' very likely, Katherine, that Marjorie would seriously take up with a minister-creature that's sprung o' the commonality, and hasna so much as a kirk or a stipend. Na! na! lass, never fash yoursel' about Mistress Marjorie. Take my word for't, ye's yet be your cousin James Renwick's wife.'

That stupid laird's would-be consolation fell on the girl's sore heart as painfully as the punitive water-drops upon the head of a victim in the Spanish Inquisition. But no sign made she of the fierce passions seething in her breast, save that her cheeks grew redder, and her foot stamped firmer and faster on the treddle of her wheel. Her fingers kept neatly twisting and drawing out the flax, her heart the while well-nigh bursting with indignant, passionate rage and love. Loathing of Marjorie! hatred of Renwick! No! no! not *that* exactly, but how *could* he actually go and make love to another when she had arranged her whole life in reference to *him;* ay! and made light too of old Dr. Fairlie's implied admiration of herself? Then hot tears sprang to her blazing eyes, but failed either to cool them or rouse Antony's sympathy.

'Is this Mistress Marjorie very beautiful?' she asked.

'Just uncommon, Katherine, else, you are quite sure, *I* would not admire her,'—whereupon he droned forth ever so many comments upon crimson lips and alabaster necks, and a crimson silk napkin.

These he backed up by strictures concerning Renwick's lack of common-sense in daring to aspire to any lady so far above his own social position. In the long-run these two persons, seated in Mistress Renwick's obscure kitchen, entered into a sort of unwritten compact to aid one another, seeing that so to do would help themselves.

Thus the days swam past! past! past!

Old Doctor Fairlie came and went with his chilblained fingers in a stoat-skin muff, and his perception of the picturesque vanishing in real concern for his patient's spiritual condition, he being of that 'black and white' school of theology which makes no allowance for shades of *lilac* and *grey*.

Excellent Mistress Renwick, looking pale in the face and

bleared about the eyes, ministered to Dorette's bodily needs, and occasionally to those of her soul, poor child.

Fat, pink and white, baby-Letty was now and again brought to receive a maternal kiss, and then remanded to the kitchen.

As for Dorettle, she lay quiet, very quiet, remembering and remembering, hoping and hoping. Sometimes bygone days in Holland seemed once more around her. Her obese parent, clad in his official gown and cap, appeared to call out, 'Come, Dorettle, my tulip, come and light my pipe.' Or Angus would be beside her, at her father's new-made grave, whispering these words of strength, 'When thy father and mother forsake thee, then the Lord will take thee up.' At other times she would fancy she saw her husband standing by the bed, arrayed in crystallized light, angelically beautiful, yet her very own Angus still.

It was this sort of sentimentality, as he considered it, which disquieted Doctor Fairlie, honest sectarian that he was. Ah! he had yet to learn that the Lord can use even our terrestrial affections as a primer whereon we may spell out the lesson of His own infinite love. He had yet to learn that it is the life, and not mere death-bed emotions, which argue a sinner saved by God's grace.

Occasionally Mistress Renwick would humbly beg Laird Baigrie to engage in prayer in the sick-room, a request he would fain have negatived, for of late things terrestrial had occupied him so much as to encroach considerably upon those hours he set apart for celestial concernments. What the

Almighty has joined in hallowing unanimity he had chosen to divorce, therefore, when the world made, as it were, a raid upon his sanctity, he opined it would be profane to approach God's footstool concerning 'special spirituals' till such time as (by his own right hand) he had driven back the intruder. The consequence was, that his long-winded petitions proved so 'dry and fusionless,' that, even while he was uttering them, poor Dorettle retired for comfort, so to speak, into the 23d Psalm, thinking it over in her native Dutch.

Thus the days kept dropping into the stream of time as it rushed past. One, two, three, four—on and on, till the eleventh afternoon, and then Dorettle's last moment arrived unexpectedly, after all the waiting for it.

One of the many mistakes of poor human nature is a tendency to erect its fleeting joys and sorrows into an institution—to expect, that as this day so shall the morrow prove.

Inside that wooden-fronted house in the Gorbals, the state of affairs, which on Friday seemed so appallingly strange, had, by the eleventh day thereafter, shaken themselves into routine. Every individual of the household knew that the end *must* be drawing near, yet each one felt as startled, when death came, as if Dorettle's demise were the result of sudden accident.

The afternoon sunshine was glinting in ruddy darts through that one of the tiny windows which was not exactly opposite the young widow's bed. As she lay on her back very still and restful, the rays fell slanting across her closed eye-lids.

Antony and Katherine were in the kitchen, yawning and arranging to help away the long forthcoming evening by a game at draughts.

Mistress Renwick, who had had a rheumatic headache, off and on, for the last forty-eight hours, was seated at the sick woman's bedside in a big arm-chair, trying, by taking a snatch of sleep, to gain strength for her prospective night-watch.

Suddenly Dorettle opened her eyes wide, looked upward, up! up! as if seeing through the flat wooden ceiling of the box-bed. A smile ripples over her face. She stretches her arms as if in welcome. 'Angus! Angus!' she exclaims in clearer tones than she had uttered for many a day, still gazing upward with a look of ineffable delight.

All in a tremble, Mistress Renwick flew to the Dutch bottle-case, poured some strong spirit into one of the queer little glasses, and held it to the lips of the dying girl.

Too ate! too late! Her jaw fell! The loving spouses, separated for a brief space here below, had met again in that better country where there is no parting any more for ever.

A couple of centuries ago, when the times were wild, transit difficult, and letter-writing rare, cousinships were apt to slide out of mutual 'ken,' especially if the related parties lived in different countries. Such had been Angus Gordon's hap, else it is not probable he would have confided so much to the tender mercies of a comparative stranger like Laird Baigrie.

Dorettle's father had been a self-made man, and not a native of Groningen, so, albeit a highly-esteemed professor in the College there, his relatives were unknown to his friends and acquaintances.

Owing to this double coincidence, Antony now entered upon his trusteeship without let or hindrance. He knew that Gordon had conveyed his entire savings to Glasgow in the shape of specie (intending to invest it in land), and now his fingers itched to count the yellow pieces.

However, for very shame, he could not do this while Mistress Renwick and Katherine were preparing to lay out the still warm corpse, and, what was worse, he could hardly forbid them to take what was requisite for that purpose out of a large chest standing near with the brass-hasped lid open. But he pocketed three or four keys, fastened together by a slender silver chain attached to the dead girl's chatelaine, and then retired to the kitchen, there to wait till the two women should finish arraying the body in fine linen of the hostess's own spinning. With a fluttering heart, that felt as if it were beating tattoos inside his throat, the 'young elder' wandered nervously to and fro the diminutive apartment. His very toes and fingers thrilled with excitement which was not exactly pleasurable, but, as it were, a sort of first-stage intoxication. Riches, and all the glory of them!

Baby-Letty, who was asleep in Mistress Renwick's dim dormitory, awoke with a shrill cry, and recalled to Antony the fact that to *her*, and not to him, appertained the money, over which he, in spirit, had just been gloating. Borne on the wings of imagination, he had gradually been losing sight of this circumstance. But what of that? Surely, surely, he being a professing Christian, could trust himself to act with integrity in all things temporal. Entreat Heaven's help so to do? Nay! For it was his inward pride that he was far too serious to spread puerilities out before the great and holy God, or bring the solemnities of religion to bear upon trifles. Therefore, all things considered, he felt confident he should acquit himself right well of the duty he had undertaken.

There is no need to enter into the details of Dorettle's burial. It was gone about decently and orderly, and Antony, as the friend of her deceased husband, laid her head in the grave.

Then the various expenses incurred for the defunct lady fell to be settled, and were paid by the 'young elder,' with a degree of justice so remarkable as slightly to resemble stinginess. On receipt of his fee, Doctor Fairlie looked disappointed, and turning on his heel, muttered some words not very complimentary to the 'paymaster;' but Mistress Renwick, albeit by far the worst used, received *her* modicum peacefully for sake of dead Dorettle's child. She felt quite a motherly interest in the little orphan girl, and aware that the new guardian was unmarried, trusted he might leave the infant under her care for a year or two at any rate. But speedily was she undeceived. Without giving a hint of his intentions, Antony, directly after the funeral, went and hired four horses, to be at Mistress Renwick's door by nine o'clock next morning, each pair of steeds in charge of a rider warranted sober and honest. Aback of these quadrupeds the "young elder" purposed conveying to Edinburgh his infant ward and her belongings. For be it understood that, in regard to baby-Letty and her fortune, he had mentally mapped out a plan of procedure, which, although involving no palpable crime, might perchance be misinterpreted by onlookers not thoroughly indoctrinated into his special line of reasoning.

People there be who would fain eat, drink, dig, and sow to the glory of God; who test their terrestrials by placing even the most commonplace of them within the bright focus of celestial light; who decline robbing Peter in order to pay Paul.

Now, despite Mistress Renwick's meek mien, Laird Baigrie suspected *she* was one of these single-eyed uncompromisers, otherwise he *would* have inclined to leave baby-Letty with her for a time,—till such time in fact as Marjorie Ker should consent to be his wife, and thus a sort of step-mother unto his orphan ward. For, to tell the truth, he had mentally arranged to oust James Renwick from the heart of his affianced love, by retailing to *her* various extracts from Katherine's imprudent confidences concerning her *own* affection for the handsome young divine. In short, he had planned every one of his projected moves as exactly as if the swift of foot invariably gained the race.

When the 'young elder' returned from ordering the horses, he found Mistress Renwick seated on the forestairs of her dwelling taking a rest and a breath of fresh air, and dancing baby-Letty up and down in her arms, ever and anon stopping that exercise to drop over her erratic snatchy kisses. Yet, serene as the good matron's face looked, framed, so to speak, in a white linen coif, her ruminations were many and solemn. She was thinking of her absent son, who, for aught she could tell, might that very moment be in the hands of those who, day and night, were seeking his life. Then she began to meditate on the providential dispensation, which, within three weeks' space, had brought from across the seas to her humble abode a happy, rich young couple, and laid husband and wife in far-parted graves; lastly, her thoughts revolved around the pretty girl-baby on her lap. Was this infant *really* a wealthy heiress? Was it likely that Laird Baigrie, with his prim mouth and hard blue eyes, would prove a loving guardian to her orphanhood?

In the midst of these cogitations the sound of Antony's voice caused her to look over the forestairs.

'Will you be good enough,' he cried, 'to pack up the bairn's clothes this afternoon? We are going away at nine in the morning. Be sure and get plenty of wraps for her, for fear she catches cold. I'm not accustomed to bairns, so I'll trust to you in respect of the wraps and such matters.'

Poor Mistress Renwick's heart stood still as she hugged baby-Letty closer. 'The laird looks sae cold and heartless,' thought she; 'God o' Israel, be the defence o' the feckless babe thou hast rendered fatherless and motherless in this wicked world.' With a tear in her eye, the worthy 'house-mistress' arose and went in-doors to begin her arrangements just as Katherine made her appearance at the foot of the street.

Antony awaited *her* approach in order to communicate the news of his speedy departure, and also, in a round-about manner, to advise her not to permit any person to interpose betwixt her and the entire possession of Renwick's heart.

'Never fear, Katherine,' said he, 'keep firmly to your purpose, and the bowls will all bowl right in the end. Sure am I that it would neither be for your cousin's good nor your happiness to hold fast that daft-like troth-plight he and Marjorie Ker have given to one another. In fact, it is a positive duty to separate them if possible. Not, of course, to do anything sinful for that end; though it is self-evident, Katherine, they're not suited, and before being man and wife six months they'd be sure to rue their bargain. Your cousin James is far from an ill-looking lad; but, as I said before, being sprung from the commonality, he is not in Mistress Marjorie's station. And what sayeth the Scripture—"Be not unequally yoked." Katherine, you and I may never again chance to meet in this world, but *if* I happen to come across James Renwick, I'll be sure to speak a good word for you, and you are at liberty to make him aware that Marjorie Ker's aunt wants her to marry *me*. I daresay that by this time she herself is sorry about the *nonsense* she spoke to your cousin. Indeed, I could gather as much from what she said to me after he had been at Greendykes.'

Katherine felt half mad with rage and regret and disappointment, and ill-disciplined love, but her natural bold persistence kept her tongue tethered.

So the laird went on maundering in a self-satisfied manner that added to her other sensations a desire to twist his neck.

'By the way, Katherine,' he added, 'ye're welcome to keep the gowns and farthingales, or whatsoever ye may call them, that ye took out of Mistress Gordon's kist[1] to hang up for curtains on the bed and windows. Ye may keep them as a remembrance o' her. They'll possibly yet serve ye for bridal buskins[2] when ye come to be kirkit[3] wi' your cousin James.'

'Ye mean, ill-legged hound!' mentally commented the irate damsel, 'it's just as weel that I had the gumption to take twa or three little things out o' the kist-shot,[4] instead o' waitin' for you to gie me my lawful dues. It's but just that my auntie should get the poor dead lady's body-clothes for the labour she has had in waiting upon her, but aunty is sae *saft*, she hasna spunk enough to ask for her ain rights. I was only

---

[1] Chest.   [2] Adornments.   [3] Churched.
[4] Kist-shot, a closed-in compartment inside a chest.

doing my bare duty by her when I took puir Mistress Gordon's red bookie and her spangled green satin pockie. They canna be worth much, tho' I confess they're real bonnie. If this knock-kneed, beggarly body, Laird Baigrie, knew I had ta'en them, it's as likely as no he could furnish me wi' Scripture-texts to prove I had done right in helping myself. I suspect he's better at *that* sort o' deil's preaching than at doin' justly or loving mercy, elder tho' he be.' For Katherine was by no means an obtuse individual, and albeit her personal standard of ethics was low, she had not failed to note the laird's oblique adaptations of Scripture.

At the specified hour, Antony and his hired cavalcade thudded away from the Gorbals, having created, whilst getting under weigh, an immense sensation in the locality.

Mistress Renwick, with a gloomy foreboding at her heart, saw baby-Letty carried away in the long arms of her guardian. The child, however, was gentle-tempered and seemed content; so her recent nurse thanked God therefor, and essayed to believe in Antony's tenderness of disposition.

CHAPTER V.

'There's rosemary, that's for remembrance ; . , . . and there is pansies, that's for thoughts.'

N that forenoon when, after hearing the news of Mistress Elspet's windfall, Antony rode away from Greendykes, he, as I mentioned, felt more really enamoured of Marjorie than ever before. The old lady's accession of fortune had, in the 'young elder's' estimation, materially enhanced the attractions of her beautiful heiress-presumptive.

And the girl, grateful for the tidings concerning Renwick's escape from her cousin and his band, had called herself to sharp account for her heretofore dislike of the identical man who now had so relieved her anxiety. Indeed, till fully certified that her betrothed was safe beyond the bounds of Tweedsmuir, she had scarcely realized the intensity of her fears. But these had at all events been sufficiently acute to damp her pleasure in Mistress Elspet's good luck, and now, in the sudden relief springing from Antony's prosy information, she felt as if *care* and herself had parted company for evermore.

As soon as the 'young elder' turned his horse's head homewards, she seized her astonished old relative round the neck, kissed her repeatedly, and ended by bursting into a perfect passion of sobs and tears.

'Losh me,' thought the puzzled spinster, 'young folks now-a-days are past my comprehension! It canna surely be that because we've gotten a' this gear the lassie's sorry for having troth-plighted hersel' to James Renwick? Or can it be, I wonder, that she's feared she's geckit at Laird Baigrie till she's putten him fairly past offering to her? I wish I kent how to help her, but the young generation have sae mony twistings and twirlings in their love passages, it's no' a bit like what used to be in my time. Weel do I remember that when Andrew Bruce sent me a valentine o' light-blue satin ribbon-knots, it was as much as my mother could do to hinder me from running that very minute to thank him, and let him see that I was clean daft about him, for I doubted not that the love was mutual. Ay! ay! it's lang syne, but to this day I can almost feel the dingle o' pain that shot through my heart when, the very next week, he came and tell't me he was about to be married! My mother was right, I daresay, and maybe the new-fangled way of making no show of a body's feelings *is* better then lettin' the men-folk see into a lassie's likings; but yet, I'm no sure either. Marjorie's so discreet for ordinar' that I canna make out the cause o' this plisky o' hers. Maister James Renwick is a bonnie youth and a godly, but I canna help thinking that it's no a fitting lot for my dear niece to be hunted like a partridge on the mountains, fleeing continually for her life, and sleepin' on whins and heather, whilk she'll need to do if she marries the young minister, puir lad. It's no' what may be termed a "grand" marriage, and yet—But losh me! it's no' possible surely that wi' all her cleverness, and her poetry, and her lang lily-neck, and her talent for pickling hams, she's fallen in love wi' that lang-leggit bogle the 'young elder' (shame on me for lightlying a door-keeper o' the Lord's tabernacle). I wish I could help my bairn at this time, but no being a married woman, of course I dinna understand rightly the outs and ins o' the affections. I wish for Marjorie's sake that I did.'

However, the kind old lady's perplexity was not of long duration, for presently her niece dried her tears, bestowed a few more embraces, and exclaimed quite cheerfully: 'Oh! aunty, I am so glad your Adonis is off at last "long sword, saddle, and bridle, and all." Now, please, do not look shocked. I am quite aware that, considering how much comfort his news of James gave me, I ought not to laugh at him, but really I feel so light-hearted I cannot help it, and, aunty, even *you* must confess he is a queer-looking bodie. But now he is away, come to the book-room and indite the remainder of your letter to the Edinburgh writer. I'll scribble it now as quick as you can speak. Before Laird Baigrie came I was so *dowie*[1] the pen seemed as heavy as lead. Puir Laird Baigrie, I'm sure I wish him weel.'

Mistress Elspet never dreamt of saying nay to any proposition of her niece or nephew either. Nay, were the plain truth told, she, in her deep consciousness of unwooed spinsterhood, rather enjoyed being ordered about by the two youngsters. Possibly it represented to her spirit (albeit dimly as through smoked glass) what *she* imagined a missing note in her life-music, the restful comfort of being the 'weaker vessel.' At any rate, by some curious process of ratiocination, the fact of being lovingly snubbed rendered less keen that inborne charge of unwomanliness wherewith ignorance sometimes debits those to whom Providence has allotted neither masculine buckler nor shield.

The epistle was duly finished, folded, and sealed, this latter operation being unintentionally supplemented by a great drop of wax which Marjorie let fall on the paper, and which her aunt declared to portend a marriage.

'Not with the Edinburgh writer surely, Aunt Eppie; that would be even worse than Laird Baigrie. Why, you think of nothing else than marriages and swains to-day. Besides, aunty mine, I shall be James's wife or nobody's.'

As the two were chatting the noise of a rolling-pin lustily

[1] Sad.

thumped on the kitchen-dresser was heard, being the announcement of dinner.

Where's Wattie? wondered that youth's aunt while walking to the dining-room. He was already there when, arm in arm, Mistress Elspet and Marjorie entered what was properly speaking more a hall than a dining-room. In its midst stood a large oaken board placed upon tressels, and around one end thereof some six or seven male and female servants were seated. They were all dressed in home-made grey cloth, but one of the men wore a flat blue cap, his badge of office as footman and butler. At the upper end of the board (where the house-mistress seated herself, flanked by her niece and nephew) were placed three platters full of porridge, each enriched with a piece of stewed pullet and a few 'plum-dames.' Similar platters of pottage stood in front of the servants, but in lieu of pullet and plum-dames these contained bits of sodden salt beef. A huge pewter salt-cellar, stationed rather more than half-way up the table, indicated where genteelity ceased and servitude commenced. Therefore did the honest folks sitting down yonder, clad in undyed woollen, know right well that though they might inhale the savoury odours of the roasted salt goose and warm damson pie, they had as little chance of tasting these dainties as of *preeing* the contents of the antique silver claret-jug set near Mistress Elspet for the use of herself and the 'twa bairns.' But not a whit did the ruddy-cheeked hungry domestics miss elegancies, for is not appetite a delicious sauce, and had they not plenty of good strong ale wherewith to wash down the pease-bannocks and cheese that supplemented their pottage?

All things being in readiness, and the outer door locked, for fear 'gangrel bodies' might pick and steal, Mistress Elspet solemnly craved a blessing on the present mercies in a grace long enough to rank as a prayer.

Eating and drinking were then set about with unmistakeable gusto, the servants laughing and addressing one another in loudish whispers, apparently not much daunted by the presence of their betters. The meal did not last above ten or a dozen minutes, after which Mistress Elspet returned thanks 'at full length.' Then the flat-capped serving-man arose, and taking a folio Bible from a *letteron* near the window, placed it in front of Marjorie, who, in regular course of morning lecture, read aloud the seventh chapter of the Revelation of St. John. Very sweetly did she read, and to a most attentive audience.

At the close, Mrs. Elspet said 'Let us pray;' whereupon everybody, turning their backs to the table, knelt where they had been sitting. A lengthy outpouring indeed did the mistress utter upon this day, which, to her in especial, was one of thanksgiving for that wonderful mercy vouchsafed since 'last the household had assembled round the board.' In the very gladsomeness of their praise her petitions were at once quaint and pathetic.

She *had* known what it was not to possess great fulness

of bread, and now the Lord had enriched her. She *had* known what it was to be solitary, and *now* she had her dear bairns, one on either hand. She *had* sometimes wished, nay longed, for only a single hour of sudden great joy, and here, in one quarter of that time, was she certified that her old neighbour in Covenant Close had bequeathed to her, not only her cash, but all the French nick-nacks she used, once on a day, well-nigh to covet.

And yet, amid this acknowledged sufficiency, there was a want. Deep down, in her spirit of spirits, a stifled cry made itself heard; a regretful cry of subdued mourning for the dear womanly instincts which had wasted their sweetness unseen and unknown. It was as if her bridal morning being come, she, before going to the altar, were laying her orange-blossoms upon a mother's tomb. A something missing in the inner life, even at its brightest.

Ah! are not the tears shed over infants' graves all the sadder because we there weep, not so much what was, as what might have been? Therefore, everything considered, one cannot wonder that Mistress Elspet, with her plain features and ugly sage-coloured gown, uttered that forenoon petitions so home-telling and pathetic that sundry of her hearers affirmed 'she wasna lang for this world, she spak sae bonnie.' Perhaps, too, the stolid rustics themselves were that day in a more thrillable frame than usual. Hearts are fat indeed that do not throb in the immediate prospect of change, and the removal of the 'Mistress and young folks' to Edinburgh would, in many respects, alter the daily lot of their present dependants.

> ' Oft o'er the soul will a sudden yearning
>   Bring back the days we are leaving behind,
> Bring back the footsteps no longer returning,
> Bring back the greeting so gay and so kind.'

'Auntie, I'm away to fish in the burn,' exclaimed Wattie, as the party was dispersing. 'I'll bring back some trouts for your supper.'

'Do that, my dear laddie,' replied Mrs. Elspet, and away scampered the boy across the hill that intervened betwixt Greendykes and the trouting stream—hurrahing, from sheer enjoyment of existence, as a cat frisks in the sunshine, or a young filly rolls on its back and flourishes its hoofs in the air. And in very truth Walter—albeit, as his aunt averred, 'no' an ill laddie'—had, in so far at least as regarded bookish proclivities, a good deal of the young colt in him. Of late years his health had become robust, but at the point where Dominie Renwick had left his education, there it remained, with little arithmetic in it, and less Latin. But even thus, Wattie, as education then went in Scotland, was by no means below par. Field-sports, however, were his delight, and print his abhorrence.

'A handsome warm-hearted laddie' he was, as Mrs. Elspet after remarked; 'albeit no skilly at his book, far less wi' his pen.'

F

But what heeded he either learning or caligraphy, so long as there were on the muir birds to be shot, or in Talla-burn trouts to be caught?

'Ye ken ye canna write yersel', auntie,' he used to say when rebutting the old lady's remonstrances. 'Ye ken ye canna write yer ain name, and what for should I scribble-scrabble like a lassie?' So by degrees the two women's attempts at inducing Watty to keep up his learning ceased, and now, with a good-bye kiss from both, that youth hied to the river-side.

Just then Mrs. Elspet chanced to have in hand a piece of work which needed much stitch-counting, and therefore in some measure precluded conversation. This artistic performance was an apron-trimming, composed of galloon-lace and curiously-knotted Dutch tape; but intricate though the pattern undoubtedly was, she made its numerical difficulties an apology for solitary meditation concerning the new leaf about to be turned in her life-chapter. Retiring, therefore, lace in hand, to her special chamber, she seated herself at the open window (for, albeit the air was somewhat frosty, she hated what she termed 'molly-coddling'), and began to muster her stray ideas.

Marjorie at the same time has betaken herself to *her* private apartment, situated at the farther end of the same passage as her aunt's dormitory. A small place it is, not above fifteen feet square, but the wainscot that lines the walls is so highly waxed and rubbed that its shine gives the effect of space. These same walls are filled with concealed presses, besides containing a box-bed, the doors whereof stand wide open, and although the couch exhibits no sheets, yet the blankets, with a great scarlet K marked on each, are wonderfully white for home-made productions. There is not much furniture, only a couple of high-backed chairs and a queer-looking three-cornered table. The chairs have stumpy, square legs, but they are almost concealed by thick fringes of scarlet and orange worsted, which depend from the black velvet seat-covers. With her own hands, Marjorie had nailed a similar fringe (by way of valance) across the outer edge of the ceiling of her bed, the doors whereof generally stood open, albeit closed sleeping-places were the order of the day. The window (a six-paned, very small specimen) being decorated *en suite*, the general effect was both quaint and pretty. Indeed Mistress Marjorie's 'sleeping chammer' was, by the indoor servants, considered so much of a sight that they now and then, on the sly, exhibited its splendours to favoured outdoor-workers, as if it were a raree-show.

To the young proprietrix herself it was an 'oratory,' but these rough rustic interlopers only noticed the tasty manner in which 'the bits o' plenishing'[1] were arranged. How could *they* know that every day of Marjorie's life there surged in her soul vague wonderments and graspings with which neither

[1] Furniture.

Mistress Elspet nor Wattie were in the least fitted to sympathize? How could *they* guess (these crass peasants) that the tenant of that comfortable little room, whose prettiness they half envied, would sometimes rush to its retirement in a sort of desperation, and, flinging herself on her knees at the open window, gaze on the wild, grand muir outside till her longings ceased to be pain, and through that visible earthly glory spread before her eyes her spirit ascended, as on a ladder of light, to the recognised presence and felt governance of God?

In the drawer of the queerly-shaped table, already described, lay a couple of volumes on a piece of blue damask.

On entering her room this September day, Marjorie takes one of these little books from its silken resting-place, looks at it for a few moments with the expression of an idolater adoring a relic, and then presses it to her lips. The so honoured volume is a small, thick, silver-clasped copy of the Sacred Scriptures in Dutch, and outside one of its vellum boards it has the letters J. R. stamped in blue paint. It has only been in her possession since the preceding 'Saturday at e'en' (her betrothal day), and, albeit ignorant of the language of Holland, she appears none the less to derive pleasure from looking at it in a printed form. By-and-by, however, replacing the volume in the drawer, she sets an inkstandish upon the sill, and then, with the other book in her lap, sits down on the window-seat. Presently she commences turning over the leaves in a dreamy sort of way, reads a line or two, stops a minute as if to reflect, scans a page, an expression of intense pleasure lighting up her face the while. Selecting from the standish one of two pens, she then writes, not currently, and by the yard, as a girl of our present period dashes off an epistle-full of flash, but forming the letters slowly and carefully, with straight, stout, short down-strokes, topped and bottomed as sharp as needle-points.

Before detailing the subject of her maiden meditations, it may be advisable to describe the volume wherein they were transcribed.

Imagine, then, a manuscript-book about half the size of a folio Bible, but not thick in proportion. It had commenced existence in common calf-leather boards, but in latter times been endued with a covering of 'wrought needle-work,' many-hued, the product of Marjorie's dexterous fingers.

Three years previously she had taken a fancy for keeping a 'diurnall,' and begged her brother's preceptor (James Renwick, to wit) would ornament the first leaf with some flourishes of penmanship.

The following is a facsimile of this initial page, the young man being at the time of writing it betwixt eighteen and nineteen years of age, and Marjorie fourteen and a half:—

My Privatt Diurnall

There's Rosemary That's for Remembrance and *There's Pansies That's for Thought*

M.K.
1679

Edinburgh. Maie The First

It would be difficult to analyse the regretfully-pleased state of mind in which Marjorie dips into some of the earlier passages of her journal. For you can easily understand that the so sudden alteration of the family plans and the immediate prospect of returning to Edinburgh, had stirred many feelings within the damsel's breast.

As she now skims over the diary, the very first entry therein calls a blush to her cheek, and something like a tear to her eye.

'*Maie the first.*—This book whilk I doe this daie begin with God his blessing, I trust, was given to mee bye my dear Aunt Elspet, and the title-page was wrott by Master Renwick, who is verie gentil and prettie, albeit onlie my Brother Walter's Dominie.

'This Morning at sunrise, Janet, my mother's tire-woman, wee Wattie, and mee, we went to Arthur his seat, to gather of Maie-dew. Already methinks my Cheeks are ruddier, because of having been washed with the Dew. I hope they may soe continue.

'Returning Home bye the Canon-gate, wee mett with Master Renwick and another young Mann, taller, but not nigh soe fresh in the Colour of his Face. Master Renwick spake verie politelie, and when Wattie (bairn-like) tellt him about mye new Diurnall, offered to ornamente it with the Penn, when he comes at six of the clock to give Wattie his Lessons.

'*June the twentieth.*—I have this daie, along with my Aunt

Elspet, been att the Grey Friar's kirkyard. We looked inn over the dyke, and saw the poor Prisonners tethered[1] there like sheep, for having fought att a place called Bothwell-Brigg. In the dyke was a little slap,[2] and Auntie Eppie and mee tried to putt our hands throw it, in order to give some Bawbees to a poor man that had butt one Arm, and was dreadfull Bloodie about the Brow.

'Master Renwick chanced to come Bye, walking arm-in-arm with young Sir Gilbert Rathillet, quite intimate-like. He likewise (Master Renwick, I mean) bestowed an Alms upon the Wounded mann. And the Words he spake! I will never forget them; neither, I am sure, will the poor Bloodie mann. Thaie were a Praier, and a Psalm of Praises, at once, also a Staff to lean uponn in passing throw that Dark Valley wee all must Tread some Daie. Yet Master Renwick, altho' so Religious, is most gentil and merrie. I think, and soe does Auntie Eppie, that if he tryed it, he could preach farr Better than even the minister of Sanct Giles' Kirk himself.

'I wish thatt mye Mother was nott soe sore sett against taking-up with the commonalitie. Nott that I desire to Lightlie the Station wherein the Lord hath putt Mee; but I cannot think it would humble Us to invite Master Renwick to take his Supper, as he ends Wattie's Lessons, at the exact Stroke of six o'clock. Butt, no doubt, it is naturall mye mother should bee somewhat Loftie, being comed of such ane hie Stock,

---

[1] Tied.   [2] Gap.

though I cannot saie that mye Uncle Andrew is more gentil in his manners than Master Renwick.

'Now, I must Stopp, lest I Sinne bye breaking the Commandemente that bidds us honour our Father and Mother. I love mye mother trulie in mine Herte, butt yett I cannott help fleeing to Auntie Eppie whenever any thing putts mee About.

'*October the Tenth.*—My dear mother has Spoken, quite humblie and friendlie, unto Master Renwick; and whatt did I doe but run straight to mye Closet, and Fall upon mye Bended knees, and thank the Lord for turning her herte. I should rather saie, for soe ordering his Providence as that the thing I most desired hath come to pass.

'It was on this Wise. Mye mother asked mee to goe with a message to Auntie Eppie's Lodging, as our Tire-woman was soe badd with the tooth-ache shee could not goe. I hadd ane ill Corn upon mye little Toe at that time, and wanted to staie att home; butt yet, thought I, mye mother's Bidding behoves to bee done, and done Cheerfullie. So I whipped on mye hood and sett out. O! trulie said Master Renwick to that Poor man that day in the Grey-Friars' kirk-yard, "In the path of Dutie-doing Wee whiles meet with deliverance from Sorrow." Thus it happened with mee this morning, Albeit to obeye mye mother was noe Verie great service to Render unto God.

'When I reached the Close-mouth, one of Lady Lawson's

swine escaped out of the cruive and rann at mee as fast as ever it could and drove mee in the mire, whilk was verie Slobberie, as it had been raining. And then came manie other swine grumphing around, till I cried aloud for Frayour.

'In this mye extremitie Master Renwick Arrived on the Spott, bye Chance, and putt the Beasts to flight, and conveyed mee home, with the dirt sticking upon mye polonese. The minute Hee tirled at our door-pinn I began to greet,[1] tho' I knew not whye; but, judging bye mye Tears, mye mother supposed I was much Hurted, and being affrighted at thatt, shee spake Soe condescendinglie unto Master Renwick, that afterwards she did not Like to withdraw her civil Behaviour from himm.

'Soe this night hee has staied Toe his Supper, after Wattie's Lessons, and I think mye mother Likes him passing well, and sees that he does not resemble the Commonalite in anie Respect.

'*Januarie the first: Nine o'clock at night.*—Of all the daies in mye Life this has been the Happiest. As it is the New-Year, dear Auntie Eppie and Her neighbour, old French Madam Rougemont, came to take their Suppers at six; likewise Master Renwick, Bye mye mother's Express desire.

'Reallie mother did look Grand with her puce satin Saque and her white damask Peticoat, the one thatt Auntie made the black and silver Scallopped Trimming for. But although

---

[1] To weep.

I insisted, auntie would putt on mye new yellow Tiffanie Tippet and apron, did she not, after all, Come dressed in her uglie Brown gown, and a Turband that is liker a night-rail than Anie other thing. I love her soe dearlie, that I was Sorrie mye mother thought her most unprettie, and that she had not on mye yellow Tippet. I had on mye best Linen gown, big scarlet roses in mye Shoes, mye hair shed off mye Brow, and hanging down mye back.

'It is verie Remarkable that Master Renwick Likewise had scarlet roses in his shoes, which looked mightie prettie with his purple stockings and doublet. His coat was Black velvet, with some silver Lace upon the pocket-holes and Cuffs, and hee wore a Falling Band made of soe verie fine real French Lace, that I saw mye mother was astonished.

'The supper was Prettie. At the head of the Table was a roast Soland goose, with sweet stuffing, and all spotted over with Stars of gold-gilt. We were most merrie, and the violer that mother had hired played at our Backs the whole time of supper.

'Master Renwick was ordered bye mye mother to Crave a blessing, and syne in came the het-pint in a great big punch-Bowl, with the steam fluffing around Katie's Head, and all the wee bits of crab-apples bobbing and dooking in the warm Drink.

'The servants were bidden come Ben, and got their share, and Wee all drank one another's good Health. Even the violer got a cup-full along with his Fee, and went away down the stairs singing like madd.

'Master Renwick gave unto Wattie a beautifull shagreen purse, because he had Learned his Lessons so well the last month. At that upp rose mye mother and kissed mee, and said "Marjorie is also greatlie improved in the same Space of Time." And then dear auntie came stepping across and kissed mee on the Cheek, and clapped mee upon the back inn presence of them All. Within my hearte I thanked God for this joie, but would Fain also have thanked Master Renwick, for I knowe well that it is onlie since mother permitted him toe come here as a Friend, forbye teaching Wattie, that I have Behaved soe Well. Hee gives mee many good advices, and almost causes mee toe greet whiles with his Stories about the poor persecuted People that at this present Time are chased upp and Down like wild Beasts. If even mye mother could Butt hear him telling these True stories, I think shee would like them! What shee admires most in Master Renwick is his merrie, Kindlie way of holding Conversations, soe she Saies.'

'*Auguste the nineth: Ten o'clock at night.*—This is the Latest hour I ever was out of mye Bed in all mye Life, but the night is nigh as Clear as daie. I have just been reading mye Chapter without anie candle or Lamp, and although the bowets are not lighted, I can see the High Street quite distinct out beyond the close-mouth.

'This daie mother and mee were at a verie grand Wedding in Sanct Giles' Kirk. It was Ladie Lawson's. She is fifty-Two years old, and a widow forbye, and is married to mye Cousin Johnnie Lawson, that might be her sonne, Albeit he is an advocate, and verie poor.

'Shee was dressed verie brawlie,[1] in a gown and saque of gold tiffanie, beautifull indeed, and shining like the sun in his strength. Her coif and veil were starred with perles, and she had white sattin Favours sewed all over her gown for the companie to pull. But yet she looked verie Frail, and her skin damp and Red like, the daie being hott, and the beard upon her upper Lipp prettie Black and thick, butt nott long like a man's.

'I had on a pearl-white tiffanie gown, tied upp with hainch-knots of silver Cord to show the white sattin furbelowed Petticoat that Auntie Eppie gave mee, and that was Her's when she was Young.

'I wonder wherefore Johnnie Lawson, who is but Ten years older than mee, and for ordinar verie kind unto mee, Lookit sae dour and gloomie at mee on this his Wedding-day. Hee often used to saie that when I grew old enough I was to bee his Littel wifie. I cannot think wherein I have offended him?

'There was present a Crowd of people, and after Johnnie was Fairlie wedded to auld Ladie Lawson, the companie

[1] Handsomely.

mounted into the gallerie of the Kirk, sitting in the front seats, whilst the minister went to the pulpit and preached a Longe Discourse.

'Auld Lady Lawson and her new husband, Johnnie, satt in the grand pew, Opposite the minister, where the king and Queen sitts, when there is a King and Queen, but the Duke of York, Hee worships nott in Sanct Giles', being a papisher, Mother saies.

'Mother and mee were next seat Butt one to Ladie Lawson and Johnnie; and after the sermon, coming down the big stairs, there being a crowd on 'Them, Johnnie took hold of mye hand and Squeezed it soe sore that I well-nigh Cried aloud, Onlie at that minute hee behoved to Lett goe, and oxter[1] toe the Door with his New wife, where the horses were waiting for us All. After wee Got home to the bride's house wee ruggit aff[2] her favours; mightie prettie ones Thaie were. I gott Five. O! but shee seemed Aged to bee Johnnie's Wife.

'I forgott to Write down in its right place that, happening to look down from our Seat in the gallerie into the midst of the kirk, I spied Master Renwick with Sir Gilbert Rathillet and diverse more young gentlemen come inn to see the Sight.

'Master Renwick lookit upp toe where Mee and mother were Sitting, and then somewaie the Eerieness I was beginning

[1] Go arm-in-arm.   [2] Tore off.

to Feel vanished like snaw aff a dyke in the sunshine. I think that what dear Auntie Eppie saies is true, "Thatt hee is a most Godlie young man," for even looking att him putts mee into a pleased frame of Spirit.

'*September the third.*—Am I in veritie the Marjorie Ker thatt onlie three weeks syne Wrott in this Diurnal? I cannot believe it, for mye hearte is broke. O! mye mother! mye mother! canst thou from yon heaven high see poor motherless mee? I now think that I might have showed more Love to you, leastwise made plainer the Love thatt I Felt. I wonder iff you sorely missed it? God knoweth, thatt in mye hearte I did love you dearlie, although I Somewaie could nott help Telling more about mye Feelings unto Auntie Eppie and Master Renwick. I am sorrie for thatt now, Verrie sorrie indeed. Sitting here with mye new Blacks on, at Aunt Elspet's in Covenant Close, I will, for fear of forgetting, note down the sadd dispensation that has made mee and Wattie motherless Orphans. Could it Bee possible that shee gott the Infection at the kirk, the daie wee Went there to Johnnie Lawson's wedding? That is whatt the Doctor Thinks, because there were manie Beggar Bodies standing around the door, and striving to gett Alms from the Companie as they passed out. But I rather suppose mye dear Parent did gett the Infection from Phemie Birlie, the watercarrier his Wife, when shee came to our house seeking some Lozengers for her Wee Lassie's cough, for that poor Bairnie died the verie next week. I am glad now that mye dear Mother gave her the Lozengers; but shee was ever kind to the Poor, whether they were deserving Persons or not, at least she never grudged giving them plentie of pills and Lozengers, soe now to us that is left Behind on Earth her Charitie is a great comfort to Remember.

'Mother could eat butt little Supper, and had a most Terrible Paine in her Brow that nicht Ladie Lawson was married, and I sat upp for hours bathing her Head with a pocket napkin trempit[1] in vinegar. Bye morning she was in a high Fever, and soon it took her head. Then did shee Beginn to sing Psalms and to Praie almost without stopping, and the twenty-third Psalm in particular. The Doctor made all the Hair be shaved off her Head, and her Eyes were shining terrible Bright. Her end Came when the Bell of Saint Giles was tolling mid-day. I was sitting on a Creepie[2] at the Bed-Corner dovering with sleep, for I was clean done out with Nicht-watching, and most dowie in spirit. Wee Wattie, puir thing, was sitting on another Creepie, sleeping, with his Curlie head upon mye Shoulder, for the Daie was warm and Thunderie. On a suddent mye mother cries out Loud, "Come here, mye dearest Marjorie!" Upp I gott and flew to the Bedd. "Come into mye arms, [mye Bairn," cries mye mother. "Bring wee Wattie too toe glorie," and with these Words shee gave upp the Ghoste. And then

[1] Steeped.   [2] Low stool.

Kate came running Ben from the Pantrie, where shee was getting some more vinager toe burn upon a Hot Shovel in mother's Room, for fear the disease might be smittle. But, alas! it was not Needed.

'I feel verie Old with soe much Sorrow, and now I wonder How I could ever Take upp mye head so much about Master Renwick, instead of thinking Continuallie about mye mother, when our time Together was to be soe shortt. But that was noe fault of his, and Hee has been a great Comfort to Wattie and mee in our Time of sorrow. Still, hee is not my mother, and I Hate mieself, because Everie time hee comes I feel Comforted, as Isaac did on meeting Rebecca after hee lost His mother.

'To-morrow Master Renwick will goe to Glasgow to visit his Mother, who is a Widow; and his own Health also requireth change of aire for a short space. This coming soe close upon the back of our great affliction causeth mye Spirit to fail, and I cannot help weeping, all things seem Soe eerie.

'Wee Wattie also is far from Well, and the Doctor saies hee must no longer abide in anie Town, but in the countrie, where the aire is pure, till such time at least as he is older. Soe Auntie is intending to take us to Greendykes, and if wee are obliged, on account of Wattie's sickness, to goe there before Master Renwick comes back it will bee a pitie.

'Dear Auntie aye refers to mee, and I am in a perplexity,

for Wattie is looking shilpit[1] and thin, and even a few daies Maie Make a difference. I love Auntie heartilie, but I wiss she would take the lead in managing things. It whiles fears to be obliged to order her, and tell her what to doe. I wish that Master Renwick, who is soe clever and good, and soe strong in the mind, was our Uncle in this time of Sorrow.

'*Greendykes, Januarie the First*, 1681.—This is the First time I have opened mye Diurnall since coming here. It is New-Year's Daie, different indeed from the last one thatt wee spent. Verie mercifull unto mee hath God been, and Greendykes is a pleasant habitation, and dear Auntie as kind as kind can Bee. Yet mye heart is Dowie; I think it will never be ony thing else, for, yestreen, when I burst out a laughing at some daft nonsense of Wattie's, I was scared at myself for doing it. The Hills around Greendykes are white with snow, and all things outside the House soe quiet that everie Daie is just like a Sabbath-Daie. The time I feel cheeriest is when I take a saunter out-bye by myself, for then I whiles in Spirit flee upp to Heaven, and I think and think about the Bonnie Angels and the Golden Streets, till I wish that all the world could rejoice in that Smile of God's, whilk makes the Bewtie of the Fair Countrie on High. And why should The Lord's Smile no make even This earth as happie as Paradise? is what I whiles ask myself. Sometimes I think thatt I would gie the whole world, if I had it, for the Companie of somebodie thatt

[1] Shilpit—pale.

could understand how Sweetlie and Holilie the Drifting Snaw and Blowing Winds sing in mye soul. Auntie cannot do this, neither can Wattie, and whatt I feel, I cannot sett down in words to make them understand. Surelie I used to bee a mere Bairn in mye waies lang Syne in Edinburgh Last Year. I now am amazed thatt Master Renwick, who was so learned, took the pains Hee did to give mee good Advices. It was a great pitie he did not get back From Glasgow before wee had to quit Edinburgh on Wattie's account.

'Verie likelie hee thinks about mee as just a foolish bit Lassie (I was onlie that when he knew mee). But, O! How often do I wish now that he was here to tell mee the meaning of mye own thoughts. Whiles, when dear Auntie and mee are sitting at the fireside, conversing upp and down, I feel as if I would Fain rend awaie an invisible Something that holds our spirits asunder. I do not know how to write exactlie whatt I mean, but if Master Renwick was here, Hee could put itt quite plaine.

'Maiebe mye notion about some folk's Spirits getting soe intimate with other folk's spirits is nonsense. And yet, when I see the Sun shining upon the pure white snow, and making it look as if it was answering Back lovinglie, I am forced to believe that in God's Bonnie Earth there maie be such a thing as two Souls Soe resembling one anither, that whatt the Bible speaks of comes True, to Wit, " One Lord, One Faith, One Baptism of human Love," given by God Himself. But perhaps

I am wrong, and Maie-bee it is a Sinn to have such thoughts. For when I am beside dear Auntie I cannot feel all this about souls to be possible, butt the moment I gett awaie bye myself, Back the whole thing comes as true-like as life.

'*August the First* 1681.—I am all shaking for joie, But it is awful to reflect thatt hee is to voyage all the road to Holland. Far beyond the Seas.

'This morning Auntie was busie making Mint-Watter, and the air was soe terrible Hot that shee bade Wattie and mee go for coolness Down to the Burn-side to pull Thrashes to putt on the passage-floor. Hardlie had Wee begun to pull when wee heard a horse neighing, soe I lookit upp, and there close-bye satt Master Renwick upon a pownie, Smiling like the Sun shining upon apple-trees in blossom. Afore going awaie to Holland, he has been visiting his old Mother, and now hath come all this road, round about, just to Saie good-bye to Auntie and his pupil "Wee Wattie." In some respects this has been the happiest Daie of mye Life, because Master Renwick hath explained to mee everie one of my thoughts, and shewed clearlie unto mee that even in This World God allows plenty of outgate for Christian people's natural feelings and their love of Bewtie. For "Whatt is Earth but the bewtifullie adorned Vestibule of thatt Lovelier Heaven, The Gates whereof Stand half open to let the Light of The Lord's Love Glint through upon red Roses, and white Snow, and happie human Faces." These Bee Master Renwick's Verie words, for I wrott them down when Dear Auntie was showing Him our New Milk-house.

'How Grand and Comfortable it was when hee said, "The Shine that floats from atween the wee chink of the Heavenlie Gates that is left open is whiles enough soe to flood the Soule with Rapturous Gratitude for whatt even the 'Natural' Eye beholdeth, and the Humane Affections imbibe, thatt there's no relief, but Sing praises Like the Little Birds among the Branches."

'I doe think thatt when I used to feel somewhatt apart from Dear Kind Auntie, even whilst sitting and Chatting with her at the Fireside, it was because I myeself stood nott far enough within the Heavenlie Vestibule to catch the Raies of Divine Light that Maiebee all the Time were falling upon her Honoured Head.

'Master Renwick is more Beautifull than hee was Lang Syne. I used to think that his eyes were Dark Blew, butt now I find that whiles, when hee Speaks Earnestlie, thaie have a purplish shade that Glorifies the Blew. It is Maiebee a Sinn to write such a thocht, Butt att these Moments Thaie seem to me Whatt I suppose the Eyes of the Holie Angells are, or maiebee it is the light from Heaven that glints out upon his soul, and thus shedds glorie upon his Human visage, as Moses his face did shine when hee came down from the Mountain.

'Master Renwick made Auntie and mee greet bye telling us about an Awfull Sight Hee Saw Last Month in the Grass-

Market at Edinburgh, and the time hee was telling us his eyes had the Purplish Angell look. He Saw ane Godlie Aged Minister, one Master Donald Cargill, gett his head chappit off for noe Denying the Lord Jesus, thatt redeemed Him from the Devil with his own precious Blood. Master Renwick was standing close bye the Scaffold, and soe Heard the old Martyr's speech, and saw his Holie, Mild countenance as hee lookit Like Stephen of Old Upp to Heaven, where he was soe Soon toe bee.

'Master Renwick saies Hee was a Noble Sanct, and Noble Looking, with Long Silvered Hair falling upon His Shoulders. His Last Words, after the Horrible Hangman tied the rope around his neck, were these, "Now Am I nigh getting my Crown, for whilk I bless The Lord, who Hath Brought me here, and Hath Made mee to Triumph over Devills and Men and Sinn. These Shall never trouble mee Anie more. I Forgive all Men the wrong thaie Have done to mee. I praie That God's Suffering Flock maie bee keepit from Sinn and Helpit to know What is Thair Dewtie."

'I hope I will never forgett the Words. When Master James said them to us, He lookit just like a Brave young Soldier, Sae firm and undismaied, albeit gentle too.

'Master Renwick did not Behold the Verie End of the terrible Sight, For he hadd to turn awaie when the dear Old Sanct his face began to goe into convulsions with the rope about his neck Beeing tight pulled, and him hanging till it upp in the Aire, and the Drums and Trumpetts causing a continuall Din, for fear He might groan aloud and the folk be scaured.

'Master Renwick was present in the crowd bye accident, and then could not win out; But he turned Sick at Heart, and had to Shutt his eyes, as verie Likelie He would have Fallen down Dead on the Spott. It behove to have been terrible to Witness. But Master Renwick said to Mee and Auntie, "That Sight fixed mye vocation. The Lord Help mee toe worthilie take upp His servant's cloak." Sae now, indeed, He is toe bee a Minister; albeit, afore that afternoon, in the Grass Market, He was in hesitancie atween that and beeing a Doctor. Hee is now going to Holland, because inn this wicked Scotland Hee cannot pass at the College, not beeing an idol-worshipping Papisher.

'I will never forgett this Daie, whilk to mee is like the Beginning of a different Life. Lord! Help mee, like Master James, to abide in His Vestibulle.

'It is now Midnight, and Everie Bodie is in thaire Bedds. It is the latest I ever was out of mine, But nigh as clear as Daie, and the Skie Blewish, Purplish, Silver-colored, Like Master Renwick's Eyes, when he speaks Earnestlie and Sweet.'

While scanning the few remaining written pages of her Diurnall, Marjorie's demeanour twice indicated a little excitement. *Ex gr.* On perusing one particular entry she shrugged her shoulders, curled her upper lip, and tossed her pretty head, as who should say, 'The idea of such impertinence!' At entry No. 2 of the apparently extra-sensational series, an expression of fear and horror flitted over her face, and she hurriedly turned the leaf. Both demonstrations were, in point of fact, referable to Laird Baigrie—the occasions being those of her first introduction to that individual and his spilling the communion cup at Talla conventicle.

After ruminating for a few minutes Marjorie took up her pen, and used it industriously during a good half-hour; for, as I before mentioned, girls of that period were not in the practice of scrawling their experiences at the telegraphic rate in which, now-a-days, they tear along the virgin page.

Our heroine's present performance was, so to speak, a compendium of 'last week's providences,' and the prospective changes impending in her usually uneventful life.

Before quoting from this summary, I may mention that between the period of Renwick's return from his six months' collegiate course in Holland, and the memorable Talla Glen conventicle, she had only met him once, viz., when in hurried and secret transit from one local Zion to another he had made a detour, for the express purpose of visiting Greendykes. 'Just a gliff an' awa',' Mrs. Elspet epitomized his stay of exactly one hour and a quarter.

Ay! but short though the pleasure was, it had not been enjoyed without trembling; for by that time persecution had waxed so hot in Scotland that no true-blue Presbyterian durst worship God after the mode prescribed by his conscience, and gospel ministers were peeled and scattered and frayed, till verily it seemed as if Elijah's days were come back again.

In these circumstances it was that the 'United Societies' wrote to Holland an entreaty to that 'most talented, learned, and godly youth,' Master James Renwick, praying that he would return home to bear up the banner of the Covenants, 'whilk, for lack of fitting hands to support it,' was like to fall to the ground and be trodden under foot.

And right willingly did the golden-haired youth of twenty respond to this invitation, hieing gladly back to his fatherland and his Master's work there.

His subsequent labours are matter of history, as are likewise his wonderful gifts of intellect. These enabled him, at an age very little past boyhood, to act as foreign secretary to the persecuted churches, besides being trusty counsellor and pastor to many strong-minded men who were hoar-headed before he was fit even to toddle at his mother's apron-string.

On the occasion of that flying visit to Greendykes, Renwick found Marjorie so improved every way that he fell in love with her from a new stand-point—this *second* attachment being, as it were, superinduced upon his original calf-love. In fact, since their last meeting both the young people were considerably altered. *He* had become a remarkably deep-thinking, wide-viewed man ; *she* a large-hearted, noble woman, one who, on fit occasion, could sink self, ay, and even true love, for the sake of high principle.

As I stated, Renwick was enraptured with Marjorie; but with such a load of responsibilities lying on him, penniless and outlawed, he felt that to utter one syllable concerning his affection would, in the circumstances, be selfish folly on his part, and cruelty to her. So he went his way, poor fellow, sorely downcast at first, despite the elastic hopefulness that usually buoyed him up in dark waters.

This melancholy frame of mind did not, however, last long, for, after all, was he not standing in that 'vestibule' whereof he had spoken to Marjorie? Therefore, ere many hours had fled, he said in his soul, 'All is well ordered,' and steadfastly faced the clouded future with calm cheerfulness.

On this afternoon, when Marjorie has been taking a bird's-eye view, as it were, of her Diurnall, her subsequent entries therein were, I must confess, slightly illogical and inflated in style.

'All of a Suddentie, Last Saturdaie, when Master Renwick was here, Auntie Bad mee convey Him upp out on the Sclates, to lett him see the prospect, especially the bit[1] called Talla Glen, where the Sacrament was to be holden the next morning. Mye Auntie went meanwhile down to the kitchen, in order to teach Bettie how to Stuff a Soland goose. Soe Master James and Mee was left bye ourselves.

'Arrived out on the Sclates, Wee stood a long time unco

[1] The spot.

quiet, because the prospect was most Bewtifull, with the Blew Skie and the Curlie Clouds that looked as if made of pearl-smoke. Then there was the Silent green mountains and the Wee bits of Lambies, that, from the high Place where Wee were Standing, looked just like Little Balls of White Floss Silk.'

When the damsel got thus far in her description, her heart —albeit she was alone in her chamber—began to beat violently, and her hand trembled so it could hardly guide the pen. In truth, the execution of the following lines was most imperfect, in an artistic point of view.

'Wee Lookit at the Farr-awaie Hills, and the Clouds, and the Lambies, and Syne Master Renwick turned round and faced mee, and then—How it came about I know not—Wee promised oursels to each other. O God! I thank thee.'

By-and-by, in a firmer hand, comes this entry :—

'And now wee are about flitting into Edinburgh town, and dear Auntie is a riche Wooman. I hope thatt I am willing to goe wherever the Lord Sees fitt to Lead mee. But Here, at Greendykes, I have had Some Daies thatt were nigh ower Happie for *this* Worlde; and alsoe I will miss the bonnie Flowers growing upon the House-Front. Out-bye in the fields, Likewise, it is Fine and quiet for Taking a slow saunter, and meditating at Even-Tide, Like Isaac of Old. Butt, as James Renwick Saies, "Onie Place Can, by God's Smile, Become the Verie Vestibulle of Heaven."'

CHAPTER VI.

'Turning around
The apple of life that "another" hath found,
It is warm to *our* touch, not with sun of the south,
And we count, as *we* turn it, the red side of four,
  O Life! O Beyond!
Thou art sweet. Thou art strange evermore.'

S was already mentioned, the deceased Madame Rougemont's lawyer entreated that lady's legatee would, if possible, repair to Edinburgh within three weeks at furthest, and Mrs. Elspet, by means of Marjorie's pen, signified her assent. But ere the missive containing the said assent was an hour on its journey towards the metropolis, the inditer thereof began to regret having timed her future movements so specifically. In fact, even while Renwick's betrothed, in the seclusion of her ornate closet, was taking, so to speak, a bird's-eye view of her personal experiences, as inscribed in her 'Diurnall,' the old lady, seated at the open window of her own room, had gradually ceased to click her knitting-needles, and gone on

thinking and thinking until the hallelujah spirit wherewith her meditations commenced well-nigh evaporated.

'Tuts! tuts!' (thus ran her cogitations) 'it's perfect madness to expect we can be ready in ane-and-twenty days. I am astonished how that lawyer body could hint sic nonsense. There's our claes to be sortit, and the winter's butter pickled. There's the swine to be hammed, forbye a tubfu' o' geese to be sautit. . . . And then Marjorie's hood'll need a new lining, and my "bon-grace" is owre shabby for wearing in a city; I'll have to get anither. A body behoves to gang decently raimented among strangers. We'll need to put on mournings of course. . . . And, losh me! I was forgetting Wattie's shirts and stockings. How, at this time o' year, when the sun has sae little strength, they are to be wishen and dried in sic a hurry, passes my comprehension. . . . And forbye, if, as this writer body says, he can procure us a tenant for this house, it maun be scoured frae tap to bottom, for my ain credit. . . . Then, whilk o' the servants to part wi' and whilk to tak to Edinburgh, I know not. . . . Really I wish Marjorie would tell me what to do.'

But after all, poor human nature is only poor human nature, and albeit Mistress Elspet was not exactly insincere in this last wish, I doubt whether, while her 'kingdom' was so new, and (despite its attendant worries) so gratifying a fact, either Marjorie's or any *other* body's orders would have been received as gratefully as heretofore. However, the spinster's capacity for carrying a full cup without spilling was not destined to be tested at present. To most of us a supreme life-holiday comes once, and only once. By a sort of noble instinct that young girl, in the fringe-bedecked bed-closet, felt that over her aunt as well as herself such a day of days was passing even then, and that the elder woman's came dimmed by a sense of disappointment. Beautiful in its unsmirched bloom, the fragrance of her own young love seemed to surround her with an aromatic atmosphere that must needs accompany all her goings, rendering her blessed and bliss-bestowing. But dear Auntie Eppie's great festival, what a poor thing it was, lacking another self to enrich *its* present, and brighten *its* to-morrow. From the midst of her clear-shining personal Goshen Marjorie gazed with immense compassion at the solitary old maid standing outside in chill darkness. Therefore she straightway resolved that if by any effort of hers Mistress Elspet's 'red-letter day' could be rendered satisfactory, it should so be. Albeit it was impossible to signalize the occasion by crowning the old lady queen of any human heart, might she not be made to experience (just for once) the delight of feeling herself, as it were, 'Queen of the May.' So, when the two females got together again, and set about arranging their flitting from Greendykes, the younger did her spiriting so wisely that her aunt ended by considering herself, after all, one of the favoured among women.

Time ran on, and there was no end of commotion in Greendykes. The specified three weeks had been over-filled with work, but now everything was ready. In bringing about this state of matters, Marjorie had the chief hand. For one does not get out of a groove all at once, and Mistress Elspet's supremacy as a rich woman once fairly accredited, she had been only too glad to subside into her position of second-fiddle player. As I said, the woman was gentle-natured, and of a clinging disposition. Woe is me! that to short-sighted humanity an ungainly exterior should render these amenities of scarcely any effect!

But this is by-the-bye.

The family transit to town was accomplished by means of nine horses, whereof four carried severally a male, with a female riding pillion behind him. On the dapple-grey Mistress Elspet rode in rear of her nephew Wattie, whose waist she clasped tightly, and who held the reins. Marjorie, who looked quite 'killing' in her freshly-lined hood, mounted the bay mare, and held on by the sturdy person of auld Willie, the Greendyke serving-man. A couple of inferior steeds bore Nancy and Betsy, both women-servants, and Habbie and Japheth, out-door workers—these last acting as escort, but bound to return to Peeblesshire after seeing the mistress safely to her destination. In rear of these four quadrupeds thudded five ill-groomed, heavy-footed animals, laden with country produce, and no end of packages and bundles belonging to the women in advance. The exodus was not effected without tears, shed chiefly, however, by the stay-at-home portion of the company. Again, and yet again, did Mistress Elspet and her niece gaze back and up at the rows of tiny windows with heart-throbs that arose partly from regret, and partly from wonder, and then launched out valiantly on the (to them) wide wide world which lay outside Tweedsmuir. Albeit the distance to be traversed was but thirty miles, the party slept two nights on the journey, and it was nigh sun-down of the third day before they entered the West Port of Edinburgh. During the last mile or two, Mistress Elspet and her niece had, from sheer fatigue, occasionally lapsed into surreptitious little sleeps. (This, however, did not upset their equilibrium, thanks to the stout leathern belt, whereby each lady was firmly buckled to her male escort). It was therefore with a start that, awaking from one of these short drowses, Marjorie once again found herself in the old city where she and Renwick had first become acquainted. Perhaps it was the damsel's own noticeable countenance, perhaps the decidedly rustic air of the whole Greendyke's cavalcade, which attracted so many glances to the little party as they heavily footed their way across the Grassmarket, and up the narrow, tortuous, steep, fashionable 'Bow.' At any rate, the two ladies felt rather uncomfortably observed, as was natural after being so long accustomed to the solitude of Tweedsmuir. At first, in the innocence of her heart, Mistress Elspet was half inclined to think that the news of her good fortune had got wind, and that in consequence she was now being ovated by a discriminating public. 'It's awfu' to see how folk actually worship mammon,' soliloquized the simple old body, with a pleasant little mental protest—'It's really awfu'!' But her rather gratifying supposition dissolved, as the string of nine wearied horses was led up the Bow. For, surely it was not possible, after all, that this crowd of people, walking in the same direction as herself and party, could have turned out solely for the purpose of seeing the late Madame Rougemont's heiress. Near the head of the ascent, exactly where the wooden-fronted dwellings were tallest and most grotesque in many-gabled architecture, at that precise point where the Bow opens into the High Street, the number of persons became such that a new idea struck the excited spinster. Were all these people assembling for a riot? O horror!—and a street riot too! Mayhap a Papish demonstration was being got up, and Marjorie, Wee Wattie and herself (being true-blue Presbyterians) might very likely be slain within a few minutes. (For you must understand that at *that* time 'big frays' were alarming things, and anybody inadvertently sucked into one might suddenly be called upon to render account of his religion and politics.) So, in a quake of fearfulness, the old lady, with Wee Wattie, as a shield of defence, steered the dapple grey, though with difficulty, through the living masses which blocked up the Bow-head from side to side. When the Greendykes folks arrived, however, at the point of junction between the Bow and the wider High Street, the cause of the great gathering became visible.

On a raised wooden stage stood a tall, stout, jolly-looking man, dressed in a fine scarlet long-tailed coat, richly ornamented with gold-lace. The powdered curls of his full-bottomed wig fell over his shoulders so as nearly to hide a falling neck-band of 'Flanders point,' of which material his wrist ruffles were also formed. White silk breeches, finished at the knee with full lace frills, scarlet stockings ornamented with gold clocks and brilliant shoe-buckles, completed his attire. Near him was a younger individual in black velvet and pink, silver-clocked stockings, and at the back of the stage appeared a tight-rope stretched betwixt a couple of poles, prepared for dancing. 'The Universallie Renowned Doktor Murdok' (so a little green flag, floating at either end of the stage, styled its scarlet-coated proprietor) was engaged, when Marjorie first sighted him, in describing the merits of his medicaments, and advising 'the sick' to approach the 'fountain of health' and get cured then and there.

During this exordium, the assistant executed a variety of dancing 'steps' to the sound of a flute played by himself. Presently, however, he laid aside his instrument, and with the 'Doktor's' assistance began doling from a hamper phials and pill-boxes. The rush to obtain these quasi-infallible nostrums became fearful, so much so that the four posts whereon the stage was erected threatened to give way.

The unsophisticated rustics from Tweedsmuir sat, meanwhile, with their mouths agape, their steeds so fast jammed in the crowd that scientific horsemanship would (even if they had possessed it) have been an impossibility. However, Auld Willie (late the Greendykes factotum) having a fixed idea that town's-folks were really *all* thieves and vagabonds, kept such a bright look-out after the baggage and sumpter horses that he let drop the reins of his own steed. Thereupon that animal began to rear in alarming fashion and a regular commotion ensued. The scared horse nearly knocked over an old beggar-wife, and her yells so frightened Marjorie that she (not seeing the *origo male*, because of the *ci-devant* butler's broad back) commenced screaming likewise. Thereupon, in a perfect frenzy of puzzlement, did the aforesaid Willie 'speak unadvisedly with his lips' to the surrounders at large. They, nothing loth, straightway took up the burden of his maledictions, and, of course, confusion became more confounded, while, glutting the narrow high-housed street, the crowd swayed, and heaved, and shoved, and swore. Jammed in its midst, the nine clumsily-limbed Greendykes horses became terrified, and neighed as if bewitched. The scarlet-coated doctor bawled loudly and yet more loudly the praises of his drugs; whilst his velvet-attired 'aide,' observing that the advance of customers was impeded, mounted the tight-rope and amused them with an aërial *pas seul* by way of advertisement.

At this juncture some miscreant in the crowd cut the leathern strap whereby Marjorie was secured unto the ponderous waist of Auld Willie, and at the same moment somebody (possibly the self-same evildoer) pricked the dapple-grey on its left flank. Thereupon the beast plunged so suddenly and violently as to hoist the quondam butler from the saddle to its neck, and cause the damsel seated *en croupe* to lose her balance and slip to the ground. To the day of her death Marjorie was never certain whether, whilst lying prone amidst uneasy feet, she had fainted or not. Her first distinct recollection was of being firmly lifted in strong arms and borne away out of the suffocating squeeze; of being carried first through a brief space of fresh air, and then into some sort of apartment where, being laid down, she opened her eyes. To see a tall, stout, 'hashy-looking,' big-featured man in spectacles and black clothes standing beside her, with an air of good-humoured perplexity, as if thoroughly nonplussed by the situation altogether.

'Oh! sir,' exclaimed she, 'where are Auntie and Wee Wattie, please?'

'Thank Jupiter, madam, that you are yourself again,' was the reply. 'Just wait a second, will you, till I communicate with them? My name is Hepburn. I'll be back in a minute,' with which assurance away he rushed.

Whilst he is elbowing his way towards the dapple-grey (neither of whose riders, by-the-bye, had observed their kinswoman's disappearance), allow me to introduce him as the late Madame Rougemont's lawyer, and the writer of that very letter which had incited the Greendykes family to migrate to Edinburgh. As regards Mr. Hepburn's personal appearance, fancy a tall, stout, black-a-vised individual, whose clothes of chocolate-coloured cloth seemed as if thrown on with a pitchfork. These items, if conjoined with tortoise-shell spectacles and a head-covering somewhat like a velvet reticule worn upside down, represent the outward man of Marjorie's preserver.

No Adonis certainly! But speak for a few minutes to him, and the awkward, impulsive kindliness of his manner makes you somehow feel as if you had known and rather liked him for ever so long. Some such notion flitted across Marjorie's imagination, when, on this her first afternoon in town, he left her alone in the dim ground-floor apartment whither he had carried her.

Yes, despite Mr. Hepburn's rough-hewn build and unconventional demeanour, there was certainly something likeable, albeit pity-inspiring, about him. Hitherto his lot had not been over happy, he being the son of a well-born 'ne'er-do-well,' who first ran through his patrimony and then tried to 'hark back' by espousing a fortune with an evil-tempered lady attached thereto. Husband and wife started in matrimony by quarrelling outrageously, but finding in due season that a reverse line of conduct would pay better in society, they conjointly got up an immense profession of super-sanctity, agreeing like Ananias and his spouse in mutual fraud, although in no other matter. Fancy the effect of this hypocrisy upon their only child George, a boy to whom the entertainment of reverential love seemed the instinctive necessity it is to some dispositions. Imagine the cruel wrong done to the boy's natural religiousness, the blighting of his upward proclivities.

When he was about fifteen both parents died within a month of one another (the mother first). It then turned out that the youth, reared in extravagant discomfort, was left nearly penniless. Poor fellow, his future loomed dark enough, but Providence proved kind. First one benevolent individual and then another gave him a hoist, so to speak, till in course of time he was fairly started as a legal practitioner *en route* to the bar, albeit not likely to reach that professional altitude in a hurry. For, be it known, in those days law-agency was entirely transacted by advocates' clerks, who trusted by-and-by (and on payment of a considerable fee) to emerge from their condition of inferiority and become brother barristers of their present masters.

George Hepburn, however, having neither funds nor ambition for such a rise, was still, in his thirty-ninth year, only a 'writer.' A gentleman in some of his aspirations. Sloughy in sundry of his tastes, possibly, as regarded these last, none the better for the general custom of transacting all business arrangements in a tavern, and there drinking affairs *in* as well as *out*.

Thanks to parental shortcomings, Mr. Hepburn had no beautiful childhood to remember, neither, since the break-up of his home, had he come in contact with much, if any, social sanctity. Nevertheless, even when lying as it were among the sooty pots, he was ever and anon visited by a wish that his wings were silver and his feathers yellow gold.

Surely, surely these were but vain breathings! when in their intervals he was perfectly happy hob-nobbing with drunken cronies in a change-house. Yet (how strange is human nature in its twists), the morning after some extra deep potation, or mayhap when the soft west wind fluffed about his hair and fanned his brow of a summer's afternoon, the longing after a wholesomer style of existence would return, and deep down in his soul would be murmured this plaintive wish, 'Oh that I had wings like a dove, then would I fly away and be at rest.' Then occasionally (not very often, but sometimes) his vague yearnings would assume a definite shape, *ex. gr.*, 'Would that some girl, lovely, talented, companionable, and pure, could drift within my *ken!* She would, I am certain, make a new and better man of me.'

Poor fellow, nobody had taught him 'the truth,' and hence, in his spiritual conceptions, he was as nearly as possible a downright pagan. Not knowing God *as* God, he waxed vain in his imaginations. But, under similar conditions, who does not?

Thus his life had run on in grossness spotted with star-dust until this October day, when, standing on the forestairs of his lodging, he descried Marjorie Ker *in* (or more correctly I should say mounted on horseback *above*) the crowd.

Ah, that angelic countenance!—its sweet intellectuality—its supreme restfulness. Gazing thereat, how Mr. Hepburn did loathe all his unvirtuous past, with its wine-bibbery and slip-shod morality. Marjorie's beauty resurrected then and there those slender spiritual affinities which the unfaithfulness of his own parents had slaughtered in George Hepburn's soul. His face flushed, his chest heaved, as if at long-last the moment for accomplishing some anticipated feat had arrived.

Could it actually be possible that that peerless damsel, seated on a pillion in rear of an old peasant-looking man, was the 'veritable she' ordained to lift him out of what at the moment he mentally called his stye?

(Understand that, at once recognising in the Greendykes party his expected clients, he knew of course that he should in all probability be soon brought personally acquainted with the young lady.)

As he was pondering, the mischievous person of whom mention has already been made pricked Marjorie's horse, she slid off her pillion, and the next minute was carried in

Hepburn's strong arms to the first accessible room of the house where he lodged.

Within a fortnight after their arrival in Covenant Close, the Kers were so snugly domiciled that the old Greendykes experiences seemed a hundred years off.

Mistress Elspet liked the change vastly, and, sundry of her quondam neighbours being still extant, she found the days too short for the consequent 'talking parties' whereat she behoved to assist. These wordy sederunts, however, very soon began to bore Marjorie a good deal, and albeit, out of amiability towards her aunt, she was often present at them in body, her spirit would the while be retrospecting 'dear, wild Tweedsmuir,' where she used to roam in maiden meditation fancy free. Sooth to say, since settling in Edinburgh, the girl scarcely knew herself. Formerly, with a child's love of sights and bustle, she remembered thinking 'Auld Reekie' perfectly delightful, and the old ladies who used to pet and give her honey-pieces very charming persons indeed. But now these same female denizens of the close appeared intolerable, albeit poor bodies they were every one, as kind and talkative as old women could possibly be. But they were always there, always (that was the nuisance) within hail, morning, noon, and night.

The close was so narrow that people living on either side used to lend and hand their soup-ladles to each other from their respective windows. And then, among its well-packed inhabitants, there were so many gossipy old maids and 'clish-ma-clavery'[1] widows, that Marjorie waxed positively nervous from feeling that her uprisings and downsittings were all being done under the inspection of a dozen or so pairs of remarkably gleg[2] eyes. But worse than this, in the dear old solitude, where there were few occurrences to divert imagination, she had gone on idealizing Renwick till he ramified in a vague sort of way through and through every hour of her daily life. But here, amid this continual chatter, and infinitesimal racketing, the sentimentally intensified love-links, that used to feel as strong as steel, seemed growing weaker day by day.

In her heart of hearts the girl loved her betrothed deeply, with an affection which (as she often assured herself) 'she could ask the Lord's blessing upon;' and yet here was this now ever-present sensation, that his image no longer formed part and parcel of her existence. This distressed her unspeakably, poor child, for she was but seventeen, and, albeit thoughtful and wise for her years, not sufficiently learned in psychology to understand that fancy alone was in fault. That in the wearing distraction of so much company, which was not companionship, imagination refused to revel as heretofore on Renwick's perfections as its sole diet. That was all; but albeit, when stated in black and white, the case may appear frivolous, to the damsel herself it felt sadly serious, and she was, as it were, oppressed with the weight of the

---

[1] Scandal-mongering. [2] Sharp-sighted.

inexplicable cloud which seemed to have dropped betwixt her and the person she loved best on earth. For, bear in mind, she had never heard from her betrothed since the day of the Talla Glen conventicle.

In those times there were no penny posts, and letters were literally events. Moreover, a wanderer with a price set on his head, be he ever so fond of his intended wife, would, for her sake as well as his own, be chary of intrusting the transmission of his love-letters to any chance-body's hands. So not even having a scrape of her lover's pen to tangiblize her present mistiness, you can easily see that the damsel's state of mind was painful, and to her a great trial. Quite as great and faith-requiring, indeed, as some calamities that bulk more grimly solid.

Mayhap the Lord, who suits His teachings to our special individuality, had some particular lesson to instil into her heart thereby. He has many ways of making us feel our entire dependence on Him, and always (with reverence be it said) 'cuts the coat according to the size of the cloth.'

Mrs. Elspet's niece was a sincerely God-fearing young woman. But youth is ever more or less gushing, and here was she, stranded, so to speak, in a colony of chattery, ancient, 'limited' dames, to none of whom, not even to dear auntie herself, could she greatly effervesce.

However, in the long-run, even this discomfort wrought for the maiden's good, by leading her to more full outpourings at the Divine footstool. It likewise was one reason why she took to writing a great deal in her 'Diurnall,' in order that afterwards she might, on reading the record of her present disquiet, see, as in a mirror, God's providential dealings displayed. Indeed, but for this very 'Diurnall,' we should not so well know to-day what 'sweet seventeen' thought and did nigh a couple of hundred years ago.

The book is now, as you may see from the facsimile of the title-page, darkly orange in the tint of its paper, and faintly pale as regards its ink, but the words are so legible still, with very few exceptions, that we can easily make extracts. The first is dated November the twenty-second, somewhat more than a month after her arrival in town.

'I have been soe verie Busie since wee came here, that till this Daie I have not wrott in this Book. But now I will doe it regular once everie Week.

'I beginn bye praising God for our Safe Journie hither, and for the Health he hath given to Auntie and Wattie and Mee. Dear Auntie is verie Happie, alwaies going to the lodgings of old friends, and thaie also come here for a continual. I, for mye part, am beste pleased when thaie come Here, for then I just sitt on the Window Seat and think to myselff. I need not to speak, for when Three or Four of them gets together and Set-to about their old Ditties, They all speak at once, or at anie rate Trie thair hand at that. When Auntie and I goe to visit att thair Houses, thaie think that Because I am the Youngest in the Companie, it behoves them, for the Sake of Politeness, to make mee Speak some, But I would farr rather not.

'Our House has six chambers, verie well furnished indeed, but the whole Half Dozen might be putt into our Dining Room at Greendykes—So Small are thaie. Indeed, the Withdrawing Room and the Ante-Chamber are so trimmed upp with French Fal-lals and Flummery, that thaie mind mee of Two Filagree Snuff-Boxes. The Funniest place is the Dead-chamber, whilk is painted Black, and for sole plenishing has a black-painted table on trestles, standing in the midst of Six Large Brass Candlesticks.

'Madame Rougemont's forebears were French papists, and shee keepit upp thair Customs, and Lay in State within the Dead Chamber when shee was a Corpse. Inn Her Will it saies that Auntie behoves to maintain this chamber as it stands, or else lose the Heritage, whilk is verie great—Farr more, three Times told, than wee expected at the First.

'Mistress Betty Grieve, that lives right opposite us here, has wormed out of Auntie that I am troth-plighted unto James Renwick, and is for ever joking mee about it, whilk is verie discomfortable; not that at Greendykes I would have minded, but somewaie, since Wee came to Edinburgh, I cannot feel that hee is all in all to mee, as I used to doe afore I was promised to be married. And yet I am sure I can lay one hand on mye heart and the other on the Bible, and sweare that I like him more than any other person alive. I wish hee could come, Even for one Hour. But that maie not bee. Where Hee is I know not; maybee in great Danger From wicked men. I wonder I can keep off mye knees about him; and whiles it makes mee most sad to think that I am easier-minded concerning his dangers since he is engaged to mee, than I used to bee when I never thocht it possible hee could fall in love with mee. . . . Oh! I doe wish he would come!

'*December the Ninth.*—Among all the acquaintance wee have, I incline most to Mr. Hepburn, the Writer; albeit hee is farr from Prettie, Being soe Dark in the complexion and mightie untidy his apparel. But yet I think I could, if need arose, confide matters unto Him that I would never dream of telling even to Auntie herself, because shee, the old Dear, could not quite understande what I mean. Also hee is an Elderly man, but has given mee such good-heartening concerning James, that I beginn again to think about him as often and as lovinglie as I used to doe at Tweedsmuir. For this, praised be God, in the first instance.

'Wattie is quite healthie now, and this day has gone to the Latin, but I doe not think he will learn much, For even when James Renwick taught him He never cared for Books or the pen.

'*December the Twenty-Fifth, being Christmas Daie.*—The snow has been soe heavie the last Week, that our Close is nigh knee-deep, and going out verie difficult. The weather is cold and the Aire thick, with Flakes as big as chickens' breast-Feathers; but for all that, it is to mee a Most merrie Christmas, as the Papists Saie, for have I not gotten a letter from James, and is nott Hee the greatest, and godliest, and Handsomest of men?

'After Breakfast, I was in the Kitchen starching Auntie's best paire of Pinners, and aye as I clappit them between mye hands, I praied inwardlie that I might soon gett tidings of him; that is, God permitting, to bee mye Earthlie Head and Husbande. The firste making of starche was not nigh yellow enough, soe I made a second cupp-full, and was just dipping the Pinners into it when there Came a Tirl at the Door-Pin.

'"Is Mistress Marjorie withinn?" I heard Mr. Hepburn asking at Betsy. "I've brocht her something she'll thank mee for."

'Soe with that Ben I ran, with mye hands all stickie and yellow, to the Ante-room, and there was Hee, holding out a letter from James Renwick to mee, and smiling his face into real Beautifulness whilst it lasted, like a sun-glint on a stormy Daie.

'"Now, mye Dear Lassie," saies Hee, "Was not I right to bid you keep upp a good Heart, and that news would soon come from your intended? His letter has come bye a verie round-about course, and to mye hand through accidente. Itt wente first to Greendykes. I wish ye joie with all mie Herte."

'With that He went awaie, but a melancholie look fell on his countenance that minded mee of the Black Frost that nipped our Bonnie Apple-blooms last spring-time. I remember how sorrie I felt for the Tender pink and White Flowers lying shrunken and withered.'

CHAPTER VII.

'Drawn away of his own lust, and enticed.'—EPISTLE OF JAMES.

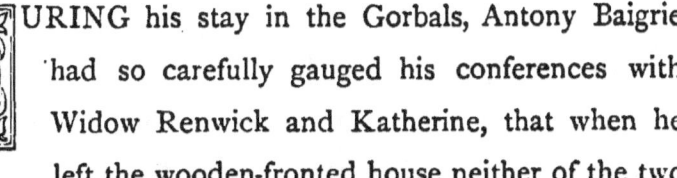URING his stay in the Gorbals, Antony Baigrie had so carefully gauged his conferences with Widow Renwick and Katherine, that when he left the wooden-fronted house neither of the two women had any fixed idea as to where he purposed conveying the baby orphan and her belongings. Indeed, beyond their more immediate bestowal, he himself had no specific plans, perhaps did not wish to have any just then. He had of late meditated day and night on the large quantity of golden pieces left to his charge by Angus Gordon, and considered (just by way of amusement) how, had they been his very own, he could have most profitably invested them, till he sometimes well-nigh forgot that these mental exercises were purely fanciful. They, as it were, floated double, like swan and shadow on a lake so calm, that fact and unreal counterpart were inseparable. The pretty, young dying widow too had inadvertently assisted in rendering hazy the boundary line

betwixt his mental *meum* and *teum*, by insisting that his trusteeship was a perfect godsend to her infant. Now, poor Dorettle was in her new-made grave, and here was the said curator jogging towards Edinburgh with the baby-heiress in his arms, and her golden money and other gear packed upon the three stout mules in rear.

It is noticeable how, sometimes, all of a sudden, events swim in great shoals into the hitherto fishless sea of some people's lives. One short month ago Laird Baigrie had no other expectation than to plod through his threescore-and-ten at Halket, with maybe an occasional field-preaching, or persecutorial looking-up by way of variety. Now, padding along in the direction of Edinburgh (for the road scarcely merited the name), his heart was so lifted up in proud amazement at the power of wealth which had drifted into his absolute control, that he really almost forgot how limited had been his aspirations four weeks back. The road between the city he had quitted and that to which he was bound was long and uninteresting, but all the more concentrated grew his calculations of merks and guineas. By-and-by baby Letty began to weep with a drawn whimpering cry that put him out of patience, by breaking the thread of a lovely mental web he was weaving, all patterned over with the Halket lands, extending ever so far beyond their present bounds. As a work of art this dream-fabric was nearly perfect, when Letty, by obtruding so noisily on the worker's consciousness the fact of her existence, tore a rent in his exquisite mammon-cloth, so he made her over, shawls, squallings, and all, to the least stolid member of his small retinue, and forthwith returned to his ruptured labour of love. By the time the cortege reached the metropolis (which was three days after starting), its principal had visioned himself into considering the little girl's existence as neither more nor less than a cross laid on his personal back for portage. Such a tiresome atom of humanity, to be keeping him out of the wealth that would be his without let or hindrance, were she but safely landed where the good babies go. But, after all, it was ten to one she would never grow up to woman's estate. Children often died quite young. Would it not be foolish to calculate upon the contingency of her surviving the many diseases to which childhood is liable? better act at present in view of the great probability that he should heir Letty, and, after all, legally enter into possession of the gold he could so delightfully and profitably invest in purchasing lands, once part of Halket, though now of Halket no longer. 'Decidedly better,' cried greed, giving a hit to the Laird's special spirituals. 'Decidedly better, and by far the most common-sense manner of procedure. So thereupon did Antony make up his mind to board Angus Gordon's infant-heiress (in the meantime) with a far-away and not very well-off cousin of his mother, Mistress Fairlie by name, and resident on the Castle Hill. Although a mere boy when he last saw her, he knew by report that she was still alive; moreover, he recollected once hearing his father laud her as being the meekest woman betwixt Halket and John-o'-Groats. By the time Edinburgh Castle and its foundation-rock hove in sight of our travellers, the mental eyes of one of them saw the baby-heiress (albeit the horse which carried her was half a hundred yards in rear of his own) safely settled under the matronly care of Mistress Fairlie (at a moderate rate of payment), and himself (backed by recent augmentation of his patrimonial acres) at Greendykes, a suitor for Marjorie's hand. For wherefore (even as matters stood) should he not lay out the little orphan's money upon land? And, if so (seeing that in case of her decease he would succeed to her earthly leavings), why not on the Halket estate as well as on any other? It would give him more importance in Marjorie's eyes, save trouble should the child die, and meanwhile do her not the slightest wrong.

In Antony's cogitations Katherine Renwick also figured extensively, for the very good reason that her promised aid towards bringing about the severance of her cousin from his affianced wife was, so to speak, a necessary *rung* of the grand ladder whereby he purposed mounting to happiness. 'I was so civil to her,' thought he, 'she'll do what in her lies to further my wishes; besides, she's actually daft with love for Renwick, and mad with jealousy of Marjorie, which is providential for me in the circumstances. Ha! ha! he! he! It's a mercy I thought of telling her about their engagement.

She would willingly kill Marjorie if she could, for a prouder-stomached young woman I never beheld. My speaking so friendly-like pleased her vastly, I could see that, and as our interests agree, I'm sure she'll stretch a point to help me.'

Oh, mole-eyed Laird of Halket! With all his fancied powers of circumvention, he had sadly mistaken the gauge of that incarnation of impetuous self-will, persistent ambition, and snaky cunning called Katherine Renwick.

At the very moment when he, on the road to Edinburgh, was, as it were, licking his thin lips over the 'nice little job' he imagined her ready to undertake for his behoof, she, in the Gorbals, was frightening her aunt and Cousin James by what the former called screeching fits, and the latter a nervous attack.

The emotional display came to pass in this wise. Aunt and niece were sitting, about five in the afternoon, at their supper of sowens and kirn-milk,[1] and, as usual, conversing about the young preacher, when a low knock at the door announced his unexpected arrival on his way to Ayrshire. He had had a run for his life the preceding evening, and the few hours he dared now remain might be the last for many a long day. So, partly with the view of showing his mother 'one bright bit' in the harassing life which caused her such constant anxiety, he mentioned his engagement to Marjorie.

A proud woman was Mistress Renwick at the notion of a 'son o' hers mating wi' real gentry;' but the intimation

[1] Butter-milk.

burned Katherine's very soul into the white heat of despair and sick rage. Generally the girl had herself so well in hand that she could conceal emotion, but in the present instance the fall from her air-castle was too complete for any strong-minded attempt at hiding broken bones. Therefore, as I said, she treated her two distressed relatives to a violent sensational display, wherein, to Renwick's sorrowful amazement, he learned for the first time the wild attachment of one whom he regarded as a sister, and a sister only. He behoved to quit Glasgow ere daybreak, but, short as his stay at home was, before it concluded his cousin was herself again, mentally and physically.

Seeing plainly that there was not a chance of recapturing the young divine, she boldly determined that at least she would not be pitied by either the neighbours or anybody else as his 'leavings.' So, almost before her aunt had ceased laving her brow with cold water, and fumigating her with burnt feathers, she resolved to marry old Dr. Fairlie, and thus get first off.

(Be it understood, in passing, that the family medical attendant had for long shown great admiration of Katherine, and been laughed at by the damsel as 'an auld gowk.'[1] Barring his sixty-five years, however, there was no conventional objection to the marriage, the profession of doctor not being at that period a very elevated one in Scotland.)

[1] An old goose.

It did not require much manœuvring to make the old man propose, and before noon of next day Katherine Renwick had agreed to become Mistress Fairlie with all convenient speed.

'If I gie mysel' time to ponder,' thought the bride-elect, 'I'll gang crazed. Since it seems love is no' to be my lot, I'll take guid care to be a leddie ony way. A doctor's widow will aye be considered a leddie. But happen what will, I'll no' be here and single next time James comes hame. I couldna thole anither time to hear him bletherin' about that Marjorie's beauty and godliness, and gudeness kens what all. If he spak' again in my hearin' as he did about her last night, it micht mak' me rin and drown mysel'. I could curse that lang-leggit idiot, Laird Halket, for blawin' a pack o' lees in my ear, and making me believe it was only a passing fancy they had for ane anither. O Jamie, Jamie! and me learning the Carritch[1] sae weel, thinking to be a minister's wife! and sma' hand o' write too!'

Thus it appears that while Antony was in the act of arranging the details of his young ward's board with Mistress Fairlie of the Castle Hill, Katherine was troth-plighting what represented her affections to old Dr. Fairlie of the Gorbals.

Had the Laird been aware of this, perhaps, by becoming less confident of winning Marjorie, he might have steered his life-course differently in some respects. Yet it is hard to tell, for there is a great deal of truth in an ancient 'saw' which

[1] Catechism.

Madge, his umquhile nurse, was wont oftentimes to din into his youthful ears :—

> 'Send your son to Ayr.
> If he do well here,
> He 'll do weel there.'

By a curious coincidence, the dwelling occupied by Mrs. Fairlie formed part of the property to which Mistress Elspet Ker had succeeded, and, till that lady's arrival in town, remained of course under the temporary supervision of Mr. Hepburn.

It being term-time, the writer behoved, for behoof of his new client, to uplift her rents, and in course of this duty chanced to call upon Mistress Fairlie whilst Antony was sitting in her tiny parlour higgling anent the very moderate sum demanded for Letty's board.

Before going on with this chronicle, however, I must state that Widow Fairlie, albeit, as the deceased Laird Halket used to say, 'meeker than Moses,' could, on fit occasion, sport her bit of vain-glory as well as anybody.

A weak, unvicious woman, her hobby was to pass as the possessor of tip-top relations and acquaintances. On these themes she was wont to descant till, warming with her subject, she would sometimes unwittingly so colour facts that the friends under discussion would have had some difficulty in recognising their own original selves in the widow's high-art efforts.

As, some five-and-twenty years before, her husband had left her in poorish circumstances, and as both relatives and acquaintances had then and since treated her to a good supply of cold shoulder, the manner in which she puffed them to each other argued either considerable Christian charity, or else a desire to gild her pinchbeck, and foist it off as precious metal. At any rate, when her cousin Antony actually called, and Mr. Hepburn met him under her roof, a right proud woman was she. The two men were duly introduced, and sat talking, till incidentally Laird Halket asked some question or other about money investments.

Mr. Hepburn, who was on his feet to go, answered freely, and then, having received the rent he had come to seek, took his leave, saying he should be very glad to do anything in his power to oblige Mrs. Fairlie's cousin.

Whilst accompanying the writer to the door a sudden impulse seized the hostess.

'Ye'll come back and eat a bittie supper wi' me an' my cousin?' said she. 'He's as rich as rich can be, and out o' pure charity is going to bring up a bit orphan lassie that was left on his hands by chance. He's to leave her wi' me in the meantime. He thinks she'll amuse me, as I was aye fond o' bairns. It's a grand thing, Mr. Hepburn, to have the love o' God in our hearts, and that's what Antony's family (and mine of course) always had.'

(*N.B.*—This last fling was owing to a conscientious desire

of pitching into her non-professing hearer, for his soul's sake.)

'Noo, ye'll come back at six, sir. Losh! wadna it be a gran' thing if ye could get haud o' my cousin as a client? It's really pleasant to see sic a wealthy young gentleman a perfect saint at the same time. Godliness is great gain, Mr. Hepburn.' (This quotation dictated by conscience in order to missionarize a man she could not help liking, and yet viewed as an outsider in the matter of saving grace.)

'Thanks to ye, ma'am, I'll be very glad to come. Good day till six o'clock.'

'And I'll invite yer friend bonnie Effie Grey to join us,' she bawled after him as he was half way down the turnpike stair. 'Ye'll thank me for asking Effie, or I'm cheatit.'

Now, be it known that the said Effie and her mother, who abode in the adjoining land, lived in a normal state of feud with Mistress Fairlie, because neither party would believe that the other's friends were high among the mighty ones of earth.

It now struck the widow that the present was a capital opportunity for showing off a real country cousin, and thus confound her opponents, whose only presentable family branch was 'a shabby creature o' a writer bodie' that held some small post in the Parliament House.

Effie Grey gladly accepted for supper, and, assisted by her mother, spent the intermediate hours in starching a pair of elbow-ruffles, and doing-up her pink silk saque and petticoat with canary-coloured ribbons, fringed and tipped with silver.

If so much preparation for a plain supper seems ridiculous, listen to the inviter, and possibly it will appear that Effie, as a bonnie lassie extremely anxious to get settled in matrimony, was only making the most of a good chance when it came her way.

'Ay! ay! Mistress Grey,' quoth the widow, after her invitation was given and accepted, 'it's an uncommon grand chance for Effie. If she could manage to catch my cousin, and be leddie o' the Halket estates, *that* wad be something worth telling.'

'It'll no' be what a body may call one o' the terrible big properties, like the Duke o' Hamilton's, or such as that?' queried the lady addressed. 'It'll just be twa or three hundred acres, I'm thinking?'

'Twa or three hundred acres, Mistress Grey! H'm! I tell ye it's ane o' the grandest estates in all Peeblesshire, and some o' them's miles broad.'

'But I'm thinking the land is no cultivate out in Peebles. Tammy Tamson, that carries up the water to our stairhead, comes frae that part o' the country, and he says it's naething but a wheen barren hills, wi' no sae muckle as a blade o' grass growing on them. Land canna be o' ony value there!'

'Oh! but Tammy Tamson is a known liar, for Halket is planted wi' fine trees, and grand crops o' barley; and there's

Halket Castle, where my cousin lives, wi' a' his men-servants and pages and women-servants, like King Solomon's for grandeur; and then he's sae godly forbye. But never fear to come the night, Effie; he'll be just as polite to you as if ye was in his ain rank. Only think! out o' the goodness o' his heart hasn't he taken on himsel' the cost o' bringing up an orphan lassie-bairn, just because he kent her father and mother! My late father was just the same sort o' gentleman.'

Thus the two gossips went on sparring till poor Mistress Fairlie was seduced into no end of flourishes, and well-nigh undertook to prove her cousin a compound of Crœsus and Saint John the Divine.

In the evening Antony arrived so unfashionably early that Mistress Fairlie had time to paraphrase Effie's exalted social position, as well as to explain how nicely she had touted him to that young lady.

The upshot of this foolish talk was that the 'young elder,' finding himself so suddenly endued with all the cardinal virtues (wealth included), and ovated therefor, enjoyed the incense offered by his admirers, and went on sniffing its fragrance till he fancied it too late to jump off his pedestal, and exhibit in *puris naturalibus*. The supper party proved a decided success. Not that it was a costly entertainment, for plum-pottage, stewed cheese, and a dish of marmalade formed the bill of fare. As for drinkables, there was both ale and claret, the first very fair, the latter indifferent; however, those who considered it thin just popped in a few comfits taken from a china box of these compacted sweets which was duly passed round the table.

Antony being country-bred, expressed (to his hostess's annoyance) astonishment at this new and *recherché* mode of preparing one's liquor. Therefore, to keep up her cousin's prestige as a man of rank and fashion, she hastily exclaimed, 'Oh, Laird, I daresay it's only among us toun's bodies that they take comfits in their claret-wine. The like o' you big gentry, that have your Canary wines, and your silver ashets, and castles, and pages, wadna be at the pains to use sweeties. It's a grand thing to be born like you, Laird, wi' a siller spoon in yer mouth,' etc., etc.

With the adoring looks of pretty Effie Grey fixed on him, what could he do but admit the superb impeachment? So, for sole answer, he expanded his lips beyond their usual pinch, and performed a deprecatory little bow, as who should say, 'Pray, don't speak of castles and silver-plate, and such trifling adjuncts of my elevated position; they are really not worth mentioning.'

Effie was asked to sing, and, incited by a mind's-eye picture of the glories attainable should she entrap the Laird, went through her rather limited musical repertory. Painfully desirous to please, and not knowing the precise style most in favour with him of the castles and silver ashets, she was at first rather posed between the serious and the profane. But recolcollecting that Mistress Fairlie had lauded him as a perfect saint, she gave forth that most nerve-racking of psalm tunes, 'Bangor.'

A glance across the table, however, soon showed that this shot had missed; so breaking off the sacred wail abruptly, she substituted an old and suggestive ballad, commencing thus :—

> ' O whistle, an' I'll come to ye, my lad,
> O whistle, an' I'll come to ye, my lad ;
> Tho' faither, an' mother, an' a' should gae mad,
> O whistle, an' I'll come to ye, my lad,' etc., etc.

A wide-awake young person was Effie, and, having an object in view, very prudently left no stone unturned in seeking to possess it. Some of her intimates used to call her rather forward, but for all that she was a good deal admired, albeit proposals of marriage were few and far between.

(As an instance how our vernacular has altered during a couple of centuries, I may here state that a 'forward' young lady of 1682 and the 'fast girl' of our present period mean exactly the same thing.)

Mr. Hepburn, as usual, made himself good company, in his own brusque, kindly manner ; but, if all were told, he was the least happy of the party. Albeit not generally considered a marrying man, he had for many a day been, as it were, spasmodically sweet upon Effie Grey, and to behold her open siege of this godly Crœsus, with the long feeble-kneed legs and minute mouth, made him feel a little downhearted.

I forgot to say that, at the proper time for that ceremony, Antony, by request, spake a lengthy, unimpressive thanksgiving, after which baby Letty, asleep and in her night gear, was carried in for exhibition. Effie kissed the fat little bundle so many times, it seemed as if she should never leave off either her embraces or laudation of Laird Baigrie's generosity towards his penniless protegée, 'the dear wee motherless lambikin. Indeed, Master Baigrie,' she ran on, 'since Mistress Fairlie spake to me and mother this forenoon o' your guidness to this orphan pet, we've telt ever so many folk about it; and depend on't, sir, afore to-morrow night it'll be the toun's talk. Mother's ten times better at sending round news than the bellman.'

Unfortunate Antony! And yet, yet how should he (being the manner of man he was) wriggle out of the borrowed plumes he all the while could not help feeling proud of?

Supper being ended, the two male guests took leave together, and in course of their walk homewards Laird Baigrie asked Mr. Hepburn whether, professionally, he could help him to a good investment for a large sum of money he had brought with him to Edinburgh. Thanks to Mrs. Fairlie's illustrations, the writer took for granted that the large sum named belonged to his present companion, and answered accordingly. It was a very great sum indeed; but luckily he chanced to know of a couple of landed bonds that between them would just cover the amount.

The night was fine, frosty, and starlit, and to discuss the business off-hand and without interruption the two men turned aside into the Parliament-House Close. There, in the quiet open Square, they dandered to and fro for well-nigh half an hour; myriads of stars glittering over-head, shining God's praises. One side of the Square was filled up by the ancient Kirk of St. Giles, with its richly-carved buttresses and spire of lace-like stone-work, in form of a bishop's mitre.

Facing round for one more turn, both pedestrians chanced to look up at the same moment, and were struck with the exquisite way in which the soft clear light brought out the architecture against the deep blue sky.

'Very fine, isn't it?' remarked Hepburn.

'Very,' answered the other.

There was a minute's silence (both still gazing up at the great mitre that looked as if all silver and ebony), and then Antony said,—

'Well, sir, it is arranged. As I am in a hurry to get back to Peeblesshire, perhaps you will have everything cut and dry for me by to-morrow evening. I want to leave Edinburgh as early as possible next day.'

'Yes, I shall,' said Mr. Hepburn; but into his face had come a softened, longing look. It came as he was gazing up through the open-work arches of the mitre at the diamond shimmer out beyond it.

Ah, that grand old steeple! It had looked down on many

a scene of festivity and battle. That night it served, so to speak, as a prayer suggested to one at least of those two tall individuals walking at its base. And Laird Baigrie—for a second of time he was awed by the felt presence, as it were, of the glittering throng shining above. Here, in the midst of a city, at midnight, the visible heavens seemed somehow more of an actual presence than they used to do in the country.

But business is business, and when one is not quite sure as to the propriety of asking God's blessing on it, why, the sooner it is got over the better. So the 'young elder' straightway left off staring up at the mitre, and told Mr. Hepburn to draw out the bonds in his (Antony's) own name. 'I can easily make them over to the infant when necessary' (thought he), 'so she'll not be a bawbee worse off for what I am now doing. Really, after all, these people have gone and spoken so much about this wealth being mine, it would be injurious to my reputation as an elder of the kirk to say I was only shamming all the time. More than likely the infant will die young, and then this will prove a wise measure; but, anyhow, I shall consider these bonds as hers, albeit drawn in my name. I don't see how, as a man with a Christian character to support, I could act otherwise than I am doing.'

That night sleep fled from the young elder's eyes. Whether owing to the indigestibility of Mrs. Fairlie's stewed cheese, or whatever cause, he remained as wakeful as King Ahasuerus. Therefore he tried to while away the weary hours, not like the

Eastern monarch, by revising the chronicle of his bygone actions, but by improving a little on the plans he had already laid for the future. In course of these premises it struck him that it would be desirable to fix Letty for five years, instead of one, with Mrs. Fairlie. Why he pitched upon five, instead of four or six, he could not tell. Why make this re-arrangement at all? he did not too minutely inquire of himself. As I said formerly, he was not much in the habit of viewing earthly things from a spiritual stand-point. Had he a presentiment that the bonds would so grow into his carnal affections that the very recollection of the young heiress's existence would prove a snare to his soul, by impeding that 'will-worship' which he fully meant to go on offering, as heretofore, unto the Lord. Wherefore blister his self-satisfaction annually, when he might just as well do guardian for the whole five years at once? On his bed, in the dark, he rehearsed the arguments he had already laid to heart, but they seemed if anything less unimpeachable than by daylight. Be that as it may, before he quitted 'Auld Reekie,' Letty's fortune was safely invested in a couple of heritable bonds in the name of Antony Baigrie, and she, poor little orphan lassie, settled with Mrs. Fairlie for five years, at a very moderate figure for bed, board, and washing.

CHAPTER VIII.

> ' We have within us warm hearts throbbing,
> Strong pulses beating, and our brains on fire ;
> We feel there is enough of music in us
> To join the heavenly choir.'

IT will be remembered that Marjorie received a letter from James Renwick on Christmas-day. He had written it at the cottage of a shepherd in Glencairn parish, and addressed it to Greendykes, supposing, of course, that his intended was still resident there. After various chance postages it at length, as we saw, reached the party for whom it was intended through the final agency of Mr. Hepburn.

In our day and generation young people's love-letters are, as a rule, sugar-and-watery productions, not particularly instructive to any save the two persons immediately interested. One or two short excerpts from ' our young Josiah's' epistle to his lady-love will give some idea how these affairs were managed in 1683 :—

'GLENCAIRN, *December the 2nd.*

'MINE DEAR HERTE,—Upon whom I think, bye Night and bye Daie, with most refreshing delight, a trustie friend will gett this conveyed to you. Would thatt I was going in its Stead. I trust, dear Love, it finds you as well as I wish You to Bee, and I entreat our precious Redeemer oftentimes on your Behalf. Sorely did it grieve Mee that soe soon after you became Mye verie own, Wee behoved to part, without anie speedie prospect of meeting again ; Yea, worse than that, for I was going awaie into probable danger, and I knew how your Herte went with mee amongst the clouds and Darkness.

'This distressed mee moche, more upon your account Than on mye own Behalf, and I Confess dimmed for a Brief space of Time the Exceeding Brightness that had, as it were, re-burnished Mye Faith in God immediately after receiving from Him the Blessed Boon of Your Affection.

'But this was onlie a Passing Trial, and soon blew bye, for The Dear Lord Kept mee in Safetie, and wrought in mee, moreover, the Night he did soe, a firm Conviction that you was even then Entreating Him on mye Behalf. And was not that Verie Feeling a Gliff of Happiness Sent by his Mercie, think ye ?

'Yea, Dear Love ! Our Experience of the Saviour's Constant Providence Should e'en Work patience in us, and that again ever Will, bye and bye, Begett hope ; Whilk hope, for time or Eternity, when founded on Him, can ne'er make ashamed them that entertain it.

'Seeing this, Sweet Herte, lett you and mee laie our mutual Love dailie upon his Altar, and then wee shall Have it Back again, Baptised, as it were, And Hee saying unto us, " Here, take *this*, and use it for Mee." O ! Should wee nott doe

Likewise with Everie one of our Earthlie Mercies? When I remember these Few Minutes Wee passed upp on the Roof of Greendykes House, it warms mee this Daie, albeit there is both Frost and Sleet here.

'I was att My Dear Old Mother's Ten Daies agone, When I told her that You had promised Your Dear Self unto mee, Shee fell upon mye neck and Kissed mee, and lifted up her voice and weeped For thankfulness.

'Yea, it was assuredly a Strange Providence that caused me Barely to Miss Meeting Laird Baigrie under her Roof. Why he came I know not verie particularlie, further than that he staied ten daies, until the Demise of a young ladie from Foreign parts. Shee was lodging with My dear Mother, and I suppose was a relative of his. But I had noe time to ask moche, as mye Cousin Katherine was ill with nerves during most of my sojourn, whilk was but shortt, seeing my errand in Glasgow was, next morning afore Dawn of Daie, to Convene a Meeting in the Lodging of Holy Ladie Caldwell, who has "testified" even unto great earthlie losses.

'Some Soules were Comforted, I truste; But unto her it proved but a Sadd meeting in one Sense. For Ane Enemie, that dwelt on the other side of the Street, spied out of his window in the dark into her window (albeit it has but Two little panes), and saw (he said) a Minister preaching by candle-light. Soe the dear old Saint and her Daughter were strait-way had to the Tolbooth, where now thaie Lye.

'I am, none can Tell, How Light-Herted, in Spite of these Troublous Times, Since I have on Earth what Schoolmen call an "Alter Ego." Find *that* out, Sweet Herte, in Wattie's Latin Vocabularie.

'Mee thinks that when this Storm is bye-past, and Fair Weather Come, If God seeth meet to Spare us to ane another, wee Will have plentie to Doe in the Waie of conversation, and will not readilie Tire of Each Other.

'Unto his Almightie Hands I committ you, Mye Beste Beloved, praieing that Hee maie right Speedilie Order Soe, that mie Duties may take mee to Tweedsmuir, a place that will Be Evermore to Mee Filled with Blissful Memories.

'If the Lord Will, I purpose being in Edinburgh, anent the Affairs of our Beloved Suffering Kirk, about the third week in Februarie. Were I att mye own disposal, fain would I goe thence to Greendykes.

'Unto his loving Hands I again Committ you. Maie Hee ever Lift His Countenance upon you, and give you peace.—Thine Onlie, Thine For Ever, JAMES RENWICK.'

Truly, if the youthful divine's converse with Marjorie generally afforded her ample matter for after-thought, this, his first and rather ponderous *billet-doux*, gave subject enough for speculation.

Antony Baigrie, the knock-knee'd 'young elder,' abiding in the house of Renwick's mother, and closing the eyes of a foreign lady there!

'It's just like a bit o' *The Pilgrim's Progress*,' quoth Mistress Elspet, Bunyan being her only available literary reference besides the Bible.

But, from commenting on Laird Baigrie, Marjorie soon fell a-ruminating about the turn of affairs which had brought her to the city where Renwick was ere long to be. How should she discover his whereabouts when there? How inform him of her own proximity?

Ah! partings and separations were terrible things in those times, when months and years might elapse without any possible communication betwixt two fond hearts, if owned (as was commonly the case) by individuals who could not write: and even if they could, dared not send a line (except by a trustworthy hand) for fear of consequences.

So down she sat on the window-seat to ponder, and at length bethought her of the rough kindly lawyer who had that very day acted for her behoof the part of carrier-pigeon.

'He'll manage it for me somehow,' thought the damsel, and thereupon a feeling of comfortable help being at hand came, so to speak, into her heart,—the same sort of feeling she had experienced when George Hepburn lifted her from the crowd that day in the Bow, and bore her in his big sinewy arms into the fresh air and a quiet resting-place.

'He'll manage it, doubtless,' and with this conviction away fled anxiety, or at least fretting care.

So, after all, Marjorie Ker's Christmas-day was a bright one, albeit the atmosphere in Covenant Close was almost thick enough, one would think, to be cut with a knife. The girl's new-born joy must have shone out surely, for cynical Mistress Clavers, sitting at her own window a couple of yards distant across the way, bawled out, 'What's that ye're readin', lassie? Wha's that letter frae? Hae ye gotten a fortin' like yer auntie, that ye're smiling so sweetly?'

To Marjorie's own amazement, the inspective, jealous

woman's queries did not this time rouse the 'old Adam' within her. How could she do aught but radiate with so much happiness coming to meet her in February? So she made answer, 'It's from a dear old friend, ma'am. Oh! I wish you were as happy as I am this day very heartily.'

'God bless the lassie,' murmured Mistress Clavers. 'It's the first gude wish I've gotten these ten years. They're an ill-natured set in this close. God bless the lassie!'

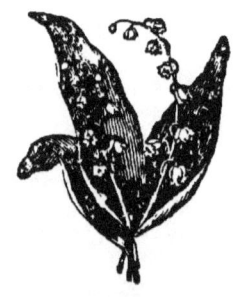

CHAPTER IX.

'Learn by a mortal yearning to ascend
Seeking a higher object. Love was given,
Encouraged, sanctioned, chiefly for that end.'

'As through a glass, darkly.'

THIS chapter will embrace the space of four years, and terrible years they were to many a man and woman in Scotland, for the period subsequently known by 'persecuted presbytery' as the 'Killing-Time,' rose then to its fiercest and bloodiest.

Pending the course of these four years, venerable and brave men, many and stately matrons, and bonnie douce maidens not a few, sealed their principles with their blood, never begrudging it, for Jesus' sake.

As may be supposed, solemnity and a serious demeanour permeated all social intercourse less or more effusively according to circumstances. Light-hearted merriment was, generally speaking, crushed out of being, but not sober happiness. It is a mistake to suppose that even the most violent religious or political contendings must of necessity turn domesticity upside down; or that, because deep feeling concerning certain matters is general, quiet-living folks become all at once public characters. It is true that, at the juncture whereof we are speaking, there were individuals who considered the imbibing of any earthly pleasure just then as neither more nor less than contempt of God's chastening rod. Just as if a man must needs cease to sing, because, having lost his legs, he is unable to walk.

Not thus, however, argued James Renwick and Marjorie Ker; albeit of late fightings without and fears within had increased greatly, and matters were at a desperate pass with the Kirk. Some of her best pastors had suffered martyrdom, others had defected, and now Providence so ordered that unto all the congregations of the faithful scattered over the country there was only one handsome fair-haired youth to minister in holy things; and a right diligent shepherd did Renwick prove, not counting his very life dear, so that he might 'hiddenly' comfort his Lord's 'harried' sheep.

Ay! hiddenly, for so his work behoved to be done, seeing that Government had set on his head the price of one hundred pounds sterling. Therefore did he continue wandering from place to place, and at conventicles preached now-a-days with a horse standing ready saddled beside him. Thus you perceive that, albeit only a few months had passed since the sacramental occasion in Talla Glen, public affairs had made a great stride from bad to worse. Nevertheless, with all this dread and all this danger, not ignored, but faced, and prayed over, Renwick and Marjorie in their several spheres ever continued to thank Heaven for their mutual love. If the powers of darkness were abroad, surely all the more precious to 'Christ's poor ones' was any bonnie blink of happiness bestowed by Providence to cheer them in the gloom.

As I remarked already, public upheavals do not necessarily imply universal domestic dislocation, and of this Covenant Close was an example in point. Albeit blocked up, so to speak, at its *off* end by the elegant mansion of a great law-lord, many of the other tenements were divided and sub-divided into very small abodes indeed. Hence probably the fact, that the bulk of the inhabitants were elderly lone females of ancient lineage and limited means, ignored by well-to-do relations, and fading or sputtering through the balance of their three-score and ten within their several tiny suites of minute apartments.

We have all our special small world inside the big ball whereon we eat, drink, and sleep; and, limited as was the social circle of Covenant Close, it had its cliques, and its petty tabooes, and its 'cream of cream,' all the same as more renowned places.

So many women, *so* many fixed opinions (especially anent matters beyond the female grasp) was, I fear, as much a thing of course in 1684 as in our own day and generation, and held true especially of the ancient spinsters amid whom for the present Marjorie and her aunt were located.

In those non-journalistic times, when even the few come-at-able books were written in Latin, it was small wonder if popular versions of current news took shape and colour from the bias of the relater thereof, or that those oral communications, after being once or twice transmitted, grew occasionally, like the bottle-imp, from a mere puff of smoke into a great ugly demon.

The long-pedigreed ladies of 'The Close,' albeit generally 'cold-shouldered' by the existing heads of their respective families, pinned their dignity to the maintaining of certain dogmas, political and religious, which it was their pleasure to call hereditary, and which, poor old souls, they squabbled about, on what was fondly supposed to be the *noblesse oblige* principle.

In 'sit-under-your-own-fig-tree' times all this might have been harmless, if foolish; but when hired spies were here, there, and everywhere, and a heedless word might chance to cost a life, the exaggerated spoken sentiments of even a set of uninfluential gossips was a thing of consequence. However, that never crossed their imagination. So, according to their special idiosyncracies, they continued using or abusing the scraps of rumour which now and again floated in from the bestead, fighting, dismayed world outside the close-mouth.

Mistress Elspet and her niece (now that the former had had

her fill of the companionship of Mistress Clavers and her congeners) drew more intimately together than ever before even at Greendykes. Walking out for walking's sake was not the mode, even had the temptation of dirty streets been greater to Marjorie than she now found it. At Tweedsmuir the girl had, so to speak, half lived in the open air, exercising soul and feeling amid grand mountain stillness, as well as refreshing her body with pure breezes. But in town it was different. She could picture Renwick in her fancy ten times more vividly when seated quietly in-doors than when picking her way over the rough causeway of a narrow street, where one could only catch sight of a patch of sky by chance. So she became quite a keeper-at-home, and as for Mistress Elspet, at no period of her life had she been a great pedestrian.

Besides their immediate neighbours, the only visitor of the Kers was Mr. Hepburn, who, by-the-bye, continued to act as Mrs. Elspet's man of business. Wattie had taken a boyish fancy for him and his anecdotive powers, and by degrees Marjorie, who had inclined to him from the start of their acquaintance, began to like him very much indeed. Not at all, be it understood, in the way of Cupidish sentimentalism, but because, despite his years and his devil-may-caredness, she found he could receive comprehendingly those ever surging fancies and suggestions that were quite too high-flown for dear auntie's mental capacity. So now and then (albeit not very often), instead of patronizing the tavern of an evening, he would pop in and take a share of Mistress Elspet's favourite supper—to wit, buttered crabs and a mug of good ale. On these occasions he used to arrive so almost sprucely attired that Mistress Clavers, spying him from her usual post of observation, spread a report that he was courting Mistress Elspet, or rather 'poor dead-and-gone Madame's siller' in her person.

Wattie, who had sharp ears of his own, accidentally overheard one version of this gossip, and told it at home by way of a joke, emphasizing the same with a loud laugh.

'Oh, dear me!' thought Marjorie, 'that heedless laddie has hurt dear old auntie's feelings with his thoughtless nonsense.'

But the human heart is an extraordinary conglomerate of sweets and sours. The old lady, instead of joining in Wattie's sense of the absurd, actually blushed like a girl of sixteen, as the faint possibility of a late 'Indian summer' dawned on her mental horizon. 'Mr. Hepburn is plain-looking, and anything but a youth! I am not yet dead-old. He certainly comes here very often, and is quite aware of Marjorie's engagement. After all, beauty is only skin-deep, and in a wife what does a rational elderly man need, besides a pleasant companion, with plenty to keep the pot boiling?'

All this floated athwart poor auntie's brain, but never a word spake she. Belief in the hoped-for after-glow was rushing over her overwhelmingly, and for the moment routing both common-sense and past experiences, albeit not her love for the right and her 'twa bairns.'

Thereafter, whenever Mr. Hepburn appeared, she would innocently slip out of the parlour and exchange her every-day 'mob-cap' for a smart pair of pinners, previously giving her face a gentle wash with sow's milk,—a cosmetic she remembered to have heard recommended as an infallible rejuvenator and depilatory.

It thus came to pass that the rough-looking lawyer was always received with open arms, so to speak, in the house of his new friends, and used to keep them posted up in *on dits* they might not otherwise have heard.

'It's very strange,' commented Mistress Clavers, who was no Covenanter; 'it's very strange that such wonderful saints as the Kers are hand-and-glove wi' sic a professed sinner as Geordie Hepburn. I'm thinking, for all their prayings and psalmings, they're Jesuits, and nothing else.'

But notwithstanding the spiteful spinster's insinuations, the writer came and went, and what was more, those visits told on his inner man. Not pronouncedly at first converting him then and there into a bleached negro, but gradually, so to speak, wholesomizing his moral requirements.

Marjorie's friendly confiding little outpourings, and her glowing, almost poetical gratitude for any scraps of news he could pick up for her concerning Renwick, opened, as it were, a new window-slit in the lawyer's soul; small, indeed, and curtained, but through which he dimly discerned how some things on earth may be truly the reflex of corresponding things in heaven.

As yet he saw not this very clearly, albeit sufficiently so to make him wish, oftener than he used, to rise up from among the sooty pots on strong pinions of yellow golden feathers! Ah! but he could not just yet, at least. So, with a sigh, he would bid 'God bless' Renwick's love, and walk right away to Bruce's tavern in the West Bow, for a night of 'high jinks' with his boon companions. Bear in mind, however, that Mr. Hepburn was not dissipated beyond the reputable average of non-serious society at that period; but the truth was, intercourse with a beautiful, talented, religious girl was gradually rousing his dormant refinement,—a something quite independent of conventional polish.

Marjorie's 'Diurnall' about this date shows how diligently he catered on her behalf for tidings of her wanderer; which catering, by the way, had, among other effects, that of leading him into contact with a different style of people from the general run of his cronies. But before extracting from the said Diary, I shall, for sake of keeping the different persons who figure in this chronicle distinctly in view, explain, once for all, where Antony Baigrie bestowed himself during those four dread years comprehended in the present chapter.

Well, after leaving baby Letty at Mistress Fairlie's, he

hied back to Halket, a very wealthy man in the estimate of Mr. Hepburn, and all those whom the old lady's tongue had been able to reach. The bonds, drawn out as they were in his own name, would not stand being prayed over; not that their existence involved any crime of commission exactly, but because, were things run up to a very fine spiritual point, some little sin of omission might have been patent to even *his* conscience. You and I are aware, however, that albeit the 'young elder' could, on fit occasions, swallow his camel, he was not accustomed to disquiet, by earthly hair-splittings, those moments allotted (in the arrangement of his time) especially to things heavenly. So onward to Halket he trotted, during a couple of east-windy wet days, feeling rather purse-proud (neither day was Sabbath), and, as he mentioned to the landlord of the 'public' where he put up at night, extremely 'groozy' all down the small of his back.

Ere he reached the mighty fortress of Mistress Fairlie's fancy sketch, the 'grooziness' had crept into his legs likewise, but Madge administered barley-gruel sweetened with honey, and next morning he thought himself better enough to ride to Greendykes.

'Best settle with Marjorie at once,' soliloquized he *en route;* 'and it's fortunate I can tell her that that forward laddie Renwick is to be married to his cousin ere long. It'll no be an untruth; for, as sure as fate, she'll make him do her will. (He would be a bold man that would 'counter yon strong-minded cuttie!¹) So I'll only be telling the even-down facts as they're likely to turn out. Ay, ay! The apostle might turn up his nose at "filthy lucre." It's no likely he ever got the chance o' much; but it's a grand thing; and then a body can do good with it. I shall now be able to stand out about getting the auntie's fortune settled, plack and farthing, on Marjorie; and that I couldna have done but for the providence that has put this large sum into my lap, as it were. The bairn may die; but yet I almost think, if Mrs. Elspet does as I wish with *her* gear, and after I'm fairly espoused to Marjorie, I'll maybe tell *her* somewhat o' Letty.'

But, alas! all the Laird's cogitations were mere wasted brain, for when he arrived at the abode of his desired bride it was untenanted; so what could he do but return whence he came? And, strange to say, not utterly disconsolate, but feeling far, far down in his heart, almost grateful that the marriage was not fixed just yet, and that, unlet and unhindered by conscience, he could now, for a while at least, rejoice in 'the bonds.'

Having, so to speak, named a day for paying-off that poor, ill-used soul's vicegerent of his, he might surely be permitted in the interim to *feel* honest. 'After I am married to Marjorie, and her aunt's fortune is made over to me, then I shall,' etc.

But the projected wedding was not, as he took for granted,

¹ Bold young woman.

only at the distance of another ride to Edinburgh, for by evening the 'grooziness' had developed into acute pain, which again brought into play hitherto unknown powers of forcible adjuration in the sufferer, that astonished both himself and Madge not a little. In short, he had a pretty sharp attack of rheumatic fever, which kept him bedfast the best part of six weeks.

On his recovery, which by the way was imperfect as regarded his left knee, he felt so cross and so greedy, and altogether so unscripturally out of amiable condition, that to go a-wooing at that particular time would have actually been more trouble than pleasure. Moreover, his aches behoved to be ousted. That was a duty he owed to himself; and fortunately, if, as he purposed, he went to try the celebrated Bath waters, the settling-day with conscience anent these bonds (seeing it depended on his marriage with Marjorie) must be deferred. So, obtaining a passport to journey into England, he appeared at Bath, and rejoiced in feeling himself a man of wealth.

'Elder' not being engraven on his face, where would have the use of 'doing' Presbyterianism in season and out, when nobody in the place belonged distinctly to that persuasion? At the same time he kept his denominational 'tally' all right, by strictly eschewing Episcopacy in all its heights and depths, its rituals, and, I fear, its charity.

At this time persecution in Scotland was waxing toward sevenfold heat, and as the Bath waters had failed in quite restoring his left knee-joint to suppleness, he considered there would be no harm in pursuing his travels to foreign parts. This project Antony duly carried out, and remained absent for the four years, anent which we shall now give some bits from Marjorie's 'Diurnall;' not, however, going at that manuscript *seriatim*, but, as it were, pecking here and there among its pages.

'*June the Twentie*, 1684.—This Daie there came a Mann to Sell some Snipes thatt he had shot on the Loch of the Cannon-Mills, and Dear Auntie bought a Paire for to-morrow's Supper. This Mann comes from Glasgow, and hath a Gude-brother[1] thatt was in Ladie Caldwell her Lodging the nicht James Preached there, when Shee was Taken Prisonner. This Mann's Gude-brother saide thatt Master Renwick looked as Bright and Heartie as the Sonne in his Noon-Daie Strength, whilk comforts mee exceedinglie. On this account did Auntie Eppie have the Snipe-Mann into the Parloure, and for A Pair paie him the Price of Three Birds, Forbye a Drink of Ale.

'It was moste Kinde of Master Hepburn to find out about this Mann's Gude-Brother, and send the Mann here to cheer mee, for I was somewhat Eerie about James, last time Mr. Hepburn came to supper.

'*August the Ninthe*, 1684.—Wattie has brocht home a pattern of His Hand-write from His Teacher, but sooth to saie, it is but verie middling in regard of the upp-stroaks, whilk are tremblie.

[1] Brother-in-law.

'*September the* 22, 1684.—Mr. Hepburn was this forenoon upp at Auntie's tenant, Mistress Fairlie's, who hath friends among Christ's oppressed People at this present time. She said The Storie goes that, not long since, Master Renwick was preaching in Carrick, and the enemie gott word of it from the Curate near bye, and them att the preaching behoved to flee for dear Life. When James was fleeing nigh the edge of a small rockie place, he Bye accident fell down to the bottom, into a snug little part grown upp with Whin Bushes. Theire hee did lie hidden, as the Bodie of Moses was bye the Lord's own Hand, and when the swearing Dragoons came, looking for him to slay, Lo! thaie saw no mann, albeit hee was keeking[1] at them through between the bonnie yellow flowers of the Whins. This was what Mistress Fairlie telled to Mr. Hepburn, and whatt does hee do afore coming here but travell out beyond the South Loch to pull a bit Whin-branch covered with bloom. When he had telt us about James's deliverance he whippt the whin out of his back pocket, and says to me, " Here, Marjorie, mie dear Bairn, this will mind you of Master Renwick's safetie. See how bright and Bonnie are the flowers whilk Frail tho' thaie bee were made as strong as Castle-Walls to him!" I'm sure no person could think Master Hepburn verie farr from the Kingdom oi God, whatever that uglie Mistress Clavers Saies. It was a kind Providence that Hee came this Night to Supper, For Mistress Clavers was out at the Vittler's paieing

[1] Peeping.

her Half-Year's Barley, and heard there that Master Renwick was taken, awaie in The West, and was to Bee Hangit without Loss of Time. Soe she came quick toe tell Auntie and Mee, and Auntie nigh fainted, and I was on Mie knees weeping and entreating for Grace to Saie, God's Holie Will Bee Done, when in came dear Mr. Hepburn wi' his News and his Whin-Branche. I think I'll keep the flowers of itt till I die, and then gett them putten in Mie Coffin. It's a Sinn of Mistress Clavers to have tell't Betty Sharpit, upp the Stair, thatt it is a disgrace For Professors like Auntie and Mee to companie with an ill-Deedie Heathen like Mr. Hepburn, and that wee behove to be Jesuites. I wiss she was half as gude as Hee is.

'1685. *March the 2d.*—Word has Come to Edinburgh that all The Advocates and their Writers are to be immediatelie regimented, and sent toe fight for the New King against the Cameronians, thatt sinful men call Rebels. O, Mye Saviour dear, Save Mee From the great Sorrow of seeing Master Hepburn going in Battle Arraie against James. Verilie this is a time of the Lord's indignation Being poured out, and noe Peace nor Reste is anie more in Scotland. Whiles I am ashamed indeed toe lie down quiet and comfortable on mie Bed here when, maybee, at that verie time, James is cowering in his plaid aside a Cold Rock for shelter. Last nicht, when a great Swirle of wind came Blowing upp the Close, and Rattled the Windows, I began thinking, and thinking, till I turned fearful with the dread of all that might yett happen.

This was Mistrustfulness, and a Snare, but I could not help itt, and itt was the verie same feeling I had that time at Talla-Glen Sacrament, when Laird Baigrie spillt the wine over mee. I'm surely to have news Soon.

'*March 30th.*—I was upp this daie, with Auntie, at Mistress Fairlie's, as Mr. Hepburn Bad us goe and see the Bunker[1] shee wants mended. Shee is pleasant, and tell't us thatt Laird Baigrie is her Cousin, and thatt Hee has a large Fortune. Hee maun have gotten itt Since wee were at Greendykes. But I wish him Weel. And, Strange to Saye, the dearest wee Lamb of a lassie is boarded with Mistress Fairlie, and is a Charitie Bairn that Laird Baigrie keeps out of respecte to its dead parents. It is a Sweet innocente, but the Laird maun be a better mann than I thocht, for in Tweedsmuir he was aye considered Close-fisted. Mistress Fairlie is bringing the bonnie bit creature to our house on Mondaie. Shee wad not quit mie knee, and keepit hold of my hand, and said, "Bonnie Ladie, Lettie's Ladie." Her name is Lettie. Mistress Fairlie saies she forgott to ask Laird Baigrie her second name, soe she just goes by the name of Lettie Baigrie; albeit is verie likelie not the right one at all.

'*April the Second*, 1685.—Kirstie Frazer, thatt keeps a Byre in Booth's Entrie, and that wee gett our Milk from, was yestreen taken upp for a Witche. Verilie these are terrible times! albeit Kirstie is faire in complexion, and not like whatt I suppose the

---

[1] Receptacle for coals.

Witche of Endor was. Thaie Saie Shee Casted ane Evil eye upon Her Sister's Bairne, and caused itt to take Fitts, She having no children herself, and jealous of her Sister's Bairns.

'*October the Thirtieth.*—The Council has ordered thatt the "Bowets" bee taken awaie, and thatt from ilka Tenement shall be hung a Lantern with a Candle inside itt. This Beeing the First night of illuminating the Citie thus, Master Hepburn came to Convoie us upp the High Street, In order that Wee Might behold the Same, and Verillie the High Street looked so brilliant it minded mee of that "Vestibule of the New Jerusalem" whereof James Renwick used soe oft to speak, and wherein hee rests continuallie, even while cruel men are thirsting to shedd His Heart's Blood. Ah! this is mie greate consolation, albeit where on Earth Mie dear Love is I know not at present, onlie this I am assured of, that He is Sunning his soule in his Saviour's Smile.

'On our waie Home, going Down the High Street, Wee begann conversing about James, and Mr. Hepburn said he Had just been Hearing from a person that it's likelie James Renwick maie Bee in Edinburgh before long, as Severals Have Kept upp their Infants without Baptism till such Time as thaie could get a right Minister to Do it. If Hee comes, Mr. Hepburn is to find out where he will lodge, and is, moreover, to convoie us to the prayer-meeting afore baptism. O! what a happiness it will be for James and mee to meet after being parted nigh Two long Years; and to Him it will

Bee a greate surprisal, seeing hee imagines Wee are all at Greendykes Still. Such a Holie life and a Noble is his! Spending and Beeing Spent for Jesu's cause. Lifting upp his preached Testimonie when manie thatt might Bee his grand Fathers are feared to saie "Cheep." I wonder if hee is now as Beautifull as hee used to Bee. Not that His handsomeness matters to mee. Mie affection is founded deeper than Eyes and Noses, albeit I am proud of his prettie well-favouredness too.

'This night, after Mr. Hepburn went awaie, I was sitting at the fire combing mie Hair and thinking about James, when all at once a burning sparke flew out and Burnt a hole in Mie Apron, also a large Mouse ran around the room two or three times. This was strange, but a more strange thing occured Bye-and-Bye, for quite Late, whenn everie Bodie was Bedded and the House as quiet as quiet could Bee, I distinctly heard three soft low knocks! These things happening just as I was thinking about James are no doubt Warnings. For God Speaketh to us in Diverse manners. Everie Bodie knows that a Fire-Spark fleeing out of the Hearth means Sudden News, and soe I take itt doe the Knocks. But the mouse running around and around the chamber, I like not thatt. Howbeit, wee are ever Safe under The Lord's Wings! As dear James once said, "Within The Heavenlie Vestibule, O! how Goodly a Lot is that, Even although att one end there Maie perchance stand a Gruesome Scaffold!"

'I hadd put past Mie "Diurnall" for the night, But when these Soe Remarkable Providences Fell out, I thought it well to Note them Down, Soe long as thaie remained Fresh in Mie Mind. Itt is now late, and I hear Betsy snoring like thunder in the Kitchen, also Auntie and Wattie, soe I will conclude.

'*October the Thirty Firste* 1685.—A most singular thing took place last night, about whilk I need not trouble Auntie's mind nor Wattie's, But I think thatt Maybee I will Tell it to Mr. Hepburn, If I cann get speech of Him alone.

'As I was jumping into mie Bedd, after Blowing out the Cruizie, I felt something just like a Waffle of Wind pass across mie Face. I cried out, Who is There? But all was quiet. O Lord! in the Daies of old a Spirit did once pass before the face of thy Servant Job, and caused him to tremble att thy presence. Can it bee thatt in Mercie Thou wouldest at this time thus certifie mee of thy immediate presence, let what Maie Bee coming to Trie Mie Faith! O! much doe I wish, in these Soe Strange and omenous Times that James Renwick himself wase Here to Stay Mie Feeble Womanhood from Beeing Soe Fear-Stricken as itt is Now and Then. Once More I am Beginning to feel Solitarie, Being parted from him whose glowing Words used toe clothe mie own Waie-Ward imaginings with such Delightful Verdure that I could rest joiefully on Them for a while, instead of Beeing Dragged bye their force Hither and Thither.

'Mr. Hepburn is a great comfort, But, albeit he can admire, So to Speak, Some Beautiful uncarnal Flowers of Earth that Auntie and Wattie consider useless Weeds; Yet when I would Fain Climb upp to those Hills of Spices, From whose Tops James used to point out "Jerusalem The Golden," Lo! Mr. Hepburn cannot follow! I think Hee fain Would Mount, tho' this He doeth not as yet, but rejoiceth in the "Breast-Posies" that grow Herebelow. O! Deare Saviour, Teach him that the Bonniest Earthlie Blooms must Die, Beeing grounded in the Duste onlie; But that, even Herebelow, there are given For Man's Solacement Lovelier Blossoms, that, albeit Rooted in The Heavenlie Garden Above, Hang down to this present World, in Long trailing Sprays, and, O! How exquisite is their fragrance.

'*November the Fifth.*—This is the Gunpowther-Plott Daie, But The Castle hath not Fired, neither have there Been Bone-Fires, Nor The Bells Ringing, as in former years. Can it Bee that the Papists are getting into Power, in Whilk case God Almightie keep Mie James and Jesu's Kirk.

'Mistress Fairlie Brought Wee Letty to visit us. I am extraordinarie fond of thatt Orphan-Bairn, Sae Sweetlie plaieful is shee, and soe Faire in the Skin. Albeit Swarthie myself I alwaies most admire Faire Persons. Wattie wants Auntie to Keepe Her here for him toe plaie with in his Bye-hours. Dear Laddie, his bye-hours are, I doubt, over manie, for hee loveth not either Books nor Pens anie more than he did long since when James Renwick taught him. It were perhaps for the prettie Orphan's welfare if some person would kindlie remove her from the care of Mistress Fairlie, who, albeit she frequenteth religious Companie, and is a Covenanter, Savoreth methinks not a little of Mistress Clavers in regard to the use of her tongue.

'*November the Ninth (a Daie much to Bee remembered bye me).*—Seeing that Master Hepburn Saies hee will to-morrow convey us to a Secret Prayer-Meeting at the Castle-Hill, in a House where James Renwick is to preach and Baptize sundrie infants (and some not soe verie young either), but their parents could not get a godlie minister of their waie of thinking before this time. I am half beside myself with joie, and thus The Lord explaineth graciously that those verie Signs, to wit (The Mouse running around our parlour, The fire-sparke that flew out of the hearth, and the Three Knocks), whilk I thought foreboded Evil, were forerunners of Good. Verilie mine unbelief is rebuked By God's love. To dear James this Meeting will doubtless bee a great surprisal, for Hee supposeth we are still at Greendykes. Mr. Hepburn is acquaint with the people in whose House hee is to staie, But O! it seemeth unnaturall for him toe bee onie place in Edinburgh Save in Covenant Close with Auntie and Mee.

'*November the Tenth.*—I know that Mistress Clavers is but a Talking Fool, but oftentimes she makes mee unhappie, especiallie when shee goes to The Vittler's, where, it appeareth to mee, they sell gossip, as well as pease and Barley. Shee hath this Morning putt mee into a cold Sweate bye Bawling across from her abominable window that it is come to light that Master Renwick is a Jesuite in disguise, and thatt now Manie of the Covenanting people want to gett him Hangit for misleading them. But not a Word of this would I credit, albeit the Apostle Paule swore it on his Bended knees. I am glad that Auntie did not hear Mistress Clavers, Being somewhat deaf with the Cold, and sitting then in the back summer parlour. The Cruel lie might Have staggared her faith, Poor dear. If I considered it would disprove this monstrous lie, and so prevent James from beeing hindered in His Master's work, I would Offer to Marrie him at once, and then Goe a-wandering on the Hills with him. If Evil doers silence his Voice, who, O Lord, is toe speak upp for thee, in all poor Scotland?

'*November the Eleventh.*—Wee have met, Mee and Mie Beautiful, Brave Hero of the Cross. O How grand hee is in Love to God and Man! The room was full, but, before entering, kind Mr. Hepburn pushed mee into another chamber, and syne brought James to mee. It was the happiness of a life time squeezed into five minutes. Hee looked like the Angel Gabriel, yet as sweet and simple, and trusting as of yore. In a few moments hee had dried upp mie tears, and, as it were, spoken mee back with him into the "Vestibule," where it ever shineth clear and Calm. It was as if wee Two had met where there is no more anie "Sea" of disquiet to annoy or drown. O He looks young indeed to have suffered soe much and done soe much. It was Beautiful to see him Baptise the children. I sat weeping in the back-most row of seats, half for gladness, half for, I know not what.

'*November the Twelfth.*—He was here verie earlie this Morning, and is now gone awaie, leaving mee trembling and downcaste, but I trust strengthened in the Spirit of mie Mind, Come weal, Come Woe. I wonder not thatt such multitudes risk dangers and death to hear his voice. Hee would cheer a Soul almost sinking in Despair. Hee saies it is quite true, after all, that severals of the Mountain-men have wickedly called him a Jesuite, because he would none of their half-measures, nor blow his Trumpet uncertainlie. Thus these persons have wrought woe and trouble unto the Kirk they profess to uphold. This grieves James to the Hearte, poor fellow.

'I marvel where Laird Baigrie is all this long Time? James was asking mee about him. Mr Hepburn and James have taken a great liking for one another. Renwick saies the root of the matter is in Mr. Hepburn, albeit as yet it is a good deal overlaid with thick clay.

'On mye finger is now a ring, with a posie, given to mee at parting Bye James Renwick. Where at thatt earlie Houre he got it to Buy I Cannot imagine. But the Posie is this, and a verie prettie one, "Yours Onlie, Yours Ever." I have kissed it manie times.

'1686. *Newe Yeare Daie.*—Mr. Hepburn Hath Most

Kindlie given to Auntie a Crimson taffetas Ribband for her Commode, and to Mee, for a gifte, a beautifull small Branche of Silvered Berries intermixed with purple Floss Foliage.

'Now-a-Daies it is a pleasure to Behold how Deare Auntie Affects Goodlie raiment, and is at pains to make herself Trig.[1] Verilie it is a prettier sight to see an old Ladie thus, than clothed (as was formerlie Her case) in an uglie Olive Saie, or the Brown Taffetas Saque thatt I used to wish I could Burn or Tear when I was young.

'I think providence kindlie Brought us acquaint withe Mr. Hepburn for our Comforte in these wearie Times when, ever and Anon, Bad Tidings come concerneing our Suffering Brethren. I sometimes long now for the blessed period when James and Mee, and Auntie and Wattie, and Mr. Hepburn shall be safe in "the House of Manie Mansions."'

In now laying aside Marjorie's 'Diurnall' for the present, I may say that, albeit sad enough in some aspects as were the four years whereof the last-quoted portions treat, they were, in one respect, the happiest of Mistress Elspet's existence. And curious it is to trace whence flowed this joyfulness, the source being, most unlikely, none other, in fact, than that ill-conditioned Mistress Clavers' unruly tongue. Her sneering insinuation that Mr. Hepburn came a-wooing her elderly, unbeautiful, kindly neighbour, had, under Providence, eventuated in that worthy spinster's unruffled placidity of mind.

[1] Tidy.

The spasmodic thrill caused by supposing that Mr. Hepburn *might* have an eye to herself matrimonially, had ere long calmed into a sort of normal pleasant little flutter of expectation, that seemed somehow to raise her to Marjorie's level in the matter of sentimental male friendship, and transfer her to the right side of that mysterious door at whose back she had hitherto stood. And then the new-born taste for making her person attractive initiated her, as it were, into the freedom of those sumptuary prettinesses she had ever since early youth considered unutterably beyond her gauge. So, albeit bloodshed and cruelty were ravaging the length and breadth of Scotland, and, as a Christian woman, Mistress Elspet bemoaned the same, yet her personality felt itself a more interesting fact than ever before. Loving and mild by nature, she now, in her gentle, vague happiness, grew yet more affectionate and easy-going, and thus, so to speak, in a glad dream of being seated on her once longed-for woman's throne, surrounded by a cool emerald radiance, her days glided into years.

Mr. Hepburn's visits became quite an institution, as did dear old Auntie's neat finery. Also a general 'petting' of her, as being, in an undefinable way, the centre of that common friendship each felt for each, under diverse modes of development. And by-and-by (so gradually that the steps towards decay were well-nigh imperceptible) Mistress Elspet's memory began to fail. To weaken peacefully, and without any temporary lucid fret, neither picturing bygone sorrow nor projecting itself into future woe, but resting with infinite satisfaction in the present *Now*. Ah! how wonderful is God's great plan of compensation! How many His ways of growing gourds for behoof of creatures we in our blindness are perchance pitying or despising!

Mistress Clavers (who had never quite forgiven poor Elspet Ker for inheriting Madame Rougemont's wealth) intended her gossip simply as a vent to her spite, but see how the Lord turned even her ill-nature into a warm *bield* to shelter His single-talented servant, when stormy winds should be let loose on the earth.

CHAPTER X.

'. . . . He saw the light
Of household fires gleam warm and bright,
. . . .
And from his lips escaped a groan.'—*Excelsior!*

THE last four years had been so filled with persecutional enormities that 'Woe-worth-the-day!' arose in doleful symphony from men of opposite religious sects, and even antagonistic political opinions. But with the opening of 1687 came a deceitful lull in the tempest, whereat some short-sighted and shilly-shallying folks rested upon their oars, wiped their brows, and thanked their stars that they had safely weathered the gale. For the lately-crowned King of Great Britain, albeit a bigoted Papist, had just issued what it pleased him to call an 'Indulgence' to his Presbyterian subjects in Scotland, which 'Indulgence' was simply a 'permit' to preach the Gospel after their own fashion, but at his pleasure. On the heels of this precious edict, however, another was promulgated, removing all disabilities from those of the Romish belief, thus doing his utmost to put Christ and Antichrist on an equal footing, but with secret intent to give shortly entire supremacy to the latter. The present quasi-liberal 'dodge' took with many who had stuck to their colours, so long as the alternative was 'pure white or coal black.' Good figs or bad figs, *tout simple*. But now that of his clemency the King had offered an opportunity of preaching and fighting for Heaven's sake under a pretty grey or lilac flag, wherefore not make use of it?

Not thus, however, argued James Renwick. With him yea was yea, and nay nay, albeit he felt none the less grieved at the defection of brethren with whom he had hitherto held communion. Nay worse, it came to his knowledge that in order to excuse themselves to themselves, divers of his heretofore coadjutors were maligning him, as being their original misleader from those succulent-soiled fields, wherein grow leeks and onions, cucumbers and barley.

(Woe's me! Woe's me! Ere many months had come and gone they knew better. But this is by-the-bye.)

As for Renwick, and those of *his* way of viewing matters, there was now only increased sorrow upon that sea where trouble enow was before. They were aspersed, as the obnoxious splinter of bone which hindered the national wound from healing comfortably; and maledictions were consequently hurled at them from right and left.

Meanwhile, God alone knew how Renwick's warm and

naturally hopeful heart was wrung by the painful complication of present contingencies. Those occasions when he could find opportunity to address his followers, and so fortify their faith, were refreshments to his own soul; but so vigilant had the enemy become in searching, that these assemblies waned fewer and fewer. Sometimes, all alone, on some wide heathery moor—and oh, so weary!—the lad (for he was scarcely five-and-twenty) would gaze up at the cool, calm, blue sky overhead, and almost wish to lie down and die, then and there. But no. For who would there be to uplift the banner he must in that case lay down? Who stand up in all broad Scotland for Christ's crown and covenant? So, 'Not yet, O Lord, not yet!' was his prayer; 'Spare me still a little longer,' his earnest entreaty.

At times, in his lonely wanderings, Marjorie's spirit would, as it were, feel close to his own, comforting, loving, sympathizing. 'Dear Marjorie, my wife "that might be;" my sister-soul "that is."' Now and then, too, fatigue of body and unrest would beget visions of terror whereat he was scared, albeit quite conscious they were only imaginary.

On such occasions, all solitary under the twinkling stars or noontide sun, he would lift his well-nigh transparent hands betwixt his face and the light, and exclaim in a very panic, 'Oh! how shall I bear having these hands cut off by the hangman's axe!'

But a greater than he had long before been also tempted

in the wilderness, and now suffered not the 'wicked one' to triumph over-much.

During this period things were going on at Covenant Close pretty much as before, though Marjorie's cheek grew thinner from constant anxiety concerning her betrothed. For, somehow or other, spring whence they might, the malign reports against him came oftener to her ears than used to be the case. Mr. Hepburn did his possible to afford counteracting comfort; but Mistress Clavers, and one or two like-minded spinsters, tittle-tattled the Jesuit fabrication till it became quite current in the Close. Ay! and travelled thence, out and back again, gathering and gathering in pungency till the superinduced spice far outweighed the original material. So, as I said, Marjorie had *her* share of anxiety, all the more that in these latter days Auntie Eppie's defective memory rendered her incompetent as a recipient of her niece's fears.

Dear Auntie Eppie! so gentle and happy! so fondled and made of! Sometimes to poor Marjorie it was quite a comfort to argue from *her* condition how God can turn even crosses into gourds, to shade tender heads that might otherwise have ached over-much in the hot east wind.

And Wattie! Well, he was just the self-same Wattie still; as rollicking and good-tempered and non-literary as of old, idling away a large portion of his time, but by no means an evil lad—rather the contrary, in fact, so far as fundamental principle is concerned; extremely fond of his two women-kind, and holding Mr. Hepburn in immense admiration because of his powers as a romancist—for truth compels me to confess that divers of the anecdotes so prized by Wattie were slightly mythical.

Baby-Letty, now betwixt five and six years of age, still lived at Mrs. Fairlie's, but was a frequent visitor in Covenant Close, a great pet of Marjorie and Wattie. The former she always called her 'own bonnie ladie,' but the big, easy-tempered boy was her delight, and to ride on his broad shoulders reward sufficient for a whole week of extra good conduct.

Laird Baigrie was understood by Mrs. Fairlie to be still abroad, but Letty's board being paid five years in advance, the old lady did not concern herself much about his present whereabouts. Regarding the said Laird, Mr. Hepburn wondered that so wealthy a man remained thus long without making inquiries concerning the security of his two heritable bonds, but having in his day come across sundry curious specimens of humanity, he made up his mind that Antony Baigrie was one such, and then dismissed him from his mind. Once, when he had by chance told Marjorie of her quondam acquaintance's large fortune, it rather surprised her, but she soon forgot all about him in her own cares and disquiets.

Whilst at this point we are, so to speak, gathering up the various threads of the human web stretched over this chronicle, it may be advisable to mention the how and where of Mistress Renwick and her niece, Katherine.

Well, within a fortnight after Laird Baigrie carried away his infant ward from the wooden-fronted house, Katherine wedded old Dr. Fairlie, of the Gorbals, and led him an unquiet life during the remaining twelve months of his stay in this world. His well-dowered widow then returned with her infant daughter to her Aunt Renwick's home, resolved to bide her time, and trust to the chapter of accidents for, even yet, getting possession of her cousin James's heart and hand; for Katherine rarely gave up her own wishes as hopeless, and now began to think that concerning the probable marriage of Renwick and Marjorie she had, after all, taken rather an extreme view.

At any rate, here, at twelve-months' end, were the betrothed pair single still, and who could foretell what the future might have in store? So years slid by, bringing to the comfortably-dowered doctor's relict suitors of diverse dates and patterns. But to none of them did she incline, not merely because, compared with her cousin, they were mostly what she termed 'sumphs,' but likewise from a sort of combative antipathy towards the unknown young lady who had monopolized what she chose to consider her own first love. Also, over and above this questionable feeling, Renwick's continual danger, his bravery, his goodness, kept up in her worldly breast a more than ordinary interest. Mistaking this chronic hankering after excitement anent a good man for personal religion, she of course cultivated the feeling, and piqued herself not a little upon the growing height of her piety.

Having thus given all needful explanations, I shall now take up once more the main thread of the narrative.

Wattie's natal day fell due in the month of November, and with an eye to the festal celebration thereof in 1687, Mr. Hepburn was supping at Mistress Elspet's. The weather was raw and cold. All the afternoon Marjorie had felt depressed, and (in consequence of the ominous and persistent howling of a stranger dog at the stair-foot) more than commonly foreboldeful concerning the safety of her absent lover. But when the lawyer arrived as cheerily imperative as usual, she brightened up, albeit he brought no news of the wanderer. Few people indeed could resist the pleasant *go* of Mr. Hepburn's kindly small chat, and to-night it had the effect of 'springing' Marjorie clean out of her dismals (for the time being), even while quite conscious that her present gaiety was but a blink between showers. To anybody peeping into the little parlour that chill, gusty evening, it would have fitly represented a model cosy domestic interior. Thanks to the deceased Madame Rougemont's somewhat *bizarre* taste in house-fittings, the low walls were covered with yellow tapestry bordered with black, a large medallion of bright blue worsted work forming the centre of each hanging. These oblongs represented severally, in severely bright colours, Saint Anthony and Saint Ursula (the patron saints of Madame Rougemont and her husband), a Holy Family, and the Rougemont coat-of-arms. There was not much furniture, only a great thick-legged ebony table and four high-backed chairs to match, but the room being small, more upholstery would have been cumbersome, and we all know that enough is not only as *good*, but sometimes *better* than a feast.

Supper being ended, the partakers thereof withdrew these high-backed chairs to the hearth, that is, placed them two at either 'ingle-cheek,'[1] the fire being just then rather fierce for comfortably sitting right in its front. Nevertheless, with the flames flickering coquettishly on the great silver claret-jug and the edges of the supper dishes, it considerably added to the pictorial snugness of the party, besides bringing out (as a painter would say) the vivid colours of their evidently holiday attire.

More by chance than direct intention, Marjorie and Mr. Hepburn were seated side by side, *vis-à-vis* Wattie and his aunt, and all four were looking their best, for say what we will about the superiority of unadorned beauty, fine feathers *do* make pretty fowls.

In honour of her brother's birthday, Marjorie wore a quilted dress of violet taffetas, made short enough to show black stockings with golden clocks, and cherry-coloured shoes, finished off with large violet rosettes. An apron, hanging sleeves, and hair-ribbons of cherry-coloured sheeny satin, completes her costume, *i.e.*, if you add thereto a blue silk cord round her neck, to which was attached, but hidden in her boddice, half of the 'siller sixpence' once given her by Renwick.

---

[1] Fireside.

Auntie Eppie was magnificent in a tawny and blue-striped saque of silk saie, and a castellated-looking cap, from which floated pink streamers.

As for Wattie, he had on his best suit, but about it there was nothing noteworthy save a 'clean Steinkirk,' whereas his ordinary style was to wear that article considerably rumpled.

But the other gentleman of the party having, out of compliment to the special occasion, endued himself in a quite new suit, is worth describing, the more so from not being naturally much of a dressy man. For so black-a-vised an individual as Mr. Hepburn, one might have supposed pale salmon-coloured raiment anything but becoming, yet, strange to say (in spite of all orthodox rules anent suitability), he had never looked half so well in his life. Not, mind you, that he had studied beautifying effect when selecting his gay garments, but as with his uncalculating dash-at-it way of going to work he occasionally happened to hit the right nail on the head, so was it in the present instance. To Wattie's delight he was in great anecdotive force that evening, so much so that, spirited temporarily out of her wearing anxieties, the girl sitting beside him, sparkling and smiling, scarcely seemed her usually stately sweet self, albeit not the less attractive for *that* perhaps.

As they were all enjoying a story Mr. Hepburn was relating, a very gentle, cautious-sounding tirl was heard on the risping-pin at the outer door.

'That'll be Betsy's sweetheart come a-courting again,'

cried Wattie, with his usual good-tempered laugh, 'sic a pair of auld asses! If Tam Ling is an hour old, he's sixty-five, and as for Bet, why, auntie, I believe, she's ever so much older than even *you*.'

Again the tirl was repeated as softly as before, and presently Betsy was heard undoing the door, and uttering her ordinary receptional salute, 'Ech! gude gracious.'

A few moments thereafter, even while a smile at Wattie's remarks anent the old servant's flirtation was still beaming on the faces of his companions, the parlour door opened, and, unannounced, James Renwick was ushered into the room.

Weary, ragged! obliged to come hiddenly, as if he were a thief! Fresh from cruel reproaches, hurled at him by a heretofore brother in tribulation. Poor fellow! the first glimpse of the happy-looking group in Mistress Elspet's tapestried parlour caused him keener pain than all his past sufferings put together. In the most trying of his many harassments, a strong sense of personal rectitude had, by God's grace, upheld his spirit—that brave 'bit spirit' so early remarked by his good old mother as ruling with indomitable force the delicate body which held it. Quite recently, his troubles had been incessant, and of a nature irritating to mortal nerves, and withal so puerile that but for the comfort of Marjorie's love they would sometimes have been in danger of foregrounding for the moment the high Christian patriotism for which apparently he got so little thanks or credit. At such seasons of temptation, out in the wilderness, Satan had tried hard to make him feel he was spending himself for a mere delusion; but even then, He who in another desert had rebuffed the Evil One's onslaught, helped His poor servant so to do likewise by bringing vividly before His mind's eye that leal maiden-heart expressly prepared for him by Providence.

Does this mode of consolation appear derogatory as bestowed by the Omnipotent upon a probable martyr for the high sublimities of Christ's crown-rights, and the freedom of down-trodden Scotland? Ah me! God's governance of His creatures is so much more reasonable than they are willing to believe! Renwick, albeit right zealous for the truth, was a young man, and almost poetically in love. Wherefore should not this heavenly reminder, that one ewe-lamb remained to him in his poverty, not prove, in the circumstances, equivalent to a 'Get thee behind me, Satan?'

During the last month the search after him had waxed so vigilant that Renwick's lot had included more solitary skulking and fewer preaching opportunities than usual, and, moreover, it was borne in upon his mind that his race was well-nigh run. In truth, this impression was partly the reason why, at great personal risk, he had come to Edinburgh, being very anxious to see his affianced once more. One may imagine one's death approaching, but one does not, therefore, at five-and-twenty, give up the sweet habitude of sinless loving, especially the woman who has saved one's heart from total disillusionment.

Coming in so suddenly from the dark little passage, with all his pent-up love and anticipative pathos leaping and rushing for immediate outgate, no wonder the scene that met the outlaw's eye caused him to start.

Marjorie ! *his* Marjorie ! the soul's-sister of his many dreary pilgrimages and starlit vigils ! his promised wife ! the woman he had loved from a child ! his very own !

Picking his way that shivery, gusty November night toward Covenant Close, he had half expected (perhaps irrationally, but we all do such things now and then) to find her in outward congruity with his own hapless condition. And what saw he ? His beautiful love, smiling *so* cheerfully, dressed *so* smartly, sitting *so* friendly, with her elbow on the great chair, occupied by a personable man in gallant attire ! In the so sudden back-rush of his surging emotions, no wonder the wanderer felt jealous. As little wonder was it that next instant, recoiling horrified from this to him strange temptation, he abhorred himself, and repented in figurative dust and ashes. It all passed in a minute, as he halted startled on the threshold. A short time suffices for a mental ebb-flood that may perchance suck in the weal and ruth of many a life.

On recognising who the intruder was, they of course sprang up to welcome him heartily, all but Marjorie, who, mazed, as it were, by the so unexpected cessation of her fears, instead of rushing forward with outstretched arms, as became a heroine, stood stock-still beside the fire, trying, poor girl, to understand how glad she was. And, albeit scarcely comprehended by herself, there was another cause for her apparent unimpulsiveness on this occasion, to wit, a suspicion that to flaunt her glorious wealth of love for Renwick before Hepburn's very face would be not only cruel, but in the circumstances wrong. Not even to herself would she have put into words an idea that had of late made her consider kindness to the lawyer a sort of mission, but none the less was a notion present to her mind that vague affection for *her* was day by day leading him nearer those paths that point to the way of holiness. Were he then, at this juncture, and especially to-night, when she had been so extra agreeable, to find himself nobody in her eyes, and the new-comer all-in-all, it might cause a desperate slide back towards the visibly broad road where formerly he had walked unresisting.

All these cogitative emotions of all these persons take a good while to detail, but the experience thereof did not occupy thirty seconds. Presently everybody subsided out of 'the intensities' into their common selves, some of them feeling compunctious for fleeting hard thoughts of others. This was poor, tired Renwick's case. While being attended at his supper by Marjorie, looking like an overjoyed Hebe, he had difficulty to keep from falling on his knees and crying, *Mea culpa! mea culpa!*

'So foolish was I, and ignorant,' this was his thought, 'I forgot all the Lord's bypast goodness, and not only distrusted

Him, but said in my haste, All men are liars. What shall I render to dear Marjorie to make up for thinking her false to her troth?'

So, thereupon, being warned and filled, did 'our young Josiah' set about love-making as fervently, and gracefully, as he did everything else. Not coarsely, as was too much the then mode with *ex-officio* swain-ish embracements, accompanied by loud assertions that they were bestowed on a goddess, but tenderly and exquisitely, retiring, so to speak, hand in hand with his betrothed and his compunction into that blessed 'Vestibule' where, in the aroma that exhales from Paradise, earthly cares and regrets lose half their sting.

By-and-by Betsy and her fellow-servant came in for worship, which commenced by the sound of 'grave sweet melodie.' For, albeit the brave young minister's very life depended on keeping his presence in Edinburgh a secret, like Daniel of old, he would not rob God of even the least shred of due honour, but boldly went through the orthodox curriculum of family-prayer, the singing of a couple of psalms included. And the after-portion,—ah me! its pithy, holy beauty lingered in the memory of some of the audience long after the fervid young speaker had gone where there is no more prayer, because all is praise. And then the servants retired to their sleeping-settles beside the kitchen fire, and the five friends in the parlour drew together for confidential outpouring, such as takes place in risky times when present meetings are likely enough to be the last. The talk was, of course, solemn in the main (for who could foretell what a day might bring forth in the way of terrors?), but yet it was pleasant too (Renwick had ever the way of, as it were, popularizing even dry themes). Judge then of Marjorie's feelings whilst with open ear she drank in the glowing words, which, as they fell from his lips, were so instinct with the spirit of Christian heroism that they served to confirm her in a project which had been (off and on) in her head for some months past, albeit she had made no mention thereof to anybody. This project was to offer to marry Renwick at once, instead of delaying indefinitely the fulfilment of her betrothal vow. What had first made her think of taking such a step was the report of his being a sworn Jesuit, which had gained considerable credence among people who might have known better had they cared to search out the facts, instead of adding gratuitous stones to the 'cairn' already so shamefully high. 'I'll disprove this lie by marrying James,' thought the ardent girl in her zeal for the Kirk, and love to its persecuted servant. But to-night, with that instinctive insight into other people's feelings which distinguished her, Marjorie had guessed pretty correctly at the state of 'our young Josiah's' love experiences, not omitting his touch of jealousy and subsequent repentance for the same. 'Oh, how dreadful it is of me,' she thought, 'to be living here at ease when the wicked are maligning James, and hunting him to death, and weakening his heart, and making him fancy things that, but for his misery, would never enter his head. I am afraid he may suppose I am ashamed of him, and the cause he serves, if—'

Out it came, by-and-by, in a little pathetic Ruth-like burst of eloquence, to wit, pretty Marjorie Ker's offer of herself as immediate help-meet to the homeless, almost shoeless wanderer. The girl's proposal took her auditory by surprise (Renwick most of all), but none gainsaid her, being tongue-tied by different causes more or less personal. As for the bridegroom-elect, recognising perfectly the reasons of Marjorie's declaration, he, poor fellow, blessed her more than ever in his heart, even while inwardly debating whether or no it was allowable for him to accept the fulfilment of his strongest personal desire. (Woe's me! earthly roses, even at their best, so rarely grow thornless, fragrant and delightsome though they be.) That terrible moment when he stood on the threshold of Mistress Elspet's parlour, the wormwood and the gall and the jealousy, his soul had them, even yet, in remorseful remembrance. How should he give up his 'only love?' How put his soul again within risk of committing such hideous sin?

As I mentioned, the talk of the little party had drifted into serious heroics, and now, screwed up to a high pitch as they were, it did not directly occur to anybody to enter into prosaic details concerning the mode in which the enthusiastic heroine should carry her non-egotistical resolution into effect. It *did* indeed flash through the young divine's brain that, suffer what he might himself, Marjorie should be kept safe and soft; but I verily believe he was more occupied admiring her self-abnegation, than calculating how they were to set up housekeeping in the wilderness. Had he possessed more of the loaf-and-fishy sort of forecast, he probably might never have climbed so far up what lukewarm professors called 'the heights,' and yet a more clever, prudent, sensible young man no one could desire to see. Letters of intercommuning being out against him, he behoved, for safety's sake, to quit the city before day-dawn, and Mr. Hepburn volunteered to escort him beyond the bounds. There is no need to describe minutely the adieus of the lovers, but I may just state, in passing, that out of very proper feeling the lawyer turned his back on their performance, keeping Mistress Elspet and Wattie in conversation the while.

And where, think you, are now those grave presentiments of speedy death which had been the chief cause of Renwick's present visit? Gone! vanished as completely as ice in the noontide sun. So utterly evaporated indeed, that till a good length on his journey he quite forgot they had ever existed. Not that the young minister was of a flighty disposition, he being quite the reverse. But remember, I pray you, he was but five-and-twenty, over head and ears in love, and, moreover, endued by nature with a temperament so springy and hopeful that even the more than commonly severe crook in his lot could hardly daunt it.

CHAPTER XI.

'Thy rod and thy staff they comfort me.'

IT was formerly stated that when Laird Baigrie found the Bath waters ineffectual in suppling his rheumatic knee, he betook himself to foreign parts, to wit, Flanders and France, many of his co-religious compatriots being then resident in those countries. In process of time the stiffened joint relaxed into its pristine 'inward-inclining' ease of motion; but still Antony continued abroad, albeit, judging by his *words*, neither foreign morals nor customs found much favour in his eyes. Indeed, his dear country and her persecuted Kirk were so constantly his themes of praise, that in a particular town where he stayed a winter, one of the magistrates (a free-thinking sort of man) used to name them 'Herr Baigrie's phylacteries.'

To hear the 'young elder' holding forth, people's only wonder must have been how so zealous a covenanter could (figuratively speaking) abide contentedly in his tent eating, drinking, and making merry, whilst the 'Brethren beloved' were gone down into the open field to do battle for the Lord of Hosts. There was no cogent reason why he should not return to the land of his fathers, yet year slid away after year and saw him still lingering on, or rather dawdling away existence upon a foreign soil, albeit not cut off from all communication with much-enduring Scotland. For, besides the fact that both in Flanders and France there were several army-regiments, composed entirely of paid Caledonians, not a few of the same nation had settled abroad as merchants and in other capacities. Hence a certain amount of news passed betwixt the distant countries, but the information thus forwarded was often so grossly exaggerated, that in practical times, such as ours, nobody would have credited one-tenth of it. But, be that as it may, there wafted ever and anon from across the sea rumours anent the outed kirk-militant, and how it had come to sore grief at the hands of 'baptized Philistines.' Such reports of course included a nominal list of '*who* turned and fled in the shock of battle, and *who* boldly and unblenching faced the foe.'

During the first three years of Antony's residence abroad the accounts thus transmitted from his native land were neither more nor less than a series of 'ill-put-together' Jeremiades beginning and ending in 'Woe! woe! woe!'

How, in these circumstances, could it be expected that a wealthy man (he had, with a certain reservation, got into the habit of so considering himself) should rush into turmoil and danger for the mere sake of so doing? On the contrary, it was simply a duty he owed to himself to remain where he was, lifting up the while no end of a vocable testimony for Christ's Crown and the Covenants.

'Storms political and religious always end by clearing the moral atmosphere.' Matters would in course of time right themselves, and then 'Oh! the immense amount of good Antony would do at Halket by-and-bye.'

About the beginning of his fourth year of absence it seemed as if his pragmatical prognostics were coming true, for the Indulgence, already described, was proclaimed in Scotland and duly bruited in other lands.

Distance lends enchantment to the view, and seen from Flanders the afore-mentioned royal edict looked somewhat like a receipt in full of all reasonable claims presentable by even the staunchest followers of John Knox. So thereupon Antony's heart waxed glad, because, to do him justice, he was wearying to commence playing the moneyed landowner in Tweedsmuir, and, moreover (inapt as he was at languages), terribly tired of being, as it were, harnessed to lingos wherein by no possibility could he go easy. His mind was therefore made up to return home in the beginning of 1688, being a full year short of the date originally proposed. It is amazing how quickly time slips past do-nothing persons, not to speak of day-dreamers, and albeit rather an adept in his own phase of this last amusement, he could now hardly believe he had been so long away.

Strange to say, Marjorie Ker's desirability as a helpmate had gradually faded in distance, but the prospect of his speedy home-going set it up as fresh as ever in the Laird's imagination. Was she still open for competition? He was fain so to hope, at least if one might draw inferences from the far-travelled hinty sketches of Renwick which occasionally came to hand. Quite recently these oral portraitures had somehow been painted in anything but rose colour, especially when designed by men professedly labouring in the same cause as himself. *Ex. gr.*,—'We should get peace now but for Renwick's absurd crotchets anent certain matters.' 'He is a good lad, but decidedly weak in the head.' 'He is evil, and a "snake in the grass" of our spiritual pastures.' 'When rational men cry for peace at any price, lo! he is all for war.' 'A seditious rebel, who tries to hinder the preaching of Christ's evangel when permission to proclaim it is offered.' 'Away with such a fellow from the earth!'

In these and similar deliverances of opinion there was never any mention of 'a Mistress' James Renwick. So doubtless Marjorie Ker was still to the fore, and accordingly the young elder generally favoured *her* with a place in his egotistical previsions. Whilst he is preparing, as mariners would say to hoist his 'Blue Peter,' let us see whether Marjorie's 'Diurnal' throws any light upon Scotland at a parallel period.

'Covenant Close, December the Eleventh 1687.—Dear Auntie Eppie, shee is So trusting, and So Helpless somewaie, Thatt each Daie I feel more and More How Selfish itt was of Mee to Saie I would quitt her. And Yett God knoweth thatt I would gladlie travell to Earth's utmost Ends with Mie Own Brave James. Yea, and shall, when he comes for mee, tho' Mie verie heart-strings should Crack for leaving Auntie, who unto mee hath been more than a mother. Att this season Mie Mind is racked with distress concerning the future, whilk is a Sinn, Seeing thatt itt is in The Lord's Hands, nott mine, and thatt Hee who Died to Save Mee From Hell can surely Manage toe carrie mee through this Present Life By the Beste Road for me. I hear no Worde of Mie Dear Since hee Left this place, nigh Three Weeks agone. I Dreamt Yester-Night that I saw a Corpse lying in our Dead-Chamber, on the Black Table in its Midst, and Wrapped upp in a White Linnen Shroud, And albeit meethought the Face was covered, I some- waie knew it was James Renwick. As I stood in Tears aside the Corpse, Three Knocks cam Toe the Door, Whilk when I opened, lo! there were the Governmente Searchers Come to examinate if the Shroud was woollen, against the new laws. I thought I flung mieself Across the Corpse to Hinder the Men from fingering itt, When, lo! One of the Searchers Turned into a Beautiful Angel all of a Suddentie, With Such Bonnie glistering white Wings, Spreckled with Diamonds, And its face was James's, with his own Dear, Blue, kind Eyes, and cheeks like Roses. This Angel put mee Back gentlie, And Saide "Bee not afraid, onlie Believe, and Thou shalt yet See What God Can Doe." Then Hee Motioned unto The Other Searcher to Doe His Dutie, And He Came forward and opened upp the Shroud to look if Wee had not putten Wooll underneath, as somewaie it was Borne in on Mee that Mistress Clavers Had given notice that wee had done. But When The Searcher opened upp the Shroud, lo! There laie Dear Auntie Eppie's Dead Corpse, dressed in the old green Saie she used to Weare at Greendykes, and When I turned round the Searcher that turned into James his likeness had Vanished Awaie. This I feare is Butt a Bad Dreame, and Therefore Am I Schooling Mieself To Truste More in The Lorde his Dailie Providence, and Also to Abide Continuallie within The Vestibule. Whilk waie to Walk in I know not. O Mie God, Bee thou for Mee the Breaker upp of mie paths, Going before thye much disquieted Handmaiden. Mie dear Auntie forgets things, and behaves just like a dawtie-Bairn.[1] How Can I possiblie quit her, with onlie Wattie to Look After Her? And How could I either Tell Mie dear James when Hee comes in Februarie, Thatt after expecting toe get a companion thatt would love and Comfort Him, Hee maun just goe awaie again all Solitarie toe His wearie Wanderings among Mosses and Mountains? I *did* think I Was Doing Mie Dutie to The Lord his Kirk When I made offer of mie hand to

[1] Dear child.

James, considering nott, at the moment, the Unmaidenlieness of thus Speaking, but sometimes now I am feared lest it was a Sinn in Mee to seek to Burden *him* with a Spouse when hee hath more than enough of Care on his dear Oppressed Back Alreadie About the Kirk and Her Down-Trodden Covenants. Onlie that night Mie Heart was like to Burste, when hee looket for one Minute as if Hee thought it possible I Could care as much for Mr. Hepburn as for Him, and love Himself less, because His Gown it was Ragged and His shoes likewise. Mie Chief Comforte in this Wearie Trial-Season is Mr. Hepburn, Who whiles Remindes Mee about God's ever-present guidance, when in Mie dismaie I am Nigh forgetting Jesus in the Miste and Waves thatt Surround Mee. I reallie am quite certaine *now* that Mr. Hepburn is a Convertit Mann. In all Mie dismaie this giveth Mee great Joie.

'*December the Twelveth.*—This is a Fine, Clear, Frosty Daie, and Soe verie Cold that When I went upp to The Wind-Mill to Order Some Ale I had toe Run Faste toe Keep Mie Toes Warme. Upon the Burrow Loch people are Skating, Likewise upon the North Loch, and from the High Street I could discern quite plain The Bass Rock, and the Blew Sea around it. The Castle on The Bass, with the Bright Sunshine upon itt, to-daie appears as prettie as if no poor Martyrs were suffering inside its Walls. In this respect it resembleth Mee at this present Time. I have no call to goe with Mine Head Hanging Like a Bull Rush, and therefore doe I seem as cheerie as Mie usual. But Everie Time Dear Old Auntie Eppie smiles att mee, and nods her Head, and Saies, "Weel, Mie Dawtie, ye'll Bee a passing Bonnie Bride," Mie heart Sinks with grief till I can hardlie Thole itt. And on the Back o' thatt comes straitwaie the Feare thatt Maiebee, att this Verie Moment, Mie Own James is lying dead on Some Snaw-Drift or Bleak Hill Side, and Will Never, Never come in Februarie. And thatt again makes mee feel as if Hee knew alreadie the agonie, the verie thoughts o' quitting Auntie and going Awaie with Him is causing mee. Verilie, O Mie Compassionate Saviour, Thou Seest mee to bee a poor, unstable Creature. Bee thou Mie Breaker-upp of the Waie, For on Thee Onlie Doe I Truste. I considered indeed that in offering to James thatt night I was but fulfilling a Christian Woman Her Dutie, Albeit I am now sometimes disquieted lest itt was human Love onlie thatt prompted mee, instead of a Single eye toward upholding the hands of thy Dear, Bewtiful, Brave, Afflicted Servant, James Renwick.

'*Decbr. Nineteenth*, 1687.—This Fore-noon A Mann called John Bold Came Selling Fire-Wood, Being Sent bye Mistress Clavers, who getts her's From his Yard. When I was paying him, Hee said, "Mistress, I ken a Friend o' yours right Weel." "Who is't?" Saies I. So thereupon hee told mee thatt Hee had once Been James Renwick his precentor, and out with him in Carrick, but hath not seen him these Manie months past, Having been compelled to quitt to attend upon his Mother, thatt then was dying here, and is since dead. It was pleasant, indeed, to speak face to face with a person thatt could tell mee exactlie whatt the people said about James on Diverse Occasions, Hee Beeing far too modeste to tell it Himself. Yett I am Sorrie thatt this Mann plainlie knows about Mee and James, whilk it is Clear Hee does. I think Mistress Clavers hath gathered it from poor Auntie (shee being now soe Unmemorable), and has repeated it unto this Mann Bold. I have promised thatt wee will Take all our Fire-wood att His Yarde, and when I goe to make paiement I shall alwaies Hear Some more about James.

'*December the Twentie-Three.*—Mr. Hepburn is grieved exceedinglie thatt the Mann John Bold gott Speech of Mee or Came Nigh Our House. He finds thatt in verie Truth the Mann *was* James his Precentor, and Beeing taken, was Sentenced to Bee Hangit, But got off bye Recanting whatt hee had before Sworn upon the Holie Bible. I will nott now goe to Bold his Yard, Nor Take Our Wood from thence. Itt will Bee noe Falsehood on Mie part, Seeing Hee is verie Likelie an Informer, and Maie all the Time Bee wanting the Hundred Pounds that Cruel and Unrighteous Men have offered as the price of Mie Godlie, Lovelie Saint his Head. Lord, Help us all in These Sadd Times!

'*New-Year's Daie, The Year of Man's Salvation One Thousand Six Hundred and Eightie-Eight.*—I arose Earlie, and Commended Mie Manie Cares unto Mie Dear Redeemer,

Thus, As it Were, Entering Anew into That Blessed Vestibule where Mie James ever Staies. Mr. Hepburn is coming to Supper, and I have just been Setting out the Table Somewhat Tastilie, I think, and helping Betsie to make Stuffing for the Flap of the Roast Mutton, as hee is fond of that Dish.

'I have been dressing Mie dear old Auntie for Mr. Hepburn's Coming, as beeing New Year it is a kind of Ploie[1] (Albeit God Knows this is no Season for Junketting, when Mie James is hunted bye night and bye daie). Dear Aunt Eppie is So pleased like, I declare shee is turning well-nigh prettie in her old Age. The Whiteness of her Hair makes her Features looke far Softer Than the black used to doe. Shee is so proud and happie this After-Noon, with the New Pearl-white Satin Streamers I putt in her Cap. Also her Crimson Manco petticoat looks well.

'*Januarie the Third.*—O Lord, Bye Terrible Things in Righteousness Dost Thou rebuke our Mistrust. Mie More than Mother, Mie Beloved, Sweet, Kindlie Auntie Eppie, that ever proved a good friend unto mee, is dead and gone, Lying this minute a Corpse. She was nodding her Head to Mr. Hepburn, and going to drink his health and Manie Returns of the New-Year, when in an instant Shee " was not," For God Took her toe himself. I am verie Sure of Her Everlasting Safetie. O! Wherefore did I crie, "Lord, open to mee Anie Waie of going to Mie poor James with a Clear Conscience!"

[1] Fête.

Where is mie Faith, that I thought strong enough to make me Rejoice in whatever was thy Will? I feel now as if I Had not loved Mie Sweet Old Auntie Half as much as She Deserved, And as if Between Her and Mee it had alwaies been *Take* on Mie Side, and *Give* on Her's. Mr. Hepburn is taking Care for the Burial. Whatt in all the World Would Wattie and Mee Doe without Him?

'*Januarie the* 20*th.*—Mie dear Auntie had never thought about Willing Awaie her Fortune, as she aye intendit it should goe to mee at her Death. Soe Wattie By Law Heirs all, Saving the Moveables, and is a Wealthie boy. Also a dear kind laddie, for hee Saies that Him and mee will just staie on here as at present, and on no account will he allow mee to go awaie. I am in a Sore Strait. To leave so young and somewhat thoughtless a laddie bye himself in a house would Bee a Sin; and yett, no doubt, in a fortnight Mie James will come for mee, if (as God Grant) Hee is Alive. Daie bye daie I miss more mie little duties thatt I did for Mie blessed Sweet Auntie. I can never remember Her doing one single unkind or harsh thing, and now her Memorie is like Fragrance poured out on Mie Sore Heart. Mr. Hepburn is looking ill, and, moreover, upbraiding himself for not having asked Auntie if she had made her Will. I am Sorrie indeed about Mr. Hepburn feeling thus, as it was nobodie's Blame, but God's Wise Providence. O! How I do wearie for a Sight of James's brave face! He always makes mee run, as it were, into the Vestibule, and there I get composed. He said He would (if Alive) Come in Februarie, and bring some Outed Minister to Marry us. Mr. Hepburn thinks that, as Madame Rougemont's Will saies, it behoves her heirs to dwell in Covenant Close, or lose the great Heritage, And as Betsy is most Trust-Worthie, The best waie will Bee just to let Wattie Staie on in the House, and let her Bee House-Keeper. Mr. Hepburn has promised mee also to give a Frequent Eye to Wattie till such Time as he goes to the Advocate's, where hee is to learn the profession for Himself. I can Now trust Mr. Hepburn Perfectly toe Keep Mie dear young brother in a Strait Course when James and Mee are far Awaie.'

CHAPTER XII.

*'The grave itself is but a covered bridge
Leading from light to light through a brief darkness.'*

SORELY did worthy Mistress Elspet's 'twa bairns' lament her decease, and many a tear they shed while recalling long obliviated instances of her unselfish kindness. Externally her demise made but little difference in the domestic economy, save that Betsy addressed her new master and mistress with due respect, and ever and anon was heard giving off loud sighs in the kitchen. These lugubrious ejaculations were persistent enough to render Marjorie quite nervous, and, poor girl, she had troubles enow of her own just then. Here was she in new deep mourning, expecting to be married in a month or five weeks, but, for fear of spies, not daring either to make any bridal preparations, or so much as a hint that such an event was in contemplation. And then, supposing the wedding safely past, what was to become of her thereafter? The more she tried to investigate the future, the more her very brain seemed to grow dizzy. She would have given almost anything just then for a true woman-friend with whom to take counsel, or to whom she might at least confide the mingled hopes, fears, and anxieties that were nearly driving her beside herself. To be sure there was Betsy, an excellent person, and as true as steel to the interests of the Ker family, root and branch. Yes, but however unimpeachable as a confidante Betsy might personally be, she had unluckily, within the last fortnight, acquired an admirer who was none other than John Bold, the firewood-seller, and *ci-devant* precentor of James Renwick. *That* was enough. Even Marjorie's inexperience understood that in such interesting circumstances it was better not to put the elderly servant's reticence too strongly to the proof.

Mr. Hepburn appeared, as usual, the 'mourning bride's' most available resource, and very helpful as well as patient he proved both to her and Wattie. Still, a feeling she could not express urged that to minutely indoctrinate him into the manifold ups-and-downs of her 'love' and its concomitants would be what modern young ladies term 'not nice,' an expression for which I am inclined to think no precise equivalent then existed. Now-a-days hypercritics laugh at the ramified application of those two monosyllables, which nevertheless sometimes help us round difficult descriptional corners, and at any rate perfectly expressed what Marjorie feared her sentimental outpourings might seem to Mr. Hepburn.

As for Wattie, although now nearly seventeen years old, he was but a big, handsome, warm-hearted boy, whose only decided opinion was that books were works of supererogation. He was, moreover, gifted with such a knack of blurting out whatever came uppermost in his mind, that, had his sister initiated him fully into the *pros* and *cons* of her intended marriage, as sure as fate Mistress Clavers would have gotten the entire details out of him before he was four-and-twenty hours older.

Thus you perceive that, albeit in constant communication with at least three persons who liked her passing well, the bride-elect was sadly in want of a useful receptacle for her mental effervescence.

The close of January was generally a busy professional period with Mr. Hepburn, and thus, on the 31st of that month in 1688, he was unwillingly obliged to forego what, since Mistress Elspet's demise, had become his regular custom, viz., to spend at least part of the evening with Marjorie and her brother.

It is interesting sometimes to track the contemporaneous goings of persons far apart, who are unconsciously being all led by the hand of Providence towards a particular centre, for a special purpose. By aid of certain items and dates, we are now, after the lapse of one hundred and eighty-two years, enabled to make out how the diverse parties mentioned in this chronicle were engaged on the 31st of January.

As Laird Baigrie has been so long absent, we shall take him in hand first, and state that, after a tempestuous passage from Rotterdam, he has just arrived at Leith, and is making the best of his way to the house of his 'far-away cousin,' Mistress Fairlie, there to take a night's lodging.

Marjorie Ker sits solitary in poor Auntie Eppie's once-cherished yellow parlour, for the great bell of Saint Giles's Kirk has rung nine o'clock, and Wattie, who, like Sancho Panza, has a talent for sleeping, retired to rest at half-past eight. Knowing the girl's peculiar circumstances, you can easily comprehend that her ruminations are somewhat perplexing, as she sits there on one of the four ponderous high-backed chairs, staring open-eyed into the fire—staring, but seeing nothing external, albeit mentally as thickly surrounded by life-like creations as was the prophet by glowing invisible horses and chariots. In Marjorie's spirit-kaleidoscope one special figure ever and anon appears, viz., James Renwick, her purposed husband, her hero, apostle, and lover, all in one.

Whilst she sits dreaming him, as it were, to her side, let us see how he is actually occupied. During many hours of that cold drizzly day he had officiated at a conventicle, held at a spot among the Pentland Hills called Black's Craig, being meanwhile under promise to fulfil a similar duty in Fife, so soon as he could repair thither. But before quitting the neighbourhood of Edinburgh (if one may so term a distance of betwixt three and four miles) he was anxious once more to see the being dearest to him on earth. Once more! Ay, for again and again since that night when Marjorie volunteered to become his wife without further delay, he had bemoaned what he now considered the cruel selfishness of taking her at her word. At the time the temptation was irresistible, but since then he had conscientiously viewed all sides of the question, and finally come to the resolution not to allow the girl to link her lot with so severe a fate as his own. In his loving estimate, the damsel's conduct but enhanced her attractiveness, and alas! the lamented jealousy episode had in truth acted as a magnifier, through which her perfections showed in enhanced beauty. But in God's sight he felt that to hold her bound by her promise was simply to endow her with long-linked distress. 'I shall soon be called to seal my testimony with my blood,' had again of late become his steady presentiment. Under this conviction, would it not be well betimes to take steps for sheltering Marjorie's affectionate heart from the awful grief that must needs be her portion as his widow?

Taken up as Renwick then was, heart and soul, with the quivering vitality of Christ's bleeding Church, inwardly premonished that his race was all but finished, does it seem out of keeping with his high vocation thus to permit a mere romance, as it were, to occupy so large a share in his actual inner life?

Ah me! as if there were not martyrdoms and martyrdoms!

As if any save God could reckon how many suffering experiences may be the portion of one individual, or say whether to the more public or private of those shall the crown be adjudged at the great day.

To appreciate the full extent of Renwick's self-abnegation (as on this rainy January night, wrapped in his plaid, he strides across the dark hills), one would require to read his inmost heart, and see how much affection for his betrothed was pent up therein. And yet he was bent not only on delaying the espousals, but in breaking them off finally, for *her* sake—for *her* sake.

We who live in ceiled houses and fare comfortably every day, may ridicule the idea of a penniless outlaw so seriously entertaining thoughts of marriage, that to abjure the same would reckon as an act of self-denial. Once more, however, I pray you to remember that even a possible martyr for a high and holy cause is not always at full tension, but being still in the body, may perchance now and then tonic his overstrained system, so to speak, with a small dose of those sinless pleasures he had found beneficial before becoming 'a man wondered at.'

Renwick was only a little over five-and-twenty, and, poor fellow! knew to his present cost whether being a devoted minister of Christ's evangel blotted out *ex officio* the old sweet habitude of loving Marjorie Ker as few men can love. By means of a man's lot in life, Providence seems now and then specially to baptize his spirit into some peculiar phase of virtue. Thus, at an age when, in nine cases out of ten, youth has still a good many childish things sticking to it, Renwick had been called to be apostle and evangelist to a scattered and numerous Church that, but for him, would have had no 'gospeller' left to do their ministry. And five years of this experience had, as the proverb says, put an old head upon young shoulders, by making large-hearted forethought for others become to him a sort of second nature. So now, as he hies city-wards, with the thick drizzle blattering in his eyes and danking his long yellow locks, there is something intensely pathetic, yet heroic, in his endeavours to forecast a safe and happy life-pilgrimage for Marjorie.

To return to that sweet sister-beloved sitting solitary in the yellow parlour, she was jerked, so to speak, out of her ruminations by a low knock at the outer door. Betsy was just lying down on her settle for the night, and had blown out her cruizie, so a minute or two elapsed before she could answer. Presently, however, the soft knock was twice repeated, and Marjorie heard the elderly maiden rattling and fumbling in the dark at the bolt and chain. The girl was getting nervous, and hence the three knocks instantly identified themselves, as it were, with those of the dream which had formerly disquieted her so much. But on hearing Betsy begin a whispered dialogue with another, evidently male voice, her superstitious fears changed into more practical annoyance at what she supposed to be another kitchen visit from John Bold, the renegade precentor, to his inamorata.

'I'm sure Betsy might have had the sense to take my hint, and not have that man coming here. There's no saying what information about James he might coax out of her.'

The door opened, and Marjorie was clasped in Renwick's arms and wet plaid.

'My poor, dear girl! My own precious wee May!'

This was all he could utter at first, from the great depths of his love and sympathy. Of Mistress Elspet's death he had just heard for the first time from Betsy, and the sight of Marjorie in mourning and solitude overcame him. It was too suggestive of what he had come to save her from, by a very agony of self-denial.

The two sat late into the night conversing, wishing (ah, me!) that the old scythesman would rest him awhile. And then, kneeling side by side at two of the big ebony chairs, Renwick engaged in prayer, uttering a solemn, yet glad thanksgiving to God for having so bound up Marjorie and him in one bundle of life, that, albeit they might be parted in time, they were sure of spending a blissful eternity together. And then, loth to separate just yet (loving one another, oh, how well!), they sat down again, stirred the half-extinct embers into a dull red glow, and got a-talking once more. Talked on, sitting hand in hand upon the same great blackwood seats whereon Marjorie and Mr. Hepburn had sat that night when 'our young Josiah's' jealousy was roused. Talked on till Renwick fairly spirited-back his companion into that 'vestibule' where even woe is burnished bright by present contentment with God's holy will. And then, when the cocks in a yard at the back of the Close were beginning to crow, and Saint Giles's bell was tolling the third watch, and Betsy and her fellow-servant were audibly vying with Wattie in sonorous snores, and the candle was almost burnt out, and the fire was no more a fire, but only a handful of soft, friable, white ashes, the two lovers (for such, near or apart, they would ever be) embraced and said farewell.

'Yes, my own Marjorie, I shall see you before leaving the city. I thank God that so sincere a friend as Mr. Hepburn is left near you and Wattie.'

'But, James, nothing is impossible. Better days *may* be coming for us all. In any case, remember I am yours, and yours only, till death. This posie-ring you gave me is my oath; it shall go with me to the grave.'

'Good-night! Good-night! The Lord cause His face to shine upon thee, my own, and give thee peace.'

On quitting Covenant Close, Renwick repaired to his usual place of stay when in Edinburgh. It was the house of a Cameronian dealer in English goods, and, all things considered, far from a safe spot for the outlawed preacher. For Government just then was on the alert to search out English articles of import that had paid no excise dues, and the subordinate officials made this quest an excuse for invading the privacy of persons who, to save their lives, would not have defrauded any one of a single mite.

Of course the religious tenets of Renwick's friend the trader, made him a marked man, although as yet nothing to warrant either fine or imprisonment had been found against him. But, nothing afraid of the King's unjust commandment concerning 'that pestilent young rebel,' as our hero was called in persecutional proclamations, he gladly, as aforetime, received him at his dwelling on the Castle Hill, accounting his visit even as that of an angel.

'It's a pleasure to me to look on his winsome countenance,' used to say the trader's worthy helpmate. 'It's a pleasure indeed; for a bonnie blue-eyed laddie he is, and aye minds me o' my sweet lassie that's been in Paradise ten years come Martinmas.'

Right hearty, you may be sure, was the welcome accorded by the honest pair to the tired young divine, who had within the last twenty-four hours gone through experiences enough to age him indefinitely, one would think. But the human heart is, and ever will be, an infinite mystery.

The state of Renwick's mind effectually hindered him from rest even after his tired body was stretched on the comfortable bed, always kept in readiness for him by his attached hosts. He had laid his self-reliance upon the altar of what he considered duty to Marjorie, and even forced himself to thank

God that so sincere a friend as Mr. Hepburn was by her side. ('Woe's me,' the very Mr. Hepburn who but a few weeks agone had roused that lamented fit of jealousy within him.) And now here he was, to his own astonishment, thrilling and throbbing in anticipation of the promised interview with Marjorie before he should go to Fife. Aspirate prayers as he would,—take his foolish heart to task as he would, was of no use,—nature *would* make herself heard, and proclaim that the human love God had given to cheer him he could not put away, but ought still to cherish as a boon. Was the noble girl's faith in Almighty governance stronger than his, notwithstanding all his overt deeds of 'dering-do' for the Covenant? In his humility he believed so now. 'She had leant on the "all possibilities" of God's power, and persisted in keeping her plighted troth till better days should come.' *He* had dared to limit Omnipotence, and so in a measure trampled out with his own heel the taper God-given to light his poor humanity in the thick darkness! Yes! yes! Marjorie's hopefulness concerning even this earthly matter was in fact sublime faith, and his forecast, when sifted, neither more nor less than will-worship. So, after tossing on his couch till dawn, he arose, fell on his knees, and praised the Lord for this new insight into the deceitfulness of his own natural man. Ah! thought he, how, with all the past in memory, how could I ever for a moment forget the perfect fitting-in of the God-man's sympathies with our sinless enjoyments. So, taking back anew Marjorie's affection as a boon and not a snare, he arose, worshipped Providence therefor, and felt new strength to go on with the work of doing and suffering in his great Master's cause.

The trader's wife, lying awake in the next room, busy with those recollections of her dead-and-gone Maggie, which the sight of Renwick's 'bonnie blue e'en' inwardly stirred in her breast, was strangely thrilled by hearing the grave melody of a sacred song rising with the first hint of coming day.

It was Renwick singing, what was to him (in the circumstances) a 'new song,' albeit an old one—

> 'Such pity as a father hath
> Unto his children dear,
> Like pity shews the Lord to such
> As worship Him in fear.
>
> For He remembers we are dust
> And He our frame well knows.'

'The whole earth is full of the goodness of our God.'

Having praised thus, the young man at length fell on sleep, it being then about the fourth hour of the morning.

CHAPTER XIII.

'Murmurs of pleasures and pains and wrongs.'

'This is the *cry*
Of souls that high
On toiling, beating pinions fly.

From their distant flight,
Through realms of light,
It falls into our world of night.'

'LAIRD BAIGRIE! Laird Baigrie!' shouted Mistress Fairlie, rapping with her knuckles on the door of the closet where, in a box-bed, Antony was sleeping as men do, their first night on *terra firma*, after nearly a week of sea-sickness.

'Laird Baigrie, are ye waking yet?'

'Yes; what's wrong?'

'Wrong! nothing's wrong, but here's Luckie Wilson, next door, been askin' us to come and get a word o' sermon from worthy Master James Renwick at her house. He aye stops wi' the Wilsons when he's in Edinburgh. He came early this morning, and is going away to Fife shortly after this meeting.

So ye'll come maybe? It's counted a great privilege to hear Master James.'

Baigrie rubbed his eyes, sat up in bed, and pursed his mouth, in token that he was considering.

'Renwick here! How very strange!'

(For Mistress Fairlie's shout had ruptured a dream wherein the 'young elder' beheld himself in process of being married by James Renwick to Marjorie Ker, with Baby-Letty doing bridesmaid, and poor Angus Gordon officiating as groomsman. The bride had on a black satin train, tucked over her arm, and filled with shining gold pieces, and all the company, save the 'happy man' himself, wore splendid glittering crowns.)

'Renwick here! How very strange a coincidence!'

'Ye'll come, Laird?' plaintively entreated the landlady, who was anxious to exhibit tangible proof of her blue blood to sundry possible attenders at the prayer-meeting.

'Yes, I'll be ready in a few minutes. How long have I to dress?'

'Nigh ten minutes, Laird; but I can run and ask if they'll put off for five minutes more, till ye get yer trunk opened. I daresay they'll do 't, for it's an honour to Luckie Wilson and her goodman to have a wealthy laird like you within their door. If I've told them once about your large fortune, I've told them a score o' times, forbye yer great kindness in keeping Letty for charity. It's what few gentlemen wad have done, I can tell you. Will I run and bid them put off the meeting?

'No, no! I'll be ready directly.'

'Thank ye, Laird; I'm sure I take it very kind o' ye. But it's bad for the stomach, to gang out fasting, so I'll just bring ye a mouthful of ale and a bit wheat loaf. Ye can swallow them when ye're putting on yer things.'

'Well, what's Renwick about since I've been away?' queried the 'young elder' of his far-away cousin when she appeared with the promised cheer. 'Is he as busy in the good cause as ever? Is he married yet?'

'Married, Laird! No' very likely! She would be a bold-spirited lass, indeed, that would go halvers wi' his chance of the Grassmarket, poor laddie! No, no; courting and wedlock is for such as you, that can afford to do as ye please, and no' for him, that's offered himself, soul and body, puir thing, for what the Scriptures call "a living sacrifice." But speaking o' marriage (ye'll no' mind an old wife like me standing beside ye when ye're tying your doublet-points)—speaking o' marriage, there's a real beautiful young lady comes here sometimes that has taken a great fancy for Letty, and often gives her small bits o' presents. Her name is Mistress Marjorie Ker, and in a sort she's my landlady, at least so I imagine, now that her auntie's dead, her that owned the property. She once said to me that it would all go to her niece. It's possible she may be at the meeting, for she "owns" Renwick; but if not, and if you could bide another day here, I'll bring you acquainted, with the greatest pleasure, I'm sure.'

Briskly bounded the Laird's blood through his veins, as with his mouth full of wheat-bread and ale, he tied round his neck the smart point-lace 'Steinkirk' he had hurriedly taken out of his trunk.

One or two indicative hints let fall by Mistress Fairlie on the previous night had made him doubt whether the exported version of the boasted Government Indulgence (on the strength whereof he had come back) was quite correct; whether, in fact, it might not have been more prudent to see how the thing would work before quitting Flanders, where one could keep up the figment of Covenantership and a whole skin at the same time. But now, as matters were falling out, who could fail to see that Providence was at work on his behoof?

Within the specified ten minutes, Antony, Letty, and Mistress Fairlie started for the prayer-meeting. The road thither was not one to admit of much colloquy (leading as it did down one turnpike-stair and up another), nevertheless the old lady contrived (with a second-hand eye to personal vainglory) to maintain a panting, jerky conversation.

'Mistress Marjorie is not quite a stranger to you, Laird, by repute at least, for I tell't her about the great fortune you had gotten (Master Hepburn says it's immense), and likewise how good it is of you to adopt Letty. I hope she'll be at the meeting.'

Oh! if vaunty frothy, talkers would but lay to heart the fact that in six cases out of ten, though speech be silvern, silence is golden. The unadvised lip-work now perpetrated by Mistress Fairlie, whilst piloting her 'country-cousin' down one stair and up another, urged him into a resolution he lived to deplore. Pending his late voyage, in the intervals of sea-sickness, he had made up his mind that in some way or other (particulars not specified) he would do the handsome thing by Angus Gordon's daughter, albeit her continuance in life had thrown his pre-arrangements a good deal out of gear. But lo! here had this woman, with her 'unruly member,' again so hedged up his path that to get into the right way was impossible. It was a repetition of the same concatenation of circumstances which had four years ago caused him to have the two heritable bonds made out in his own name instead of that of his ward.

'If Mistress Fairlie has told Marjorie that I have heired a large fortune, and praised my charity towards this orphan, how can I possibly do otherwise than go on appropriating the imputations? I trust Providence will point out some *other* manner of showing kindness to the child, poor thing, albeit in these times money only brings a woman into trouble. I wish Mistress Fairlie had kept her information to herself, and left me free to do as I chose. But since she has spoken, I see it would do infinite injury to the Covenanting cause were I to brand myself as having betrayed trust. I did not do that, but ill-natured maligners might say so. The woman thou gavest to be with me, O Lord, she gave poor me the apple, and I did eat.'

The meeting was delightful, and Renwick looked inspired. 'Trust in the Lord at all times.' This was the gist and essence of an extempore discourse that made the men feel heroic, and some of the women burst into tears.

It was a picture worth seeing, that noble, graceful, albeit of late delicate youth, so earnestly pleading with the fifteen persons crowded into a stuffy little apartment, half-filled with bales and boxes of the landlord's traffic.

'Trust in Him, dear friends, at all times. He'll never forsake you; never. And then, up yonder! up yonder! Oh the bliss of being for ever up yonder!'

In stating that Renwick's address fascinated his hearers, I should have excepted Laird Baigrie. True, when the young divine first opened his discourse, Antony, like the rest of the company, was, so to speak, drawn away by the intense eloquence of the appeal. But presently his attention began to wander from the pleasant song unto the singer thereof. The years that had passed since his last sight of 'Our young Josiah' had evidently enhanced the good looks of the latter. All at once, in the midst of his mental vagabondage, this fact struck Laird Baigrie. (Ah! Mistress Fairlie, sitting over there so placidly on a sack of English hops, listening a-gape to the gospel of peace, if you but knew the rut your morning's chatter is cutting in the smoothness of your boasted cousin's future course, it might shake your self-esteem a bit.)

'Yes,' reflected the provoked Laird, 'he *is* very handsome, now that he's a grown man, and although that idiotic old babbler insists nobody would marry him, I'm not so sure of that. She says Marjorie is quite daft about his principles anent kirk affairs. Very likely; she used to be firm enough that way; and if she is such a regular frequenter of Renwick's meetings here, and they occur very often! whew! I daresay she's his attraction to Edinburgh. Saints are pretty much like their neighbours, I take it, when there's a handsome heiress in the way. He is too beautiful for a man, but women have often atrociously bad taste.'

By the time Renwick concluded his exhortation (which he did in a burst of grand pathos that lingered in some memories for many a day), Antony's old jealousy had resurrected in its pristine venomous strength. Still, on went the preacher's touching tones, but he heard them as in a nightmare, being now busy about much mental evil in the midst of the solemn little congregation.

'And doth the grave affright you, with its chill darkness? Ah! remember, dear friends, that our blessed Saviour hath Himself lain there, and now it is scented with roses, and illumined with the hope of glory. Amen, and amen!'

As Renwick stopped, exhausted, an early sunbeam struck crosswise in at the window and around his head, lingering there like an aureol. After many an affectionate handshake and fervid blessing the assembly separated.

As Mistress Fairlie was leading away Letty, Renwick patted her on the head, saying, with one of his unforgetable smiles, 'My dear little Letty!'

Giving him a trustful look with her large, calm, blue eyes, the child placed her plump hand in his, and said, 'Letty loves you, and her bonnie lady too.'

'What nonsense was that child speaking to Mr. Renwick about a pretty lady?' asked Antony of Mrs. Fairlie, as he toiled at her heels up the long roundabout stair which led to her abode.

'Oh, Letty's a queer lassie and uncommonly noticing, although so quiet. It's the bonnie Mistress Marjorie Ker that I tell't ye about that she means. I must confess she was wonderful fond o' Mr. James's doctrine, even the bairn saw that. When her auld auntie was alive they never missed a chance o' hearing him. But you can judge o' her beauty for yourself, Laird, if, as I hope, ye intend staying with me till to-morrow.'

'Thank ye; yes, I'll be very glad of a day's rest, I have not gotten over the effects of my sea-sickness yet.'

Arrived at Mrs. Fairlie's door, the 'young elder' fumbled in the pockets of his cloak, and then announced that he had stupidly left behind him a handsome Holland linen pocket-napkin, quite new, and wrought at the corners with gold thread. 'I would be loth indeed, ma'am, to lose this napkin, as I paid a heavy price for it in France; I think I must have dropped it where I was sitting, so I'll just step back to the spot, and be here again before breakfast is on the table.'

As was already mentioned, the tenements containing the abodes of Mistress Fairlie and Wilson the trader stood side by side, their respective entrances being separated by only twenty or thirty yards of street. Whilst the 'young elder' is traversing that short distance, it is needful to explain what had transpired in Covenant Close since Renwick quitted it five hours previously.

It so happened, that at the very time he and Marjorie were saying adieu in the yellow parlour, Mistress Clavers was seized with such a dreadful fit of toothache that to remain prone in bed was a physical impossibility. So she arose, intending to pace her narrow chamber and try if perchance weariness might induce sleep. But before commencing her perambulations, she very naturally took a look out of that tiny window which 'the Close denizens' sneeringly used to term her 'watch-tower.' (Not that at four o'clock of a dark February morning it was likely anything worth noting would be visible.)

I may here observe (in parenthesis as it were) that having at one time *herself* expected to heir Madame Rougemont, Mistress Clavers had always entertained a secret grudge against the Kers as interlopers, with no objection to pick any possible holes in their envied coat. With her tortured head swathed in a flannel petticoat, the spinster glances aimlessly across the narrow close, expecting only to behold tiny darkened windows set in a mass of gloomy wall. But lo! what tableau is this which meets her entranced gaze, and drives away her agony as effectually as the exhibition of a dentist's forceps? A golden-haired young man, with the countenance of a Saint John, embracing that 'upsetting' creature Marjorie Ker! 'It must; yes, it must be the outlawed preacher, "owned" by her and her daft auld auntie that's away.'

All the suggestive hints expiscated from poor, guileless Mistress Elspet in her latter days of weak perception, now arranged themselves in the spiteful spinster's mind as logically as if she were getting up a case of circumstantial evidence.

'Can it be possible it's to be a marriage after all? It looks like it. And yet, to think o' her, wi' her genty airs and graces and her by-way-of godliness, marrying a beggar, wi' a hundred pounds offered by Government to anybody that can catch him dead or alive! Covenanters! hem! let them alone for knowing what side their bread's buttered on. Here's this lad Renwick yelping about being persecuted, and yet willing, I make no doubt, to draw in his stool and sit down snug for life at the fireside that should by rights have been mine, if that false old papist, Madame Rougemont, had done as she ought. I wonder how such unco good folk as the Kers, and this minister o' theirs, could in conscience enjoy gear gotten from a bigoted papist. Oh, there he's away at last. Down on her knees at her prayers. She's made well out o' her everlasting prayers first and last. My teeth are easier; I'll just take a mouthful more brandy and go back to my bed.'

Mistress Clavers awoke early, and so free from pain as to be seated betimes at her usual post of observation, to wit, the small window facing the Kers' yellow parlour.

Presently Betsy, in fulfilment of her morning duties, flung open the said window, nodding at the same time to the old lady, and saying that it was a 'fine caller morning.'

'Ay, a braw morning, Betsy. Ye had a grand visitor last night.'

'Wha?' queried the handmaid.

'Oh! ne'er plead ignorance wi' me, Betsy, for, where ye stand, I saw your godly Master Renwick wi' my own eyes kissing Mistress Marjorie this morning, long afore day-dawn.'

Betsy was too dumfoundered to throw the 'wicked, ill-tongued wratch o' an auld maid' off the scent, so she merely snorted and retired, trusting that since Renwick had gotten clear off no harm was done.

Neither of the women had observed John Bold standing down at the stair-foot, listening open-eared to their colloquy. He had arrived with Mistress Clavers's weekly supply of firewood, and now, having laid it within the entry, was drinking in every word bawled across the Close. By-and-bye he waylaid Betsy, and by dint of much loverly talk expiscated from that elderly maiden the additional information he desired. 'Yes, Renwick must still be in the city. John Justice is safe to give me half of the prize-money. Fifty pounds hard cash! why, it's well worth taking trouble for.' (Now John Justice was Bold's second cousin, being by profession a 'toller'[1] of English goods.)

You can easily imagine the rest. Marjorie up betimes, the long-lost light of happiness in her face, attiring herself carefully, for was not Renwick coming this day, albeit only to say farewell? John Noble, the 'man-sworn precentor' incensing his cousin, the exciseman, into his suppositions anent 'our young Josiah's' whereabouts, and the two men's subsequent paction to divide the price of innocent blood, share and share alike.

Returning now from this long discursive explanation, let us rejoin Antony, whom we left going to Goodman Wilson's in quest of his fine Hollands napkin. (No possible amount of possessed wealth could oust from the Laird's heart the greedy spirit that bare rule there.) Arrived at the foot of Mistress Fairlie's stair, he noticed a knot of men gathered on the street a little beyond the entrance-door whither he was bound. Stepping onward to hear what was the matter, he saw a man in the uniform of a 'toller' lying on his back. He had that minute dropped down dead, and at the edge of the crowd three of his comrades were now disputing under their breath with a fourth, whether it were best to leave the corpse for a

[1] Exciseman.

few minutes and prosecute their present affair without delay, or first carry the dead man to the guard-house. They spoke very low, but Antony gathered that the urgent business in hand was to catch Renwick. Should he run directly and warn that hapless youth of his imminent danger? 'Am I my brother's keeper? Mistress Fairlie said that Marjorie's so daft about him the very bairn Letty sees it.' There was a terrible, albeit momentary, struggle in the 'young elder's' soul, as he stood there irresolute, staring in the dead 'toller's' face—pale to the lips, quivering from top to toe, agonized with mental heavings. No! no! not calmly and wittingly did he now commit sin. *Only*, knowing to do good, he did it not. (Alas! the Laird was still at his old 'Lunes;' for what else than spiritual phrenesies were his persistent attempts to hoodwink conscience by looking at right and wrong round a corner instead of straight in the face.) 'I wish I could even yet—' Too late! too late! the time for action is past. For as he stands biting his lips, and nervously patting one foot on the ground, the 'tollers' leave their still warm fellow prone on the street, and hurry up the stair to search Wilson's house for unexcised English goods,—that being their pretext for intruding. Wishful to flee, yet, as it were, glued to the spot, horror-stricken, remorseful, Antony remains alone, gazing upon the dead man's wide-open eyes. Oh that the last five minutes were to be lived over again! Listening, listening, listening through what seems an eternity of miserable waiting, then so to speak, taking comfort in the fact of his present wretchedness. 'Verily I am distressed for thee, my young brother. I suffer agonies for thee! But what, O God, can I do for him now save lament?'

Listening, still listening, as if all his senses had become one great ear.

'My God! My God! Surely that was Renwick's voice? Strange, that none of the men have re-emerged from the stair. No mistake about a fight *now*. Hark! That's a pistol shot.'

People hurry past, calling out, 'Catch the thief! He's gotten out by the back door, and is off down the Nether Bow.' With a long breath of thankfulness the 'young elder,' feeling thawed, as it were, goes back to Mistress Fairlie's and his waiting breakfast with what appetite he may. The meal has not had time to cool, it being only ten minutes since he told his far-away cousin he would go and fetch that fateful Holland-linen pocket-napkin of his.

'I thank thee, O God!' (this was his hallelujah when re-mounting Mistress Fairlie's stair)—'I thank thee, O God! that after all the young man hath escaped, and I am free from any uncomfortable reflections.'

'Have ye gotten your grand napkin, Laird?' queried Mistress Fairlie.

'No,' answered he, cheerfully. 'There seemed to be a commotion of some kind with the guard. I heard them calling out to "catch the thief;" so thinking it best to keep out of harm's way, I just turned my steps home again.'

A first-rate breakfast Antony made, and, being lightened in his mind of what he feared, he duly repeated a double-strong grace and wiped his mouth, glad he had done no overt wickedness. There was a fearful tragedy being even then enacted not far off in the back street; but Mistress Fairlie's sitting-room was to the front, and so high in the 'land' that it would have required a 'roar of many waters' to break the silence which generally reigned up there.

CHAPTER XIV.

> ' . . . Death, who comes for me
> From regions of the blest afar,
> Where there is nothing to deceive,
> Hath left his iron gate ajar,
> And rays of light you cannot see
> Are flashing through eternity.'

DIRECTLY after the prayer-meeting, it was Renwick's intention to repair to Covenant Close, and spend in Marjorie's company the short remaining time he dared at present risk staying in Edinburgh. Having arranged his plaid muffler-wise, so as partly to conceal his face, he was standing in the house-passage taking leave of his host, when a loud knock, as if with a stick, came to the door. Wilson opened, and, lo! there stood three 'tollers,' who said they were credibly informed that there were some 'uncustomed' goods in the house, for which search behoved to be made. Two of the men then entered, without leave either asked or obtained, and went straight to the room where the preaching had been. John Justice remained standing on the threshold, and challenged the minister, saying, 'My life on it, this is Master Renwick.' Thereupon came the other two back from the apartment to keep watch at the outer-door, but John Justice went away down-stairs. In a few minutes, however, he returned, bawling loudly, 'All within this house must go to the guard, that it may be proven what trade they are of.'

Renwick made answer, 'I shall soon show you what my trade is!' Upon which John Justice did once more run down to the street, crying for help to carry that 'bloody, rebellious dog, Renwick, to the guard-house.'

Meanwhile, the young preacher tried to escape by another door, but when he, with great force, tore it open, lo! there were more 'tollers' lying in wait behind it. Seeing the imminent danger of 'our young Josiah,' Wilson, albeit a man past his prime, tried to aid his escape by fighting the watchers, and so leaving a free passage. But one of the enemy, a lusty young giant of a fellow, dealt the old trader so merciless a blow on his mouth that a couple of teeth were broken and his upper lip frightfully gashed.

This roused Renwick's protective instincts, which were ever notable; so he discharged his pistol in the air, to frighten the assailant, albeit not with intent to kill. The report of the fire-arm caused the 'tollers' to scatter backward in terror, and thus unintentionally to open up a way of escape for the bestead youth himself. So down the winding stair did he rush, out into a small square court that opened into the Castle Wynd. Onwards he fled, in panting perturbation, yet very calm of spirit, as one who feels his hour is nigh, but fears not to shake hands with death. He hears his pursuers' steps gaining ground rapidly, their threats and curses hurtling in the air like jostled red-hot bullets. The hue-and-cry is up, and from sheer idleness many persons join in the chase, though quite unaware of its object.

As Renwick turns out of the court, a chance passer-by, who happened to be carrying a long dyer's pole, hit him therewith a heavy stroke on the breast, and thus caused him to stagger and grow faint. But, to quote once again his worthy mother, 'Though James's body was but middling strong, the bit spirit o' him was undauntable ;' and, moreover, life is sweet at six-and-twenty. So up he got to his feet again, and being a peculiarly swift runner, soon distanced his original pursuers. Indeed it is likely he would have gotten clear off, but for the effects of that unlucky stroke with the pole, for more than once after receiving it he fell and vomited blood. Still, still on he sped valiantly, down the Castle Wynd, along the Grassmarket, up the Cowgate. There a sudden gust of wind blew off his hat, which, in the circumstances, was a great misfortune. For you must bear in mind that, having turned round a sharp corner into another street, and left his former following considerably in rear, as well as out of sight, the chances were he might presently have slunk away unobserved. But, a handsome young gentleman running hatless, with his long yellow hair streaming behind him! Why, there must surely be something a-foot. So one man and another followed, and some cried this, and some cried that, till the crowd and clamour waxed very great indeed.

About half way down the Cowgate, not far from the Magdalene Chapel, 'our young Josiah' was gripped by a drunken fellow of the baser sort, who then learned to his astonishment and delight that for simply behaving like a *brute* he had gained a prize of one hundred pounds sterling. Within a few minutes the God-serving, man-loving outlaw was manacled and lodged in the guard-house.

Poor fellow! his pursuit and capture had not taken long, for rude hands were locking prison chains upon his wrists before Antony Baigrie had quite finished breakfast. A few minutes! Ah me! does even one ever flit past uncharged with some human joy or sorrow? These last ten or twelve, so fateful in issue to Majorie Ker's two lovers, let us see what burden they brought for the maiden herself.

She had arisen betimes, and attired her person with even more than customary neatness, for was not *he* coming, albeit only to say farewell? But away with that sorrow, she would not think about it yet;—could not, in fact, with all the intermediate delight in prospect. To tell the truth, the girl was this morning what old-fashioned folks in Scotland used to call *fey*, *i.e.*, unnaturally gladsome. Fix her thoughts on the adieu, or anything sad, she could not, but set about arranging the breakfast-table in a spirit of quivering gaiety that, so to speak, dazzled her into yet more flashing brightness.

Wattie, having amply broken his fast, had gone away to shoot water hens at the Borough Loch. (He was ever an obliging lad, and Betsy wanted aquatic fowls' feathers for some purpose or other.)

Marjorie's little preparations being completed, she, with flushed cheek and beaming eye, took her Bible and sat down on that of the four big chairs farthest from the window, intending to read away the time till Renwick's arrival. Her purpose was to peruse the chapter which came in course of her regular morning lecture, but the book (lying on her lap) fell open of itself at the twenty-third psalm. In default of anything more solid, drowning men are said to clutch at straws. Launched unexpectedly away from our every-day jog-trot condition of mind, and so affrighted to find ourselves floundering in space, we all wax more or less superstitious, and cling to any object which represents standing-room.

The twenty-third psalm. (Two hundred years ago, as I said before, to discredit omens argued carnal unspirituality.) The twenty-third psalm. Oh! how happy felt Marjorie as her eyes fell on the first verses thereof! Surely not for nothing had the volume opened at that particular page. Her pulse throbbing, her heart beating lively, her eyes shining. All alone in the little yellow parlour. 'James is coming soon.' This was the light in which she read—

> 'The Lord 's my shepherd, I 'll not want.
> He makes me down to lie
> In pastures green : He leadeth me
> The quiet waters by.
>
> My soul He doth restore again ;
> And me to walk doth make
> Within the paths of righteousness,
> Ev'n for His own name's sake.'

Yes! assuredly to have hit by chance upon this especial psalm was a capital omen. In an instant, just as she was about to peruse the fourth verse, there fell over her spirit, as it were, an immense chilly darkness, entering which cloud she feared : 'Yea, tho' I walk through death's dark vale.' Not a word more could she read. Tears rushed to her eyes. All her pleasurable excitement was suddenly gone, like a dream of yesterday. Trembling, clenching her hands, with prophetic yet shapeless agony grasping her heart, she sits listening to the vacant air, cowering inwardly, as if a spirit were passing before her face. By-and-bye the horror wore off, and with a quiet acknowledged trust in God's immediate presence, instead of the wild inflation that had blown her, so to speak, hither and thither all the morning, she finished the remaining verses of the psalm—

> 'Goodness and mercy all my life
> Shall surely follow me :
> And in God's house for evermore
> My dwelling-place shall be.'

Borne, as it were, in the arms of these last four lines, she re-entered then and there that 'Vestibule,' where, as Renwick often said, 'grief itself is transmuted into joy.'

Such, dear reader, were the experiences brought to Marjorie Ker by those very ten minutes already described in their manifestation towards Renwick.

Do love-linked souls feel simultaneously, albeit divided by distance? It is hard to say. But how else account for the fact that the mysterious cloud of horror enveloped Marjorie's spirit at the very minute when her beloved James was being 'gripped' by that drunken evil-doer in the Cowgate?

About a quarter before ten o'clock, the damsel, still resting, so to speak, upon that last cheering verse of sacred song, thought she would make some little alteration in the table arrangements. With this intent, she had just risen from her seat, when a loud hurried tirl on the door-pin froze her to the spot where she was standing.

Bigger, more recklessly protective-looking than ever, in rushed Mr. Hepburn, to take her in his arms and hold her tightly there. His pale face spoke plainly enough. She understood it all.

'My poor child! God help you, my poor little Marjorie!'

'Where is he? Oh, take me to him at once!' This was all she could say.

No tears, no interesting screams or fainting. Time enough for that in the possible long, dreary, lonely years to come.

'Oh, do take me to him at once, Mr. Hepburn! He was to be my husband. I know I can comfort him. Oh, do take me to him!'

Just then Mr. Hepburn was so completely projected out of his individuality into the misery of those two young people, that I do not suppose any distinct personal wish mingled with his thoughts. Yet, unrecognised by his own perceptiveness, he had the sensation of looking, so to speak, over a wall into a garden of delights, and feeling how blessed it must be to be there. 'Was there ever sorrow like unto this woe that has overtaken Marjorie and her betrothed? Ah! behold how these two love one another.' The great rough man admired their mutual affection, as he reverenced their sanctity. Something beautiful viewed from over the wall. Something so sacred as to be scarcely appreciable by a grovelling, gross creature like himself.

Poor fellow! High self-appraisement was certainly not his forte; and yet he was, as we know, sometimes fain to rise up from among the pots and mount away into the blue ether. But the wings with which to flee? Well, Marjorie represented them to Hepburn's mind's eye; had so done, off and on, ever since that day when he saved her from being trodden under foot in the Bow. There are so many different ways of doing good in this world. An aged divine used to aver that some people did it by effluvia; to wit, the silent effect of their daily life, walk, and conversation. In this fashion, Marjorie had certainly atmospherized Mr. Hepburn for good, and his very soul clave to her, as you can imagine, with an intenseness that savoured more of reverence than love. But, as I said, on this eventful morning he never thought about his own sentiments at all, being utterly taken up with the tragedy then going forward.

'Oh, do please take me to James, Mr. Hepburn. I don't care who sees me. I glory in being his intended wife.'

Alas! he could not at once conduct her to Renwick, probably not for many hours. Not till permission was procured from the authorities. Poor girl! how shall she remain within that confined small-roomed house, waiting, waiting, waiting, with every nerve quickened and every pulse beating like thunder. (This was how he viewed the more immediate foreground of Marjorie's dark future.) Had she been away out in the country, she might, by hard walking, have worked off some at least of her mental misery. But mewed up here in Covenant Close, oh, it is too dreadful! Fain would he have administered religious consolation, but so graceless and coarse and unspiritual as he was, how should he dare intrude into sacred mysteries? And yet, poor fellow, to ventilate his own unexpressed upward longings would have been to speak of things 'within the veil,' had he but known it.

'My poor, dear child, would to God I could help you!'

His very presence was comfort to the stricken girl. He had always proved to her a trustworthy stay. In this so agonizing time of waiting he certainly was her sole earthly helper. Wattie was away at the Borough Loch shooting water-hens, and as for Betsy—well, Betsy was reputed an experienced Christian woman, but somehow (albeit, did not feel quite orthodox) Marjorie preferred, just then, Mr. Hepburn's humble attempts at proving the union of God's love and wisdom, to a repetition of the elderly handmaiden's cut-and-dry sick-nursy Scriptural truisms.

Neither that day, nor the next, nor the next after that, was access allowed to him, who lay fettered and closely warded in the Tolbooth. Solitary within his cell the brave young martyr flung himself on his knees (albeit with difficulty, because of the cruel bonds), and prayed unto Him who seeth in secret. He offered his life freely unto the Lord, and entreated the gift of 'through-bearing grace,' both for himself and those dear ones whom his violent death must needs plunge in extreme woe. Before being served with his indictment he was removed to the lodging of Viscount Tarbet, and there examined as to whether he owned James Duke of York for his lawful sovereign, and likewise, whether he considered it right to pay cess, and to carry defensive weapons at field-preachings.

On each and all of these points he spake his mind with so much composure and staidness as to astonish many then present, and disquiet one or two not a little.

Upon Friday the 3rd of February he again underwent a

preliminary examination, whereat it was demanded by the Chancellor 'of what persuasion he was?'

'Of the Protestant Presbyterian persuasion,' says the prisoner.

'How cometh it then to pass,' asked his lordship, 'that you differ so much from other Presbyterians who have accepted the King's toleration, and owned his authority? What think ye of them, Master Renwick?'

'I am a Presbyterian, and hold by the ancient Presbyterian principles which are embodied in the Covenants, and were generally professed by the Kirk and nation from the year 1640 up till 1660. Those who, for the sake of a little very uncertain liberty, backed out of these principles, have not gained much. Neither have those of yourselves (looking straight at his interlocutors) who apostatized to acquire worldly honours.'

The Chancellor, as well as several of those sitting with him on the Bench, applauded, saying that 'These were the real Presbyterian principles, which all Presbyterians would openly acknowledge had they but the courage to do so.'

Divers of these same judges afterwards mentioned privately that 'that pretty lad Renwick was of old John Knox's principles, principles both tolerated and approved of in former times, albeit now, by the new law, declared to constitute treason.'

Being remanded to the Tolbooth, Renwick was there served with a copy of his indictment. A most wordy, circumlocutory composition this indictment was, albeit the tenor thereof was condensible under three counts—to wit, Do you own

King James the Seventh as your rightful sovereign? Do you consider it lawful to pay cess? Do you approve of wearing defensive arms at field-preachings?

Renwick's trial was fixed for the 8th of the month, being the fifth day after the indictment was served, and meanwhile much energy was displayed in hunting up witnesses likely to bring damning testimony against him.

And how all this time was the so-called 'Head of the wild Whigs,' the 'bloody dog Renwick,' engaged? Loaded with irons, immured in a dungeon, meditating, praying, praising. This last most frequently. Noble young hero! So warm-hearted, and truthful, and pure. He bore no ill-will towards any of God's creatures, not even to those whom conscience forced him to withstand. But you can easily fancy how it wrung his heart to think of the terrible calamity impending over his dear old mother, and the girl he loved so deeply. Yea, in the presumable present dismay of the latter, he was so intensely afflicted, that hour upon hour did he spend in commending her pitiable case unto the Saviour, whose sympathies are so infinitely deeper and stronger than any man's. Thus, albeit alone and in prison, Renwick had perhaps better company than his cruel jailors.

But oh! those three days were unforgetable days to poor Marjorie, knowing, as she did, that James's life was at stake, yet neither allowed to see, nor in any way communicate with him.

Mr. Hepburn was indefatigable in his efforts to gain admittance to the prisoner, but without success. 'After the indictment is served on him he may see his friends, not sooner.' This was all the reply obtainable. And then, in his great anxiety to be of service, he bethought himself of Renwick's mother. Really, considering how imperfectly his own parent had done her duty by him, the lawyer's intense appreciation of the 'mellow loveliness' of true motherhood was quite marvellous. 'Poor Renwick's mother! Yes, she must at any cost see her noble son once again. Ay, and that son's intended wife. Surely it is fitting that in this season of mutual grief the two women should mingle their tears together, and mayhap thereby lessen the after-loneliness of both.' Arguing thus, Mr. Hepburn lost no time in despatching a trusty messenger to Glasgow, with instructions to return accompanied by Mistress Renwick, but not to detail *all* the sad necessity for her immediate presence in Edinburgh.

If ever a stalwart, black-a-vised, matter-of-fact-looking man filled the post of ministering angel, Mr. Hepburn at this juncture did so toward the sorrow-trysted maiden of Covenant Close. His perpetual comings rippled the dead sea of her grief, and she used to watch for his 'tirl' as they that wait for the dawn. Having, of course, no good, or indeed any, news to communicate, he was occasionally driven, poor man, to what is medically termed the exhibition of rather weak mental medicaments; and sometimes, in the immensity of his pity, he would actually so far outrage his humility as to venture on little goodyisms. These were often pathetically childlike, from their unquestioning simplicity; so childlike, indeed, that, less extremely circumstanced, Marjorie might perchance have found fault that, having begun to read God's alphabet, he rested there. But a poultice, and not a gemmed bracelet, is the prime necessity of a festered wrist, and the girl's heart was aching too consumedly to make casuistical theology a *sine qua non.* Be it understood that, being a Christian, she of course confided, first of all, in Jesus; but at present I am speaking of her only as a young girl with an adored lover, about to be tried for his life, and a probable long series of regretful solitary years before herself.

I daresay you already comprehend how it came to pass that, even to so high-toned a person as Marjorie Ker, Mr. Hepburn's first little efforts at religious consolation were grateful, because of their very unpretentiousness. As for him, poor man, with an ingrained belief that both Renwick and his betrothed belonged to a higher style of creature than himself, he made his hourly offerings of sympathy and friendship, much as a heathen beggar might lay his handful of common wayside-flowers on the glittering taper-lit altar of his bejewelled patron saint,—lay them there, that is to say, not as being intrinsically valuable, but just because his feelings of worship need embodiment.

As was already stated, the legal indictment was handed to

the prisoner upon Wednesday, and by dint of bribing the officials, Mr. Hepburn had got permission for himself and a friend to visit the Tolbooth soon thereafter. Early on Thursday morning, accordingly, he arrived at Covenant Close, pale with suppressed excitement, and, as calmly as he could, bid Marjorie throw on her plaid and come away. An order had shortly before been issued by the Council, forbidding to street pedestrians the use of plaids as mufflers, but he forgot this, and only considered that it seemed to his masculine perceptions the easiest and speediest mode of dressing for a walk. The unfortunate damsel being, as it were, 'confused' out of the power to think for herself, just did as she was bid, and presently, leaning upon the lawyer's arm, was on her way to prison.

(Mistress Clavers observed the couple emerge from the stair-foot, and, strange to say, felt more personally aggrieved by the apparent fact that 'that minx Marjorie Ker had acquired an oldish swain,' than even by the loss of Madame Rougemont's lamented heritage.)

The distance was not great, but Marjorie shivered and trembled so exceedingly that Mr. Hepburn feared she would not be able to make it out. Therefore, in order, if possible, to divert her mind from its agonizing fixity upon that distressful meeting now close at hand, he began to speak of Mistress Renwick.

'She will be here by to-morrow evening, I hope. Poor

woman, this is a sad journey for her, but, please God, will in any event prove a comfort both to herself and her noble son. By all accounts, she is a person to go Christianly through any emergency.'

'Mr. Hepburn,' said Marjorie (just as they reached the gate of the Tolbooth), 'will you bring her to Covenant Close, instead of letting her stay at the Wilsons'?'

'Yes, my dear, gratefully. It has grieved me very much that, passing through all your present sorrow, you should have no female friend fit to sympathize with you. Yes, I'll bring her to the Close.'

Once inside the prison walls, Marjorie's temporary nervous weakness vanished. Rather, should I say, it was ruthlessly crushed under the heel of her woman's love, than which the Bible itself tells us there is no more potent affection. Like that fair young Lady Graden, who four years agone had comforted her brother-in-law in his dungeon, and only took leave of him at the gallow's-foot, Renwick's betrothed would now forget self, and think of him only.

When the allotted hour had expired, Mr. Hepburn came to fetch her, half recoiling, were the truth told, from the expected scene, with its tears and sobs of despair. Ah, no! The two lovers had gotten within the 'Vestibule.' A lump rose to the rough-looking 'writer's' throat when he saw that beautiful youth and maiden sitting there, hand in hand, so calm, so sweet, poor creatures! He felt assured they had faced the worst that might be coming. And yet! yet! surely there must be some element in this holiness of theirs which, while beautifying earthly things, so linked them on to heavenly concerns, that even their loss could not cause despair, as if all were gone.

(You perceive how Mr. Hepburn was once more peeping over the wall, but into a different part of the Garden of Delights, perhaps the very spot where grew the choicest flowers.)

To save his life, he could not have written or spoken this, but, nevertheless, these ideas kept floating in his mind, as he stood upon the threshold of that dungeon, gazing on Renwick and the lovely girl who should (but for those so terrible times) have been his wife.

'God Almighty reward you, dear friend, for all your goodness to us,' said the prisoner. 'How to thank you for your kind forethought about my dear old mother, I know not. Marjorie must do it.'

Ah me! man and wife they would never be *now*, and there was something exquisitely pathetic in the young man's 'Marjorie must do it.'

Next day the visit was repeated, and likewise the loving pain, the clinging, the lingering. Neither made a feint of hope, in so far as regarded Renwick's chance of life. Verily none too soon, young though they were, had they taken shelter within the 'Vestibule.'

When, on this second day, Mr. Hepburn came for Marjorie,

he was struck with the almost glad expression that beamed on the fair faces before him. The two had just been speaking of 'up yonder,' till, for the moment, the passage thither was forgotten.

Her mother-in-law (who should have been) was expected to arrive in the evening, so all that afternoon Marjorie was busy preparing for her reception. Indeed, she compelled herself to bodily activity in order to keep down great floods of dismay that were ever ready to surge over her soul, save when beside yon bright, gentle, brave, praiseful martyr, lying so heavily ironed within the grim Tolbooth.

Wattie, like the amiable lad he was, did what he could to lighten his sister's grief-burden, and even proposed trying to buy off his former tutor by the sacrifice of all his property, Greendykes included.

'They 're a set of greedy wretches, these Counsellors, and will no doubt be glad to take my offer. So cheer up, May, we 'll all three go to Holland, or France, or some quiet place; and I 'm such a great strong chap,[1] I 'll work for you both. Now, come along, and show me where you want the pin for your old lady's cloak to be nailed up.'

Considerably before the hour at which Renwick's mother was at all likely to arrive, Mr. Hepburn was in waiting at the West Port, that gate through which five years before Marjorie and the Greendykes party had entered Edinburgh. In the so

[1] Fellow.

terrible intervening times, many a fair face, and many a sad one, had doubtless passed under that high-towered archway, but none more Madonna-like in mild, fair, simple goodness than that of Mistress Renwick. As Mr. Hepburn had judged from report, she looked just the woman to go Christianly through any emergency, however dire. One of those alabaster-complexioned, grey-eyed, gentle, rather slow-spoken persons, whose immense resources of hidden energy crop up in some astounding crisis, to the astonishment of all but themselves.

From choice, her manner of life had always been secluded, and thus, albeit her sphere was humble, her manners were rather quaintly simple than vulgar. Among her few acquaintances she had ever been considered a 'superior motherly religious woman ;' and as for her late husband, he used often to declare that if anybody wanted to see his wife's picture they had only to read the thirty-first chapter of the Book of Proverbs. But her boy! her boy! On him was lavished all that intense lovingness of which natures like hers are sometimes almost poetically capable. At any other time the idea of visiting that 'grand young lady,' to whom James was engaged, would have deeply commoved the modest, humble, 'stay-at-home and read-your-Bible' woman. But as mighty griefs are said to swallow up all minor annoyances, so do they, by the grand immensity wherewith they as it were surround us, dwarf those conventionalities that at other times seem insurmountably high. With her precious boy's life hanging by a thread (for despite Mr. Hepburn's precautions his emissary had told her how matters stood), with her whole soul seeing him only, feeling him only, what to her were externals? And yet, seated on a pillion behind the messenger, how calm she seemed in her paleness, how unwearied looking! But, ah me! if her body had travelled over more than forty weary rough miles, her spirit had not wandered far, not farther than the bounds of a dark narrow dungeon, where her dear one lay awaiting his doom.

Mr. Hepburn took a liking to her at first sight, but not to the smartly attired natty little fair-haired woman, who came riding in her rear, mounted on a tall grey horse, and carrying a four-year-old girl in her arms. Who could she be? Evidently they were travelling in company. He was not long of being enlightened by the lady herself.

'I am poor James Renwick's cousin Katherine, of whom I daresay you have often heard him speak. I am a widow, my husband was a medical man, and left me a fortune. This is my only child.'

The writer was dumfoundered on his own, and annoyed on Marjorie's account. It would never do to billet this additional female and child in the Covenant Close house, which was anything but roomy. And besides, what he had reckoned on was the comfort of a quiet, motherly inmate, who might help the poor girl to 'rub through' those eerie days and nights that seemed coming to her.

Katherine, who was as sharp as a needle, observed his perplexity, and soon set it at rest. 'There's a cousin of my late husband,' she said, 'who abides on the Castle Hill, one Mistress Fairlie. He used to say she was very hospitable and meek-minded. I'm certain she'll be glad to receive me and my infant, as I can pay handsomely for our keep.'

The lawyer was free of his quandary, but ashamed that she should have noticed it, and more than half provoked at her cavalier mode of arranging what was best to be done. Scarcely, however, had he got off one horn of his dilemma than he was impaled on another. Both these women, being strangers in town, and he the only squire present, whilk of the twain should he first escort to her place of abode? But again did that 'sharp-set' looking cousin of poor Renwick read Mr. Hepburn through and through, and after putting sundry pertinent questions in local geography, decree that he should first set down her and her child at Mrs. Fairlie's, and then deposit her aunt in Covenant Close. (It is certainly pleasant to have the burden of decision lifted off one's back, but I am not sure that, as a rule, men folks like to have it done for them by the weaker sex.)

'Not an ill-looking little woman by any means,' soliloquized the writer, as in humble obedience he accompanied the horsewomen along the Grassmarket; 'not by any means ugly; but oh, how the deceased medical man must have rejoiced when he reached his *hic jacet*, poor fellow! How in the name of all that's wonderful comes she to be of kin to that angelic youth James Renwick?'

Whilst the little party is jogging slowly towards the Castle Hill, up the very wynd adown which, but a few days before, Renwick had run for his life, let us precede them, and inspect the interior of the dwelling whither they are bound. The present occupants are four, viz., Mrs. Fairlie, that woman of 'meek repute,' Letty, Laird Baigrie, and a 'lassock,' or maid of all work. Scattered over the biggest apartment (which in virtue of its size and a box-bed did duty both as guest-chamber and withdrawing-room) were divers trunks and packages, and male garments, that looked in the dim twilight like so many hobgoblins. On the bed lay Antony, just awakening out of a sound sleep, the first he had enjoyed during the best part of five days and nights, to wit, since his arrival from abroad.

You recollect that whilst Renwick was fleeing from his pursuers and being taken captive, the 'young elder' sat comfortably at breakfast within Mistress Fairlie's elevated residence, where no hubbub that might occur on the street was likely to sound. Perhaps you remember likewise the short, sharp soul-exercise he had experienced a few moments previously as to whether or no he should hie up-stairs and warn 'our young Josiah' of his imminent danger, and the private reasons why this waverment ended in letting things take their course. But before his morning meal was half digested, or Mistress Fairlie had meekly maundered through a third of her hazy comments upon the sermon they had been hearing, in dashed goodwife Wilson, with a face as white as a sheet, and a heart-rending account of 'our young Josiah's' misfortune. Now, if there be any truth in that proverb which maintains the best physicians to be Drs. Diet, Quiet, and Merryman, it holds to reason that severe sea-sickness, supplemented by battened-down qualms of conscience, must have a bad effect on the digestive functions. At any rate it proved so in Laird Baigrie's case, and a pretty smart bilious attack was the result of those tossings, physical, mental, and moral, he had undergone. Hence the five dreary days, that had defiled so sadly past Renwick and Marjorie, did not 'dance with winged feet' past the 'young elder.' But on Friday evening he, as I said, awoke out of sleep like a giant refreshed, and, in reply to meek Mrs. Fairlie's suggestive inquiries, said he 'would just fling on his night-gown and creep into the parlour for a wee bit o' supper.'

'I'm real glad, Laird,' quoth she, 'that ye feel somewhat appetized. What would ye think o' trying a crumb o' tripe? It's fine and light for the stomach. There's a potful ready boiled, so I'll away and see that Mattie dishes it nicely with onions and milk. That and a drink o' strong ale will make you as sound as a— In all the world, wha's that tirling as if they intended to risp off my door-pin?'

You already guess, dear reader, that Mr. Hepburn had

come as forerunner of Katherine and her little girl, who were sitting on horseback at the stair-foot, in company with pale, patient Mistress Renwick, and the conductor of her steed.

So right ably did the writer special-plead the merits of his case, that Mistress Fairlie considered Providence had taken to *pouring* instead of simply *dribbling* grand connections upon her humility.

'Ou ay, Mr. Hepburn, often have I heard him that's away speak o' his cousin the Glasgow doctor. A terrible genteel gentleman, worth oceans o' gold and silver. And ye say his lady says she'll pay me handsomely. Dear me! (as that puir lad Renwick would say) I wonder what God'll do next? I'm proud, I must say, that the connections on baith sides o' my house happen to meet under this roof. It's wonderful! It'll make that spiteful body next door lose her senses. I think I'll ask her to her supper to-morrow. Will the lady and the wee bairnie soon be here, sir?'

With poor Marjorie waiting in Covenant Close, and mild Mistress Renwick on horseback in the street, Mr. Hepburn was not likely to make long work of the sharp-set little widow's introduction to her late spouse's cousin's wife, and he hurried the latter down-stairs as fast as possible, with the 'lassock' at her heels to carry up the baggage. Within a very few minutes the acquaintance was accomplished, the tall grey horse unloaded, and 'the writer' himself mounted thereon, riding away with 'our young Josiah's' mother as gallantly as if he were a professed squire of dames, instead of an ill-brought-up, rough, creature who had never, in all his days, come in contact with an admirable woman save one, to wit, the affianced wife of poor James Renwick.

Antony was always remarkably slow at dressing, and albeit, on this his first convalescent appearance, he did not contemplate making any great toilette, yet he fiddle-faddled so long with tags, and laces, and buttons, that when he shambled slipshod into the parlour, Katherine was there. In her 'flustration' his hostess had for the moment forgotten his existence, and was now again below-stairs directing Mattie in the matter of baggage-conveyance.

Katherine's hands felt chilled with holding the horse-reins, so she drew in a low stool beside the fire, and sat down to warm herself. In the hurry-skurry Mistress Fairlie had carried off the small oil-cruizie which usually illuminated the room, thus leaving the fire as its sole light.

The relicit of Doctor Fairlie was, as you may remember, short of stature, and very slender, and hence you will not be surprised that Antony, whose vision was of moderate range, should mistake her for Letty.

Imagine the astonishment of all parties, especially of Mistress Fairlie, when the re-appearance of the cruizie deprived her of the glory of making her fine relatives known to each other. Imagine the Laird's amazement, and Katherine's, and the old lady's wonderful 'touting.' Imagine the two children asleep in bed, side by side, quite sister-like, or rather, I should say, the new-comer locked in Letty's plump, white little arms (she was such a loving, small mortal was Letty, that no live creature seemed to come amiss to her affections).

'Much more genteel in consequence of having travelled.' This was the sharp young widow's private note on Laird Baigrie.

'Rather distinguished-looking, and prettier than I used to fancy,' was Antony's *mem* concerning his *vis-à-vis* at supper.

Yet, were the truth told, neither was glad to see the other, but the reverse. Perhaps this was natural enough, when we call to mind the purport of their former confidences and communings. The clever match-making plans had failed, and the preconcerted alliance for affording tit-for-tat assistance in counteracting the arrangements of Providence had proved a myth. Each was, moreover, conscious of present personal projects, which rendered the other's clue to the past an odious entanglement. Of course neither hinted at this, but with due regard to propriety, filled up the gaps in Mistress Fairlie's 'puffery' with lamentations concerning the state of the Kirk in general, and Renwick's plight in especial.

By-and-bye they all retired to rest, and during the silent watches of the night both women were awoke by a loud cry proceeding from Laird Baigrie's chamber. At first they thought the house was on fire, but on inquiry found the 'young elder's' repose had been disturbed by a dream. He did not enter into particulars, and was very cross when questioned why he had roared 'No! no! no!' so violently. The said vision was on this wise, and really not worth making a mystery about. He thought he had just been espoused to Katherine, and was sitting beside her on a high throne topped by tall green crystal antlers, when in danced the widow-bride's little girl (after the manner of Herodias's daughter) offering to him (Antony, that is) on a golden plate the heads of Renwick, Marjorie, and Letty. No! no! no! he seemed to exclaim; and it was the sound of his voice uttering these words which alarmed the two ladies.

Let us now take a peep into Covenant Close. On his way thither Mr. Hepburn often turns in his unsuitable and incommodious side-saddle to gaze at his companion, and every time he does so feels ready to thank God aloud. He had not, as we know, been much in polished society, but being of gentle birth, and endued with no small pride of caste, had an innate sense of the fitness of things. Marjorie, albeit far from haughty, was a highly bred girl, and he somehow felt that it would distress him were even grief to subtract one item from the entire refinement of her associations. Hence after proposing to domesticate the Glencairn tailor's widow with her son's intended, he had felt doubtful whether the toe of the peasant, so to speak, brought into such close proximity to the heel of the courtier might not after all give to the latter more pain than stay. But as he ambled beside his protégée those fears fled, and he felt proud both of her presentability, and the fortunate hit he had made for behoof of poor lonely Marjorie. He had the tact not to remain long, but took leave after arranging at what hour he should come on the morrow to escort them to the Tolbooth.

'Would it trouble you too much, sir,' said Mistress Renwick in her usual serene, dignified, humble way, 'to call upon my niece, Mistress Fairlie? It is but right she should see her cousin. They were brought up together.'

Of course it was right, and by unmitigated rectitude gentle Mistress Renwick tried to steer her life-course, but on this occasion, had she consulted her own feelings, I scarcely imagine Katherine's company would have been desired.

Mr. Hepburn was no little annoyed at the request. His in-born conviction was that the 'all alive' young relict's presence would at that sad little reunion be like Satan's when he attended the assembly of God's sons, and therefore he had privately resolved not to go near Mistress Fairlie's till it was over. But now he stood rebuked and self-reproachful, poor man, knowing nothing experimentally of life's goodnesses or its family proprieties. What were they to him but a demi-coagulated chaos, where he floundered in search of solid ground, and for want of light sometimes mistook land for water, and water for land. So, as I said, he felt conscience-stricken by Mistress Renwick's petition.

Next day at noon was the time specified for visiting Renwick, so at half-past ten the writer called at Mistress Fairlie's to fetch Katherine, and was astonished to meet his rich client Laird Baigrie, whom he imagined to be still abroad. While the young clever widow (who by-the-bye was, notwithstanding her grief, wonderfully costumed) retired to make ready for her walk, the two men fell a conversing up and down, as the saying is. First the bonds were discussed, and favourably reported of as still first-class security, and then our 'young Josiah's' terrible predicament came on the tapis. But Antony, for special reasons, was disinclined to go minutely into the details of Renwick's capture and consequent danger of death, so led the talk to Marjorie, more for the sake of shirking the other subject than because he particularly wanted to speak about her to Mr. Hepburn. But she being a theme whereon that poor creature (whom his companion considered to be in the gall of ecclesiastical bitterness) never tired of dilating, he waxed fluent in loving expatiation of her and her position. He pictured so touchingly her forlorn state should her only love be slain, that the Laird rushed to the conclusion 'the uncovenanted dog' had an eventual eye to her and her tocher for himself.

'If the young man suffers,' said Mr. Hepburn, 'she won't survive him three months, take my word for it.'

('Cunning, greedy rascal,' thought the addressed. 'Those writers all are. Wants to throw dust in my eyes.')

'I never imagined,' went on Mr. Hepburn, 'that affection

like theirs was possible, though they make so little fracas about it. Yes, sir, depend upon it, Renwick's death means hers.'

'In case of her demise, her brother would of course inherit all that property she has from her late aunt?'

'Property, my dear sir! Why, she hasn't a bodle that I know of, or if she has anything it must be the merest pittance. I believe the old lady intended it should all go to her, but she died intestate, poor body, and was weakly in the mind for years before.'

'Dear me! I wonder you did not make sure about the old woman's will.'

'Well, to be candid, I have bitterly reproached myself for not doing so; but when I first got acquainted with them, Mistress Elspet often spoke of her niece as her heiress, so I stupidly took for granted that all was right, and afterwards her mind dwindled away so gradually that—in short, till the day of her death, I always thought Marjorie richly endowed.'

'Providence,' said the Laird, 'is very mysterious in its workings, and our duty is to bow submissively. Had James Renwick been aware how this matter stood, I scarcely think he would have been so persistent in holding the girl bound by a trumpery troth-plight given years ago when they were little more than children. These ministers, even the best of them, are but human. The man who is willing to undergo persecution for the Kirk's sake, may see his way to prefer a rich wife to a beggar. It would have been a poor marriage for both of them.'

'Poor! poor! good God!' exclaimed that benighted uncovenanted writer to Antony's disgust. 'Poor! poor!' He was remembering those peeps over the wall, you see.

'Do you think of leaving soon?' Mr. Hepburn was asking, when Katherine re-entered, smartly dressed for her walk. 'If not pressed for time, you'll surely remain and see us safely out of this hideous business. As an "elder" you may perhaps have it in your power to help the poor lad' (Mr. Hepburn had unlimited respect for phylactery-wearers), 'one never can tell. I'm no better than I should be, but God knows, if my life could stand for that of yon brave, holy youth that poor Marjorie is so bound up in, I'd gladly give it. Do say you'll remain, sir.'

The Laird assented, sending a long-winded message to the prisoner, and then Katherine and her escort departed. It would be difficult to analyse her thoughts as she walked out for the first time in Edinburgh, albeit only in the direction of the Tolbooth. All the way from Glasgow she had, so to speak, inflated herself with a wild, foaming hope that now she should be all in all to her cousin, and thus, even if his life (which Heaven forbid!) were taken, have the satisfaction of knowing she had achieved her desire at last. And with all the ill-regulated love, and the pity, and the wish to fling herself scenically into the martyr's arms, there mingled quaintly a fierce delight at this wonderful providential break in the monotony of her existence, and a thrilling shiver of ecstasy at approaching that metropolis where real high life was lived, and where weighty matrimonial fish might be caught.

But alas! that innocent-minded, uncircumcised Philistine, Mr. Hepburn, who albeit he had tasted the sours had never sipped the sweets of family relationship, entertained, nevertheless, the delusion that congenital links were, *per se*, pure and non-egotistical. Therefore, *en route* down the High Street, did he pour into Katherine's indignant ear a really eloquent account of her dear cousin's fathomless love for beautiful Marjorie Ker, and that peerless damsel's unparalleled affection for him. On he went fluently, and receiving neither reply nor comment, the ignorant social outsider fancied Mistress Doctor Fairlie, having been inside 'the wall' (as, of course, being a widow, she had), was mentally and mournfully taking note of the woful difference betwixt now and then.

Some folks, who pretend to be wiser than their Maker, deplore occasionally the present necessity of wearing vile bodies, and conclude that the flesh is merely a cumbersome cloak wherewith the spirit is weighted. Just as if it were not a blessing to frail humanity that it is frail humanity. Just as if this world would be fit to live in did spirit discern spirit unveiled.

Could Mr. Hepburn, whilst expatiating *con amore* on the love-passages of those admirable young persons, have seen

Katherine's soul, the words would literally have been horror-congealed upon his lips. The smart little widow's disembodied spirit would, just then, have been an ugly subject to contemplate. Rage, jealousy, hungry wolfish love for Renwick! Hatred of him, hungry love again! Despair, furious detestation of Marjorie! A sort of murderous hope that that admired damsel's betrothed might perish, in order to swamp her happiness! A cowering fear that she should find the said Marjorie as pretty and as good as Mr. Hepburn had described her. A choking at the throat; a vain desire to weep; a swelling at the heart.

Woe's me! Thanks to these sensations, it was indeed a seething fume of sin and wretchedness which entered the yellow parlour that morning inside the well-got-up fleshly tabernacle which announced itself as Mistress Doctor Fairlie.

They all four walked together from Covenant Close to the Tolbooth, Mr. Hepburn and Mistress Renwick in front, the girls silently bringing up the rear.

The writer's instinct advised him to remain during the interview, and try his possible to annihilate Katherine's presence, by monopolizing her attention. Little, indeed, did he know about the persistence of a strong-willed woman. Turn Katherine aside from her aim! Turn the sea back at half-tide!

Her excitement pained them all, poor Renwick most. Perhaps he read it in the light of that day five years ago, when he first told his mother about being engaged to Marjorie. He pitied his cousin, felt annoyed, and was angry with himself for being so.

Thirty minutes, sharply told, was the time allowed for this visit, and Katherine's selfish cruelty was frittering them away unenjoyed. It was long since the prisoner had had a quiet talk with his mother. He knew his decease was at hand. He wanted so very much to be alone with her and Marjorie. Twenty of the allotted thirty minutes were already gone. Katherine's unholy selfishness had somehow knagged her aunt, cousin, and Marjorie into a strange feeling of apartness from one another. Poor Mr. Hepburn, in his own illogical way, arrived at this conclusion, and tried to mend matters by retiring. Renwick, who knew every expression of his dear mother's countenance, saw she was distressed by an idea that he was not utterly at peace. He took her hand, and looked in her kind pale face, adown which quiet tears were trickling.

'Mother, I can hardly pray since I have been in prison,' said he.

'My Jamie! my own Jamie!' she cried, looking upon him with an affrighted gaze.

'Nay, nay, dear mother,' said he, with his own beautiful smile, 'I can hardly pray, because I am so much engaged in praising, and ravished with the joy of our God.'

And then Mr. Hepburn came back, and then Renwick delivered his mother to his betrothed. Poor lad! he was anticipating for those two dear ones long days of grief when they would need one another's sympathy.

Why or wherefore, they themselves knew best; but that very afternoon the authorities issued peremptory orders that no access to the 'rebel' Renwick should be given, on any pretext.

On the 8th instant he appeared before the Justiciary Court, where, after his indictment was read aloud, the Justice-Clerk asked, 'Whether he adhered to his former confessions?'

'Yes, I do.'

'Do you own King James VII. to be your lawful sovereign?'

'I own all authority that hath its prescriptions and limitations from the Word of God. But this usurper I cannot own as lawful King, seeing that both by the Word of God and the ancient laws of the Kingdom such an one is incapable to bear rule until he swear to defend the Protestant religion. This a man of his profession cannot do.'

The next question put was, 'Do you think it wrong to pay cess?'

'Yes, when it is levied for the express purpose of suppressing the pure gospel. Would it, think ye, have been lawful for the Jews, in the days of Nebuchadnezzar, to have brought every one his lump of coal to augment the flames of the furnace wherein were the three Children, supposing the tyrant had so commanded?'

Then came the third question, as stated in his indictment, 'Do you approve of wearing defensive weapons at field-preaching?' to which, it is needless to say, answer was made in the affirmative.

According to the usual form, Renwick was bidden sign these his confessions, which he did, saying, 'I would willingly seal them with my blood.'

Sentence being pronounced, that he should be hanged in the Grassmarket the Friday following, to wit, the 11th instant, Lord Linlithgow, the Justice-General, asked him 'whether he desired a longer time?'

'It is all the same,' responded 'our young Josiah,' with cheerful calmness. 'If it be protracted, it is welcome; if shortened, it is welcome. My Master's time is the best.'

He was then remanded to prison, but divers both of the judges and assizers said privately that never had they beheld a more beautiful, clever, pious-like youth, if only he were less stiff about following old Knox, step for step.

Being now, as he supposed, within three days of eternity, Renwick entreated that his personal friends might be allowed to visit him. This request was negatived, albeit sundry priests were thenceforward made, so to speak, free of his dungeon, tormenting him by arguments and oblique persuasions. Some persons who felt interested, after a fashion, in the 'pretty young man,' tried to persuade him into petitioning for a reprieve. But to all these entreaties and cajoleries he replied that while grateful for the kind-heartedness which prompted them, he behoved to keep to his principles, adding, 'and never, moreover, did I hear of any martyr begging for his life. Will a man rob God's truth?'

Yet, strange to say, without either the prisoner's consent or permission, he was reprieved until the 17th day of the month. But this was no true kindness, seeing the interval was so filled up with enforced abstract discussions and tempting offers from his antagonists that the poor lad, so far from possessing his soul in quiet, was well nigh harassed into a nervous fever. The only wonder was that he stuck to his colours with such unwavering fortitude. For remember, as I said formerly, that at six-and-twenty life is, humanly speaking, all before one, and who could predict with certainty that a change in Government might not occur? Besides, the actual 'three points' for which he proposed sacrificing his life were not, *per se*, and apart from present circumstances, vital articles of Bible faith, albeit at this precise juncture they certainly involved Christian ethics. But were the times to alter for the better—why then, etc., etc.

Lastly, being 'deep in love,' and naturally a youth of vivid, ay, poetically brilliant imagination, how could he help now and then figuring existence as it might be were freedom of conscience restored and Marjorie Ker his wife. Perhaps none of these spiritual glozings were sufficiently definite to rank as 'potent seducements,' but they rendered that narrow cell in the Tolbooth a representment in some sort of the great open desert, where the God-man entered experimentally into some of His infinite sympathies with us children of clay. Ah, have we not each his special desert of temptation, albeit our nearest and dearest sometimes fail to recognise it as a barren wilderness, and imagine it a land flowing with milk and honey. 'Soul-geography' is but little understood here below, more's the pity. Jesus, who once was tempted, remembers and comprehends that the glossy, cool, translucent waters of a mirage-lake may be intensely inviting to thirsty man toiling over burning sands, even while he is aware they are only passing shadows. God alone knew the peculiar trial through which (after so nobly testifying) Renwick passed within his prison solitude. And all the while outsiders (ay! even his foes) supposed him borne, so to speak, aloft into the third heavens on the wings of stern duty fulfilled.

CHAPTER XV.

'My soul among fierce lions is,
  I firebrands live among ;
Men's sons whose teeth are spears and darts,
  A sharp sword is their tongue.'

IN Scotland, during what emphatically used to be termed the 'Three Killing Years,' divers legal routine usages were set at nought, but as yet, *i.e.*, in 1688, it remained a thing of course that the relatives of a prisoner under sentence of death should have access to him without let or hindrance. Directly after James Renwick's condemnation, however, a new order was issued for his special benefit, to wit, that no private friend of the prisoner should be admitted to his cell on any plea whatever. It is surmised that this doing of evil, in order that supposed good might eventuate therefrom, was brought about by the mistaken kindness of Bishop Paterson and another. The former, a clever, easy-tempered, sensuous sort of man, had been at the trial very much struck with Renwick's comeliness, piety, and earnest conviction of the vital importance of some little matters he himself considered perfectly immaterial. Therefore, to prevent any interference with his purposed sapping of 'our young Josiah's' belief, he and a like-minded friend (Doctor Munro by name) used their influence to rob him of all human consolation. Cruel of a verity are the tender mercies of the wicked. During six of those nine days the condemned-cell was converted perforce into an audience-chamber, where everybody entered appearance save they whom the unfortunate occupant longed to behold. Papists and Malignants, in they came, treading, so to speak, on one another's heels, and well nigh taking the scold and the scoff out of each other's mouth. Some went away in a rage, and divers returned confounded, forced to acknowledge that God was with him of a truth.

Two Papist priests in especial were very persistent in their abuse, for the curious reason that those of his own persuasion who had deserted, spread abroad the bruit that he was a Jesuit, and hence were the Popish clergy enraged that he should be called of *their* principles. Others of the same body argued with him, quoting many Fathers, but no Bible, unto whom his only reply was an indignant 'Begone!' (Indeed, for many a year afterwards, this expression 'Begone, as Renwick said to the priests,' passed into a proverb in the Tolbooth. However, all did not rage and storm thus. Divers of the 'indulged ministers' got access to converse with the prisoner, and confessed that albeit they condemned his judgment anent various matters, and his persuasion concerning others, yet considered him a godly youth, and spake much of his calmness and beautiful composure of spirit.

Bishop Paterson was assiduous in endeavours to win him over, and by dint of making interest in high places, got a written pardon, whereto, almost with tears, he begged Renwick would adhibit his name, or, failing that, even only let one drop of ink fall on the spot marked for signature.

But 'No, no; thank you all the same,' was still the youth's answer.

'Think ye, my lad, that none can be saved unless they hold your principles?'

'Nay, I never said so, never thought so ; but these truths for which I suffer I have deliberately considered, and not taken them up lightly.'

'I am right sorry to see you so tenacious, and casting away your own life, my poor child,' said the Bishop, 'but from my heart I wish you well.'

Renwick then thanked him for his courtesy, and the churchman took his leave, saying it was a great loss that he held such principles, for 'indeed he was a pretty lad.'

No sooner had Bishop Paterson quitted after one of his visits than in came one professing Reformed Presbyterianism (in whose company 'our young Josiah' had, more than once, gone to field-preachings), reproaching him rudely for 'companying' with prelates.

'Ye behoved to have sent for him, Master James. When, I pray you, did ever bishops, before this, visit folks in the Tolbooth?'

Another day one M'Naught, a curate, came to discuss 'The Toleration Act' with the poor lad that was nearing another world, and would fain have had quiet, as he said, to think over his 'flitting.' M'Naught laid off his arguments to the best of his ability, and inquired what he thought of the 'Indulgence,' and the men who accepted it.

'I am against it, but judge many of those who have accepted Toleration to be godly men.'

The curate retired, commending the youth's gravity and sincerity, and admiring that he spake with such Christian charity of those who opposed him.

Nearly his last visitor, if we except some foolish young officers of the Guards, was the King's Advocate, Sir John Dalrymple. He came with a troubled countenance and some small show of conviction, appearing regretful for having had a hand in his death. They two had a very long conversation, for it could hardly be called argument, and Sir John ended by saying that he was most sorry Renwick's death should have occurred during his own short tenure of office.

By-and-bye, to see their loving and mutual embraces, who could have supposed it was the official accuser and the accused who were taking leave of one another?

By these specimens, some notion may be formed of the

manner in which poor Renwick passed the first six days of his remaining nine on earth. Had he not, so to speak, been firmly anchored in faith, such side-blasts might perchance have somewhat drifted him from his moorings, whereas the more he was storm-tossed, the deeper struck his flukes into the sea-hidden but solid ground, to wit, Christ Jesus.

Upon the seventh day, thanks to various strong representations made to the Court by influential parties, Mistress Renwick and Marjorie were admitted. Mr. Hepburn accompanied them, but only stayed to embrace the prisoner, and then left directly. Why Katherine was not present, involves too long an explanation for the fag-end of a chapter, more especially as Laird Baigrie figures therein, no little to his own astonishment. I shall therefore devote one division of this chronicle to these two, who, you will please bear in mind, used to plot together in Mistress Renwick's semi-dark kitchen concerning the best method of making Marjorie and her lover forswear their mutual troth-plight.

CHAPTER XVI.

'Confusion and dismay together mingled,
Forced such a feeble "Yes" out of his mouth,
To understand it, one had need of sight.'

REMEMBER, I pray you, that, albeit till ushered that morning into the yellow parlour, Katherine had never set eyes upon Marjorie, her jealousy of that young lady was cruelly chronic. Of course Mr. Hepburn's comments while escorting Mistress Doctor Fairlie to Covenant Close did not mend matters, but still she clung desperately to the hope of finding her rival nothing 'so very wonderful after all.'

'Men-folks are but indifferent judges,' soliloquized the widow, as she walked silently beside Mr. Hepburn, to meet the object of Renwick's love. 'They don't know a really pretty face when they see it. I daresay James's admiration was partly vanity at being "taken up with" by anybody higher in rank than himself. I expect she's a proud creature, but if she shows any airs to me, I'll settle her.'

Alack-a-day! a single glance at Marjorie brushed away

Katherine's vain hopes as if they were a spider's web. Beautiful! elegant! Yes, yes, there was no gainsaying those obnoxious facts.

And to hear James's mother, a tailor's widow, coolly saying, 'Marjorie, my dear,' to that set-up minx, and to see her own aunt as much at home in that fine tapestried chamber as if she had been born and bred among gentry! Why, it was enough to provoke a saint. And then the daughterly way in which the said 'Marjorie, my dear,' helped the meek, pale-faced old woman on with her hood.

'It is positively indelicate,' thought Katherine, 'thus to appropriate my aunt as her mother, when she is not married to James. I wonder such a holy angel as they make her out can do anything so barefacedly impudent. She has stolen even my poor vulgar old auntie's heart from me,' said the smart little widow to herself, with mingled regret, rage, and spite. 'I'm *nobody* now-a-days, it seems.'

Marjorie's reception had, however, been unimpeachable; but Katherine's cravings were as difficult to satisfy as those of the fallen angels the poet John Milton has described as wandering through the length and breadth of their newly-reached hell.

'Even this big swarthy scrivener forgets my presence, now he is in hers! I call it disgusting of James's mother to sit quietly and see her flirting with another man, while he, poor fellow, is in jail.'

She had not much admired Mr. Hepburn before, but now his indifference added to his charms, and was set down as another item in the long list of Marjorie's sins against herself.

The prison interview has already been described, and Katherine's state of mind on quitting the Tolbooth; whence it appears that the family distress had not proved a mollifying ointment to soothe the inflammation of her sinful soul. Poor woman!

After handing in his two friends at Covenant Close, Mr. Hepburn volunteered to see the widow home to Mistress Fairlie's. He had an intuitive dislike to discussing her unfortunate cousin with Katherine, albeit she ever and anon held a pocket-handkerchief to her eyes, and drew her hood close, as who should say, 'Come, see, was there ever sorrow like unto mine?' So, as the two walked towards the Castle Hill, their conversation branched and diverged, till at length the lady's present fellow-lodger became the subject of discourse.

'A lucky man he is,' quoth Mr. Hepburn, rejoiced to show off the style of his clients before this disagreeable, unabashable little woman from outside the metropolis. 'A lucky man he is! As rich as half-a-dozen Jews! Your friend, Mistress Fairlie, has seen his castle and lands with her own eyes, and can vouch for them. *I* can only answer for the investments I have made on his behalf.'

'Are you quite sure about his wealth?'

'Of course I am, madam,' answered the lawyer, indignantly, under the idea that she wanted to pooh-pooh what she imagined his boasting. 'Of course I am. Why, this time four years, independent of what he had before, he succeeded to an immense fortune in hard cash. I myself drew up a couple of heritable bonds for him, worth a duke's ransom, as we say.'

'I should fancy him a stingy sort of person,' remarked Katherine (in vivid recollection of Antony's payment to her aunt and self for the death-bed expenses of poor Angus Gordon's child-relict).

'Stingy, madam!' responded Mr. Hepburn, irate at what he considered another peck at the wing of his show-bird. 'Well, if it be stingy to adopt an orphan girl, and out of pure charity to maintain her, just because he happened to be acquainted with her parents, I should like to know what generosity is; that's all.'

I daresay you remember that during six days (thanks partly to Bishop Paterson's mistaken kindness) none of Renwick's relatives were admitted to see him, but painfully from hour to hour waited in hopes of obtaining admission to the Tolbooth. We saw how this interval was spent by the prisoner. Let us now, if possible, discover how it passed with his nearest and dearest.

Marjorie, and her once intended mother-in-law, spent the hours in, so to speak, growing into each other, mutually astonished the while at the entirety of the 'graft,' and praising Heaven therefor. Mr. Hepburn kept coming and going—longed for, relied on, confided in, valued unspeakably. As for Wattie, he behaved admirably; and to show his love for dear May, was gallantly attentive to the mother of his former dominie. Sincerely distressed also for James Renwick, whom, even in the wearisome days of spelling-books and dictionaries, he had always been fond of.

'Ye're a dear laddie,' would the martyr's mother sometimes say to him, with unshed tears in her eyes, ay, and sad thoughts in her heart of another youth whom she had once fondled as probably she never would again. 'Ye're a dear, kind laddie.'

So much for the Ker domicile in Covenant Close. Let us now, Asmodeus-like, lift the roof off Mistress Fairlie's habitation, and discover what is transpiring there.

Mr. Hepburn's chance-announcement that Marjorie was no heiress, but the very reverse, so disgusted Antony, that he felt quite annoyed at having promised to remain in town till Renwick's fate should be settled. Indeed, but for the 'writer's' assurance that as a 'covenanted elder' it behoved him to stay and see how the matter should end, he would at once have packed up his traps and padded off to that ancestral castle of Halket, in whose praises Mistress Fairlie had so successfully exerted her magniloquence. But flight from Edinburgh at this precise juncture might argue lukewarmness in the covenanting cause, and now that he was back in Scotland, the 'young elder' owed it both to himself and the Kirk not to lose religious 'caste.' Therefore did he linger at his far-away cousin's, feeling meantime rather flattered by the constant pæans she sang before Katherine concerning his riches, and godliness, and generosity to his dead friend's orphan. Thus, by a quaint dispensation of Providence, were the 'young elder,' Katherine, and Baby-Letty once again assembled together; albeit the pet name of Baby no longer fitly described the latter, she being now a great girl, rising seven years of age.

When the inducement was sufficiently strong Katherine *could* make herself agreeable, and now, satisfied of Antony's wealth, she did her possible to attract him, and make the time pass pleasantly. In the latter effort she would have perfectly succeeded but for an unuttered query which haunted the Laird, to wit,—'How much or how little does she know concerning Letty's affairs?' Try as he would, he could not distinctly recollect what she had told him in Glasgow as to the extent of the communications made to her by Angus Gordon's youthful widow previous to his own arrival at the woodenfronted house. Of course, being the 'young elder,' he did not, in so many words, tell himself that he purposed countering any one of the cut-and-dry rules laid down in the Bible for man's guidance. But he ignored the fact that (when one comes to think of it) the number of Scriptural 'shalls' and 'shall nots' is very limited compared with the amount of cases of conscience daily starting up for solution. He forgot that God places us, each man, in the midst of his own special set of entanglements and circumstances, with the Bible as a general index only, the Lord himself being sole referee in regard to details. Indeed, when properly sifted, Antony's gauge of perfection was simply the letter of the law, not only as regarded temporals, but spirituals likewise, according to his interpretation of things divine, and (more was the pity) he tried hard to keep the two separate, lest by running one into the other he should make a mess of the whole,—a creed, this, very apt to lead its holders much farther 'off the straight' than they intend to go. But at present, the Laird did not opine that the question which vexed his spirit was one which demanded classification, either under the heading of matters relating to time, or those specially concerning eternity. He was neither going to commit highway robbery nor murder, but he fervently wished to know if his free agency was intact, or whether Katherine had a hold over him in the matter of the late Angus Gordon's trust. All this mental disputation imparted to the Laird's manner a sort of nervous distractedness, which gave Mistress Doctor Fairlie the impression that he had really fallen in love with her this time, and thereupon she quickly built a splendid future for herself, when she, as Lady Baigrie, should reign in Halket. Perhaps, had he been aware how little she actually knew concerning his young ward's affairs, he might have proved less obsequious; but conscience makes cowards of those who don't keep it clear and bright.

Thus—albeit she was not one whit in what is properly called love, and he thought her terribly strong-minded, and rather sly—the first three days under old Mrs. Fairlie's roof were, on the whole, spent agreeably.

Upon the morning of the fourth day Mr. Hepburn called to ask if Katherine would like to go and see her aunt, offering to escort her to Covenant Close. It was fine sunshiny weather, and thinking to make herself very smart for her walk, she put on the gay green satin 'pockie' taken four years ago out of Mistress Dorettle Gordon's trunk by Antony's implied permission. It had never been worn hitherto, but being by far the most *recherché* article in her wardrobe, she had brought it to Edinburgh as an off-set, seeing one could never tell what chances might turn up when one went a-travelling.

The visit was duly paid, and right glad were all parties when it was over. On Katherine's return, when taking off the pretty gold-embroidered green satin pocket, she began, in a dreamy sort of idle way, to turn out its contents, just, as it were, to while away the time. Antony was out, so was Mistress Fairlie. Her own little girl and Letty were playing at housekeeping inside their box-bed. There was nobody to speak to. So, as I said, in very *idlesse*, half-undressed as she was, she set about investigating the forgotten contents of the 'pockie,' which had not been unbuttoned for ever so long. They were not many. A few cloves, a scrap of pink taffetas, and the small 'bookie' that had once belonged to poor Dorettle

Gordon, and lain in the pocket when it changed hands. Down sate Mistress Doctor Fairlie upon the front of the bed to examine her treasures. The book was really a gem, albeit only a small toy affair, bound in ivory, and studded with minute garnet-headed nails. 'It'll be the very thing to use when I become Ladie Baigrie,' thought she, turning over the little blank pages; 'I'll write in it then to show off my accomplishment of penmanship. It's remarkably pretty. I suppose Mistress Gordon, poor thing, couldn't write, since there's nothing marked in it. It is really very beautiful. I don't—' Ah! what is this written on the penultimate page? Not much. Only a short list, in the late Angus Gordon's handwriting, of several moneys left with his wife at the Gorbals, when he quitted that place for Peeblesshire. Back, back, into the past flew Katherine's sharp wits, piecing together this little incident, and that hinty speech, until, from the whole, she twisted a pretty strong rope wherewith to tether Laird Baigrie should he pretend to over-scrupulosity.

'Christian charity forsooth!' said she to herself with a sneer, while replacing the tiny jewelled tell-tale in its receptacle. 'Christian charity! why, every plack of this grand fortune that Mr. Hepburn makes such a to-do about belongs, of right, to wee Letty Gordon. An elder! Humph!'

(A very clever woman was Katherine Fairlie, not beset by the common female infirmity of wandering from her point. Only let her mind be fixed upon a specified subject and at it

At present her intention was to marry Antony, or rather his wealth, so, though the discovery above noted was certainly startling, yet where would be the use of publicly exposing his 'shady' conduct?

Riches, and all the glory of them! The castle of Halket, and the liveried pages, and silver ashets; the banquets of wine and mirth; the lords and ladies assisting thereat as her guests. Oh, 'twas an entrancing vision! Surely its possible fulfilment was worth any amount of painstaking, even should that comprehend genteel resetting of stolen property.

The 'young elder' was no doubt a hypocritical rascal, and Katherine's associates had ever been of the serious order. But, to be what old Mistress Fairlie called 'Lady of Halket,' she would even stretch her moral gauge a trifle!—buy her leg of mutton, with its imperative make-weight of what French butchers term *garnaison*, *i.e.*, inferior bits. (One can't expect perfection in this world, can they?)

Whilst the widow was immersed in these meditations, Antony returned from his city stroll, whereupon it all at once struck her that there was no time like the present for trying the bold stroke for a husband she had in her eye. Therefore, without more ado, she commenced preliminaries then, and in Mistress Fairlie's parlour. It was rather a ticklish affair, managed, as you can imagine, with considerable tact on the lady's part, and a hidden wish for escape on that of the gentleman. But see what a firm hand and head can accomplish. Nothing was further from Laird Baigrie's desire than marriage with Katherine. Yet, within ten minutes after she had fairly laid siege to him, he had plighted to her his troth. She was aware that the 'young elder' guessed her to be cognisant of a certain little transaction of his, which, if bruited abroad, would not only give occasion to the ungodly to triumph, but cause the wealth and honours she aspired to share to flee away like a vapour.

Antony felt intuitively (without a single word being spoken concerning Baby-Letty's fortune) that his alternative lay between immediate matrimony with this most inquisitorial of relicts, and being 'had up' before the uncircumcised for fraudulent breach of trust and embezzlement. One may like partridge pretty well without relishing to have it thrown in one's face. Half-an-hour ago he considered Katherine a comely, dapper little person. Now, the consciousness that her knowledge of the bonds had bound him, as it were, to her chariot wheels, made him for the moment actually hate her.

The bargain was concluded; but how felt the successful mooter of it! Successful? Say rather wretched and empty in the midst of her sufficiency. Of gaining Renwick's heart, even were his life spared, she knew too well there wasn't a chance; but all of a sudden this conviction stung into fierce vitality the old, feverish, imperious love that used to sway her. For a moment or two, oh how utterly did she loathe Laird Baigrie, herself, and Marjorie! The last most

But for that damsel's handsome person, might not she herself be now feeling womanly and gentle, instead of devilish and hungry-hearted? Presently, however, Katherine was herself again, and turned her soul to gaze on riches, and all the glory of them. Ah me! how few of us, after all, can quite resist their spell?

When, at the end of six days, the authorities relented so far as to permit the admission of Renwick's relatives to his cell, as I mentioned, Marjorie and his mother visited him, and to their satisfaction, but amazement, unaccompanied by Katherine. Her absence from this interview was by her own desire, and in arranging this she had, as usual, a decided motive, besides strong nerves to carry her will into operation. The fact was, Antony had volunteered to accompany her on the occasion, and recollecting how, four years agone, he used to rhapsodize concerning the perfections of her special bane, Marjorie, she thought it safer, in the circumstances, to withhold her so slippery *fiancé* from any temptation to resile from his engagement.

'Cauld kail is soon het again,' says the proverb. Best run no risks, seeing that at the best men-folks are but 'kittle cattle.'[1]

True, Renwick was still in the body, but in all human likelihood behoved to 'dree his doom' very shortly, and then his affianced would be free for competition.

[1] Ticklish subjects.

Mistress Doctor Fairlie did not care three straws personally for her betrothed, and felt sometimes half-mad with grief for Renwick; but if a thing *has* to be done, there is no use sticking at obstructive trifles, and to become 'Leddie Baigrie' her mind was made up.

So, instead of hieing to the Tolbooth, escorted by the 'young elder,' she pocketed her natural regrets, and made-believe her feelings (forsooth!) were too sensitive to undergo the ordeal of beholding the friend of her childhood shackled like a felon.

Antony did not credit a tithe of this, but pretended to do so, being privately very thankful to avoid seeing the martyr. He had done the correct thing in offering to go with Katherine. It would tell well afterwards, and now he almost blessed his intended wife's hypocrisy for saving him an interview with the man his inner conscience told him he had helped to a cruel and untimely death.

CHAPTER XVII.

'The grave itself is but a covered bridge,
Leading from light to light, through a brief darkness.'

JAMES RENWICK was appointed to die on the 17th of February, and on the 14th he behoved once more to appear before the Council concerning the 'Informatory Vindication,' a paper he had written and published a couple of years previously, in order to gainsay the calumnies that were spread abroad by spies and informers.

This meeting being with closed doors, what passed is not known, but the prisoner returned to jail extraordinarily cheerful, rejoicing that he was counted worthy to suffer shame for the cause of his Redeemer.

This being the first day when the embargo was removed, imagine his delight, on arriving at his cell, to find his mother, Marjorie, Wattie, and Mr. Hepburn awaiting him there.

'How are you, dear friend?' said the writer.

'Very well,' answered 'our young Josiah' cheerily, 'and within three days I shall be better.'

Mr. Hepburn then essayed to go away, saying he would come and fetch the ladies when the appointed hour finished, but, to his astonishment, Renwick, with a strangely sad, yet happy smile, begged he would remain.

(Ah! poor lad, he had reasons for this request that none of the others comprehended till many a year had come and gone.)

As from a deathbed, he was trying to arrange what would most contribute to the happiness of his mother and bride, in the long, long years that might yet be their portion here below. Of the many whom he had called friend,

> 'Some had defected, some had fled,
> Some were scattered, some were dead;'

and not one was there whom he could elect to supply his vacant place towards his dear ones, save this comparative stranger, this Mr. Hepburn. Being, however, an acute judge of character, he had read the rough-diamond of a man with deep interest, and liked what he read; noted his capacity for high spiritual polish, and the innate humility that made him ready to esteem almost everybody as better than himself. And then his kindliness!

Yes, the brave, warm-hearted lad, taking thought for the beloved friends he was about to leave, desired to associate Mr. Hepburn in their now short intercourse with himself, to the end that by-and-bye, when all was over, they should lean on him as a sympathizing strength. Mayhap, poor youth, he even looked forward to a time when the beloved of his youth should not forget himself, but be calmly consoled by this friend known in the present deep adversity. It is hard to tell. And yet never, no, never had he loved Marjorie so much as now, never so clearly discerned the beauty of the life they two might have led together had the times been different. Ah! well, by-and-bye, 'up yonder' will make amends for all.

Another interview took place next day, tender and thrilling. Katherine was present, and took a final leave of her cousin in a wild passion of regretful tears, ending hysterically.

The last meeting but one of Mistress Renwick and Marjorie with James was on the night before he suffered, being the 16th of February, and his twenty-sixth birthday. You must imagine its pathos, for I cannot adequately describe those two leal young hearts cleaving so utterly to one another, and yet saying to the voice that bids them sunder, 'It is well, Lord; yea, it is well.'

When his mother was weeping, he sweetly exhorted her thus: 'Wherefore grieve, dear mother, that your own laddie is going a short while before you to enjoy what eye hath not seen, nor ear heard, neither hath it entered into the heart of man to conceive ?'

'My own, my very own!'

These were his last words to Marjorie.

Upon the morning of the 17th, the chief keeper of the prison, called the 'Goodman' or Governor of the Tolbooth, went to Renwick and desired that at the place of execution he would refrain from stating the cause of his death, or expressing any reflections that might be irritating.

'What God gives me to speak, that shall I utter, and nothing else,' said the martyr.

'Ye may even yet get your life,' answered the 'Goodman,' 'if ye'll only sign this petition,' offering him the paper.

'Nay, friend, what would that be but declining from a testimony for Christ ?'

He then asked if his mother and two others might come in to take leave of him, but to this the 'Goodman' objected, saying he would perhaps give them seditious papers to carry out.

'Search and see,' was the reply; and so leave was granted.

Poor Marjorie trembled from crown to toe. Shivering, half-fainting, inwardly entreating God for strength to hold out to the last, she could not lift her eyes off the beautiful hero of her childhood and youth. The past kept rising before her bit by bit. It seemed but yesterday that Renwick had rescued her from being trodden under the swine's feet; and that hour of hours passed on the roof of Greendykes, how present it appeared ! Her heart was well-nigh breaking.

It wanted exactly two hours till the time of execution, and the 'Goodman' kindly prayed Renwick's friends would join him in his last meal, which (in form at least) they did.

Being seated at table, in giving thanks he said, 'O Lord! now that Thou hast brought me within two hours of eternity, I thank Thee that, through grace, it is no more distress to me than if I were to lie down on a bed of roses,' etc. He exhorted them all to prepare for death, 'which,' said he, 'is in itself the king of terrors, albeit not to me now as it used sometimes to seem during my hidings and wanderings.'

They would fain have joined together in singing a psalm, but first one gave way, and then another.

Whilst Renwick was praying for their happy reunion beyond death and the grave, a drum beat loudly outside the Tolbooth. It was the signal that the guards had come to convey him away.

'I am ready!' he exclaimed, as if in a transport of joy. 'I am ready. Behold, the Bridegroom cometh!' He clasped his mother and Marjorie alternately to his breast, kissing both tenderly again and again.

'Mother dearest! Marjorie! My own Marjorie!' These were all his farewell words, poor fellow! for his heart grew suddenly full, and, for the first time since his capture, the salt water stood in his eye.

Being led away by the guards, he looked back on the two women with an expression of love that brooded in their souls until they too went to the hereafter and met their lost again. After the usual custom, he was taken to the Town Council, and told that if he had anything to say it behoved to be done then and there.

'I have nothing to say to you,' answered he, 'save what is in Jeremy the prophet, at the 24th chapter. "Know for certain, that if ye put me to death, ye shall surely bring innocent blood upon yourselves and upon this city."'

He was then informed that he would not get leave to be heard upon the scaffold for the ruffling of drums, and that therefore he had better pray where he was. But he refused, saying, 'I will not be limited by *you* what to speak.' Mr. Hepburn (who was suffered to be present) was requested to beg his friend would do as commanded, but declined with tears—those terrible tears that a strong man sheds only in extremity.

One of the magistrates asked the prisoner if he was personally acquainted with Mr. Hardy or any other of the town clergy, and desired their attendance? But he replied, 'Had I taken them for my counsellors, I should not have been here this day. I will have none, save this one man,' meaning Mr. Hepburn. He then went cheerfully to the scaffold, amid a greater crowd of on-lookers than had ever been seen at any execution in Edinburgh within the memory of man. The continual ruffling of drums was deafening, this being purposely done to prevent the spectators hearing the martyr's dying speech.

He sang the 100th Psalm, sweetly and composedly, whereby one or two of those nearest the scaffold were deeply affected. Then he read the 19th chapter of Revelation, and afterwards prayed with much enlargement and unction, thanking the Lord for honouring him with the crown of martyrdom. 'An honour this, O Jehovah! which even the angels are not privileged to enjoy, seeing they cannot lay down their lives for their princely Master.' Prayer being ended, he spake shortly to the multitude as follows :—

'Friends, I am now about to lay down my life for three things, to wit,—*First*, For disowning the tyranny of James Duke of York. *Second*, For preaching that it is unlawful to pay cess, enacted expressly for bearing down the gospel. *Third*, For teaching that it is lawful to carry arms for self-defence, when persecuted at gospel ordinances. I think a testimony for these worth many lives, and had I ten thousand I should not begrudge them in this cause.'

He was at this point rudely interrupted and bidden have done, but gently replied, 'I have almost finished.'

'Whatever ye do, O dear friends!' he said (again addressing the crowd), 'make very sure of your interest in Christ. There's a storm coming that shall try your foundation. Scotland must be rid of Scotland before the delivery come.'

They then ordered him to mount the ladder, which he did, after warmly embracing Mr. Hepburn, and commending his mother and Marjorie to his care, saying, 'You know how I love them, poor darlings! Farewell, dear friend, till eternity.'

After the napkin was tied about his face, he called aloud

to the crowd, 'Dear friends, keep your ground, and the Lord will provide you teachers and ministers.'

Then he was turned over the ladder with these words in his mouth: 'Into thy hands I commend my spirit, for Thou hast redeemed me, Lord God of truth.'

CHAPTER XVIII.

'What silent depths this life may show
 'Mid all this whirling, gasping fever;
Single hours drip dull and slow,
 But time runs on for ever.'

THE judicial murder of 'our young Josiah' had, to all appearance, silenced the last voice in Scotland that dared be lifted up for freedom. The scared remainder of Covenanted Presbytery cowered into darkling corners, dismayed and coerced, howling, 'Woe worth the day!' The bigoted Jesuitical King waxed fat and kicked, like Jeshurun of old, saying, 'Aha! aha! now shall I set up Popery through the length and breadth of the land.'

Young, and in one sense uninfluential, though Renwick was, he had been a stumbling-block in the way of absolute power; and now he was removed, the King became absolutely infatuated with the lust of proselyte-making. Verily, albeit for the present scaffold-testifyings in the Grassmarket were out of fashion, it was nevertheless a cloudy and dark day for Christ's few starved sheep left in the bleak wilderness.

This was the state of affairs from that memorable 17th of February up till November. Before, however, describing the strange governmental changes which then took place, it may be advisable to see what our old friends, the Kers, Fairlies, etc., are doing in the interim.

Laird Baigrie and Katherine being (not to put too fine a point upon it) less morally pleasant than any of the others, I shall, following the approved nursery maxim, 'Pills first, sweets afterwards,' give them the precedence.

In due season, *i.e.*, as soon as possible after Renwick's death and their own engagement, they were married at Edinburgh, and forthwith set up their household gods, not in the Halket Castle of Mistress Fairlie's imagination, but at Greendykes, which Antony had rented from Wattie Ker, through his man-of-business, Mr. Hepburn.

Letty, and Katherine's child, Hetty, accompanied the newly-espoused pair, and when it became known that the bride had been a widow, it was generally taken for granted that both little girls were hers by her former husband. Antony and his wife allowed this mistake to pass uncontradicted, for reasons tolerably understandable, perhaps, but which the 'young elder' declined entering in his spiritual diary.

The *ménage* was handsome, and pretentiously well ap-appointed; but truth compels me to own that the domestic circle lacked that affection which is popularly supposed to render home an antetype of heaven. The fact was, that very shortly after 'being taken in and done for,' Antony discovered his neat little grey mare had a strong tendency to act the better horse,—an inclination he strenuously strove to resist.

Resist Katherine! And besides, hadn't she 'a hair in his neck' anent that trust of Angus Gordon, deceased? Being himself slightly inclined to stiffneckedness, of course for a while there were domestic wars and rumours of wars, but in the long-run he had to succumb to the godless little helpmate, whom he could not honour, but whom, to his sorrow, he found himself bound to obey.

But all this was only the experience of their start in connubiality. Even the devil is not all black. Given that Katherine's interests and yours coincided, and that you elected her sole manager of you and your affairs, she would wear thick mittens over her claws, and not scratch your eyes out. If her better-half would but consent to go easy, surely, surely it was for her delectation, as well as his own, that his go-to-meeting garments should appear spotless, and the finger of scorn be prevented from pointing out the tainting fly in his box of moral ointment.

So, by-and-by, things shook themselves into their places, as it were, and ostensibly the Greendykes household was most respectable.

The two little girls got on tolerably together (thanks to the sunny temper and loving disposition Letty inherited from dead and gone Dorettle). Hetty, Katherine's child, was her mother's own daughter in selfish, head-strong ambition, but gave promise of great future beauty. Adding that Letty indicated merely an average share of forthcoming good looks, we shall leave the quartette singing their life-song in proper time if not perfect harmony, and return to Marjorie Ker and Covenant Close. For nearly five months after her lover's martyrdom she lay on a bed of weakness and suffering, ill of a sort of intermittent fever, which utterly prostrated her strength, and baffled the doctor's skill. In God's wise providence perhaps this very sickness was the means of saving Mistress Renwick's reason from reeling, by giving her an immediate duty of love to fulfil towards the afflicted girl, and thus, in a measure, withdrawing her mind from the exclusive contemplation of past horrors. Very assiduously and fondly did she watch beside the bereft young bride, who feared not to die, but shrank with terror, poor child, from length of days. Thus weeks slipped by, and grew into months, but they brought little change in the condition of the invalid, who, save during the accesses of fever, lay pale, shut-eyed, and motionless. Nurse and patient grew fonder and fonder of each other, but rarely ventured to speak of him on whom their thoughts ever rested. Wattie used to sit beside poor May's bed, and pat her hand, and slip on tip-toe about the house, and go a-shooting at the Borough Loch and Canonmills Water, and eat, drink, and sleep as well as any healthy, clean-conscienced lad of seventeen, with no fixed calling in life, is fit to do.

But the bright star of the rather gloomy family firmament was Mr. Hepburn. As brusquely gentle, as kindly imperative as ever, there had come through the man an inexpressible refinement, as if a clay vessel were changed into fine porcelain, albeit unaltered in shape and colour. Had anybody told him he was more than fulfilling the charge committed to him by the 'martyr,' he would have thought it gross flattery. Yet, in very truth he was to the stricken women a son of consolation; the kindest of sons and brothers. Even Betsy (who, since the martyrdom, had turned John Bold to the right-about, and subsided contentedly into her former state of hopeless spinsterhood) declared, that but for the writer's comings and goings the house would be as eerie as a kirkyard. 'And really,' added she mentally, 'I think he's kind o' religious-like, though he's gotten a trick o' ordering a body about as if he was master and mair in this house. Well, well, this is a shifting world—we're here the day and away the morn. He was an uncommon fine young gentleman was poor Mr. Renwick, that's now in glory, and fond was him and Mistress Marjorie o' ilk ither, but I'll no lose my senses wi' amazement if some time Mr. Hepburn comes to be master here in downright earnest. But I declare there's the auld wife knocking again on the wall for me to take ben Marjorie's broth, poor lassie.

I'm a havering fule to think about Mr. Hepburn being her joe. Na! na! I believe her first joe will be her last, and that's James Renwick, wha's now in glory— Coming this minute, mem. I'm just ladling Mistress May's broth into the bowl.'

It was August before Marjorie was fit to leave her bed, and in August the atmosphere of Covenant Close was generally so ill-aired as to be anything but a restorative. A mere shadow of her queenly self looked the 'martyr's betrothed,' but the patientest, gratefulest, gracefulest ghost conceivable. The first day she sat up on a chair, instead of lying prone on a mattress, was quite a little fête in the household. A very staid, serious fête it is true, yet still a day of rejoicing that she had, as it were, come back to their midst from the borders of the grave. But it struck Mr. Hepburn that true and deep as her grief undoubtedly was, there was something unnatural in the dead-sea despondency that seemed to isolate her even while sitting beside those who were now her dearest on earth. In one sense none of them had got over the dire distress of their loss, but six months' work of 'time the healer' tells somewhat even on feelings the keenest and most retentive. The more Mr. Hepburn pondered the case, the more was he convinced that what Marjorie required was free-spoken sympathy in her recollection of the more insignificant every-day sayings and doings of him she mourned. That she needed somebody to converse about him, not as a dead hero or even a glorified spirit, but to linger tenderly over his *littles*, and thus, as it were, link on the warm, human, sensitive *then* to the quivering human *now*. (From pure respect to what they fancied the specific sanctity of each other's affliction, Mistress Renwick and Marjorie, when weeping over their departed, had scrupulously steered clear of everything suggestive of his endearing intimate personality, and opened thus, so to speak, a chilly gulf betwixt the man they had loved and him they were now lamenting.) How to break down the cold wall these two Christian women had unintentionally erected betwixt themselves and their 'dead in Jesus,' that was the difficulty Mr. Hepburn set about overcoming. 'I'm sure,' thought he, 'he himself, poor fellow, would have been the last to snap asunder even the thinnest threads of old associations. Why, he used to say that in heaven we'll enjoy remembering even the clothes we wore here, if so be we served God in them.'

It was really marvellous how clearly Mr. Hepburn recognised Marjorie's exact state of feeling, and how successfully he hit upon an expedient for 'filliping' her stagnated energies. Never in his days had he travelled a score of miles beyond the city walls but once, when on the occasion of precognoscing a witness in a case of disputed succession, he had gone to Broughton, a village about a couple of miles out of town. Albeit this peep at rurality had taken place in the old rollicking days, when his upward longings were fewer and farther between than now, he had often since remembered how the artless complaint of the newly-made widow with whom his business was had affected him.

'Ay! ay! sir, folk is a' very kind to me in my sorrow; and I ken my dear man is in glory, but I canna help wishing in my puir torn woman's heart that onybody that him and me knew when we were young and blithe was here just to speak to me about what we used to do and say then. It puts him and me sae far asunder someway when they tell me it's no right to connect him, noo that he's a spirit, wi' eatings and drinkings, uprisings and downsittings. Oh, if onybody would but speak wi' me now and then about what he liked me to make for his dinner, it would ease my heart.'

Summer was on the earth, Broughton still extant with its cottages, and apple-trees, and lowing cows, and unsophistication. Mayhap the poor widow was there too. But at any rate, to exchange the yellow parlour and stifling atmosphere of Covenant Close for pure air and village sights and sounds, would assuredly be good for Marjorie's body, if not for her spirit also.

Having come to this conclusion, the writer literally, as well as proverbially, took the 'first boat across the water,' and before six next morning had been rowed over the Nor' Loch, and walked from its opposite shore to the village. He was rather disappointed to find the widow had consoled herself by giving Tam a successor, but glad that her cottage might be rented for a month for a 'consideration.' So it was all settled without more ado, and you may imagine the astonishment of those two quiet women in the Close when that evening he told them they behoved to 'bundle and go' to-morrow at noon.

'Go where?' queried Marjorie for information, not to gainsay any proposal he might choose to make. (Nobody in the house ever thought of saying 'Nay' to the good-tempered imperiousness that sprang generally from a humble conviction that other people's welfare must be seen to, at any cost of his personal comfort.)

'Why, to Broughton, to be sure, to stay there a month. It's as warm here as an oven. You'll both be the better for a sniff of cool breeze and the sight of green grass.'

Do not, I again pray you, suppose any of the party in the slightest degree really oblivious of their common grief; but what with Mr. Hepburn's anxiety to see things set *en traine* for the temporary 'flitting,' and what with Wattie's delighted anticipations of endless birds to be shot, and endless honeycomb to be eaten; and what with Betsy's instant commencement of bustling preparations for going to the country, the two chief mourners were that evening actually seduced into a fleeting but lively interest in the programme of next day's proceedings. True, the smile was quickly succeeded by a tear, and both women mentally rated themselves 'callous monsters' because of having (even for a few seconds) allowed their affliction to retire into the back-ground. In order, therefore, to get reinstated in their own esteem, they endeavoured to make things square by looking (ay, and feeling) ten times sadder than before their most innocent little escapades.

Viewed in the light of the tears wherewith Mr. Hepburn's 'Good-night' was received that evening, it did not at first sight seem as if his experiment were successful. Nevertheless, the primary step in his purposed task had been taken. Subjects outside the realm of gloom wherein Marjorie had dwelt ever since the 17th of February had been introduced, and she interested in them, albeit only for a moment.

'See if I'm no' right,' soliloquized Betsy. 'As sure as a green grosel[1] is a green grosel, Mr. Hepburn will be my young mistress's husband yet, little as either him or her is thinking about it at this present time.'

With the aid of a pair of safe pads, and a broad-backed baggage-mule, the removal to Broughton was duly accomplished, Mr. Hepburn doing the distance on foot, and acting as pioneer and general care-taker. Their road skirted the eastern side of that great blue-green sedgy moor whereon the New Town of Edinburgh now stands, and its free, smokeless expanse reminded the 'mourning betrothed' of her native Tweedsmuir. The sun shone bright, and a coquettish but rather stiff breeze gave her no end of trouble to keep her riding-hood in its proper pose, but made the

[1] Gooseberry.

blood course through her veins as it had not done for many a day.

Mr. Hepburn walked at her saddle-bow, holding a bearing-rein for fear that, in the rider's weak condition, any highly improbable display of spirit in the steed should startle her. Not insisting that his charge should talk against time, but just allowing her to drink in the soothing influences of nature as she listed. Indeed, sooth to say, he himself was not very conversationally inclined that morning. His good Samaritanship had prospered to a wish, and poor Renwick's love was looking somewhat like herself again, so queenly, so sweet, so pure, and oh! so grateful for the present treat.

Yet, yet, when are people quite contented?

By some inexplicable mental process he was again peeping, as it were, retrospectively over the wall which separates coarse harum-scarum solitary creatures like himself, from the tender glorious life leadable by superior beings such as Renwick had been, and Marjorie was.

'... A vague unrest,
And a nameless longing filled his breast.'

'A wish that he hardly dared to own,
For something better than he had known.'

'Of all sad words of tongue and pen,
The saddest are these—"It might have been."'

'Ah well! For us all some sweet hope lies
Deeply buried from human eyes.'

'And in the hereafter, angels may
Roll the stone from its grave away.'

Mistress Renwick rode considerably in advance, urged thereto by natural refinement and tact, besides the desire to meditate and pray. Betsy walked near the old lady's horse, thus sequestrating the other couple, so to speak. As for Wattie, he was like a chained bird let free, scampering hither and thither off the line of march. Hallooing after an expeditious hare, or flinging a stone at some energetic snipe that never stopped to say, 'Don't,' but fled incontinent.

'Hurra! isn't this a fine place?' he asked again and again of Marjorie, bolting away, however, without giving her time to answer. 'A rover's life for me!—what say you, Betsy? This "open" is almost as good as our own Tweedsmuir, isn't it? You'll say so, old woman, when you see how I'll fill the pot with hares and grouse, and what not. Just you wait a little, and I'll astonish you. See if I don't.'

A very happy month they all spent at Broughton; Wattie being engaged in what he called 'peppering' the birds from morning till dewy eve. Everything felt so fresh and new, and far-away out there among the orchards and villages, and yet one could so distinctly see Edinburgh-walls standing on high, over yonder, to the south-west.

After his day's 'worry' in the hot moiling city, Mr. Hepburn would frequently walk of an evening to the cottage, and be refreshed with curds and cream and honey cakes, in the most primitive style possible. And then, when the setting sun was purpling the moor, and making the distant castle look as if it were one great blazing ruby, they would all go out for a stroll, while home-wending bees hummed their 'song without words,' and aërial regiments of crows cawed overhead, speeding away toward the golden-clouded west. On these occasions, however, Mistress Renwick, albeit a model matron, would generally, about five minutes after setting out, find herself too tired, or too warm, to proceed further, and so pray them to have her excused. She had as great a dislike to making herself *de trop* as if she had been a gentlewoman born, and while loving Marjorie with all her heart, never forgot the original difference in their position. As a walking companion, Wattie was utterly untrustworthy, so it came to pass that his sister and the lawyer were left pretty much to entertain one another. And very often their converse was concerning him who was gone, at every meeting, in fact, after one particular evening, when Mr. Hepburn took the initiative in starting the subject. He did so, however, with fear and trembling, poor man, dreading lest, after all, he might foolishly be rushing in among the footprints of angels.

A new light shone in Marjorie's eye, fresh comfort filled her soul when once she could speak unreservedly of Renwick, as he used to be in the dear old days when he came on New Year's Night to supper dressed in velvet with scarlet rosettes in his shoes; or when, later in life, he and she walked hand in hand to Talla Glen conventicle, etc., etc. It was marvellous what a transformation had been wrought by Mr. Hepburn's intuitive conception of that queenly damsel's craving for small sympathies at this epoch of her life. Verily the severity of her heart's winter was over and gone, and spring greenerie had come instead of ice and snow. Having, so to speak, received at the writer's hand her dead back from outer darkness, she felt very grateful, and (albeit Renwick's memory filled her soul) began to reckon time by Mr. Hepburn's visits.

CHAPTER XIX.

'Sometimes in the hearth's bright glow
She watched a picture come and go.

A manly form at her side she saw,
And joy was duty, and love was law.

Then she took up her burden of life again,
Saying only, "It might have been."'

HERE follow some extracts from Marjorie Ker's Diurnall :—

'*November the First*, 1688.—Uponn this the first daie of Winter I sall Again write in this Book, whilk is, by the Handwrit upon the Title page, sacred ever more to mee and mine.

'Since last I took upp the penn, Great and Swelling streams have flowed over Mie head, and the Lord Hath written mee desolate, and a Widow Woman in Verity, Seeing that mie Beloved and mee were as Gude as Married. For long after that never-to-be-forgotten Daie, when Mie Precious Dear, the Lord his Valiant Servant, ascended from The Scaffold inn the Grass-Marcet Here to that Citie whose Gates are of Pearle and her Streets of Fine Gold, I praied God would Mercifullie Stopp Mie Breath, Seeing it behoved evermore toe Bee Spent in Lamentation. Thus Spake I in Mie Haste, unadvisedlie, For whatt Right had I to Dictate unto the Lord of Hosts, whose I amm, and for whose service I am Spared a little longer. But O! Mie Dear, Dear James, What an emptie World this is now unto Mee. Upp till the time Wee all went to sojourn in Broughtoun, meethinks I was well nigh beside mieself, Repining against the Lord his Providence Night and Daie, albeit not by Word of Mouth. I felt hardened up in my mind like as Lot's wife was in her body. Shee could only gaze towards the ruins of Sodom, whereto her heart clove; I could think not a Moment of Ought else but Mie Dear's Cruel Murder. Upon mie Bedd did I lie Weeks and Months, with this one terrible thought eating into mie verie Soul, and to Mie Shame Bee it said (seeing I profess to Bee a Christian) instead of humblie asking the Lord to Carry mie Burthen, I set mie face towards his dispensation as hard as a flint, and gnawed, so to speak, mine own tongue to try if therebye I might better thole Mie sore pain. And all the Time I was thus Misconducting mieself under The Chastening Rod, Mie dear Gude-Mother (So I consider her to Bee) and Kind Wattie and Master Hepburn, and Even Betsie, Were tending mee as Constant and Tenderlie as though I was a Queen, poor Dear James his blessed Mother foregoing even the Indulgence of her Own Grief in order to the easement of Mine. Yet, albeit I blame Mie behaviour att that time Toward Mie God and these Dear Friends, I know, as none else can, How dreadfull was the Agonie I felt at the thought that haunted mee continuallie, To Wit, " Your Love is Murdered For Serving the Lord."

' When in August Mr. Hepburn took us to Broughtoun, and on the Road spake now and again just a kindlie word about the Wildflowers on the Muir, or Such like, the quiet Place and the Sunnie Air and all that, made mee feel as though I had been in a bad dream for Months past.

' It was on the Whole a Happie Month We spent at Broughtoun; for Mr. Hepburn and Mee Spake verie often about Langsyne before I knew him, but when James and I were Daft about one Another, Afore the Trials of Life Had Brushed Away our Belief in its Perfect Bloom. Now, Thank God, I am Content to Abide here below, till it pleases him to permit Mee to Meet James in Glory. I trie to Bee cheerful when Beside the others; But all the Time, albeit I smile Whiles, Mie Grief, Mie Sore Grief, Keeps Running on, Softlie and Hiddenlie, Like the Uglie Feet of a Pure-White Swann paddling Below the Blew Watter.

' *November the Sixteenth.*—How thick the Snow is falling; and Albeit only Two Of the Clock, it is well-nigh Dark, So that Wee have the Parlour Cruizie Lighted and a Big Fire. Wattie went out at noon to Skate on the North Loch; But the Snow and the mirkness will Stop that. Mie Dear Gentle

Mistress Renwick is Suffering somewhat from a Pain in the Shoulder, And After Applying a Cataplasm thereto, has lain down on her Bedd.

'For a wonder, Mistress Clavers is not in her parlour; at least I observe no Light in it. So being Solitarie and unobserved, I Will think a little over the past, and try, as it Were, to re-people this Parlour, as, alas! it Never can Bee again on Earth. Dear Kind Auntie Eppie Cometh in Mie Vision, and Sitteth upon one of the Great High-Backed Chairs, and on another, My Own Love, That is now a White-Robed Angel! Oh! Sometimes even Yet it rendeth mie heart to fancy how verie, verie happie wee might have Been here below as Man and Wife, but for the Bloody Crueltie of that Tyrant, James Duke of York and his Brother, who was quite as Bad, Whatever people maie Saie. Yea! Wee Would have Been as Joyous as Humanitie could Bee, If God's Will had seen Fitt; For Mie Dear Had not a Fault Thatt ever I could find out. No, not one! Mr. Hepburn Was Saieing so Last Night. In this, as in Most things, I find His Mind agrees Much with Mine. How Fond Hee was of Mie Dear! Well, Well, Bye and Bye we Shall all meet in the Home where no going out can part us.

'I wiss Wattie would come back. It is turning So Stormie, I am feared for Some Accident. Hee is a Kind laddie, but somewhat fond of Roving, whilk after all is maybee natural in a youth.

'I Stopped writing, for Mr. Hepburn came in with the Most Wonderful news, to wit, That the King hath Run away out of this Land, and that His Nephew is to Bee King in his Stead. God Send this Bee Trew, for Mr. Hepburn Saies the nephew is no idolator, but a Covenanter like ourselves, or something similar. O Mie Bonnie, Holie Darling! why hath this Blessedness to Poor Scotland Come too Late to Save Thee?

'*November Twenty-thrid.*—Wattie hath been att a wonderful Sight this daie. He beheld, when he was upp Buying some little nails at the Tinman's in the West-Bow, diverse Men, Sent Bye The Council and Their Bishops, who Climbed upp on the Port, and Took thence, off the iron spikes, the Heads of the Martyrs for Truth that have Been Bleaching There Years and Years. Often have Mie dear Gude-Mother and I praised God that our Beloved's Beautiful Head was allowed to be laid quietly in the Ground.

'Mr. Hepburn comes in Shortlie after Wattie with the Same news, But adds, that it is thought the Bishops and Council are now (in this changing time), affrighted lest it Should be asked, "Who Set upp These Bloodie Heads there, and Why?"

'1689. *March the* 14*th.*—Mr. Hepburn Came this forenoon, albeit hee was Verie Occupied otherwise, to take Mistress Renwick and Mee upp the High Street to See the Thousands and Thousands of Covenanters that have come Flocking into the Town, to Bee here pending the Sitting of Convention, partly to protect, if need Bee, the Duke of Hamilton, who is no Friend to Papists. Mistress Renwick did not wish to go, So I went alone with Mr. Hepburn, whilk I did enjoie, Seeing he Converses So pleasantlie about James and Heavenlie Things, Not in formal, Stiff Texts, But so natural like and easie. It was Verie prettie indeed to See the Fore-Stairs covered with folk Sitting on Carpets, and some pieces hanging over the Windows for honour of the Covenants, whilk is a change indeed. Wee took a turn (it Being fine and Sunnie) round Bye the Bow, past the Verie Spot where Mr. Hepburn lifted mee upp when I fell off Mie Beast the first time Wee met. It is noteworthy, as a providence, that Mie Glorified Dear should likewise have saved mee from being trodden under foot, and that also on the occasion of our first meeting. I can only see this co-incidence as through a darkened glass, but somehow I feel as if Mr. Hepburn's friendship to Mee was a last gift from Mie Dear. Hee was So lovinglie tender in Making over to him the charge of his Mother and Mee.

'*April the Eleventh*, 1689.—A Great Day for Scotland. The Tyrant is putt Away for ever, and his Married Daughter and her Husband are to be our King and Queen, By the Name of William and Marie. Our Folk are running about the Town, Mr. Hepburn Saies, Shaking hands with one Another, with blew Knotts in their Bonnets, And Shoving the Papists off the Calsey.[1] Oh that Mie Beloved had lived to See this Daie! Yet wherefore wish So? His prayers are

[1] Causeway.

answered. His Martyrdom hath helped to Bring Freedom to God's Kirk, And Hee from the Blessed Land on High Seeth it all, and rejoiceth.

'I caused Mr. Hepburn Stop, whilst I went into Luckie Watson her Booth and bought an Ell and a half of Blew tiffanie Ribband, and when Wee went home I made us Everie One a little Knott in honour of this Daie. Wee all wore them at dinner-time, and then read the 124 Psalm of triumph, yet were there tears in all our eyes, because One Brave Young Soldier, who had fought right valiently, was not with us to join in the Doxologie. Mr. Hepburn asked mee to pin his Knott in a Bit paper for him when he took Leave, "As," Said hee, "I'll Aye Keep it in Memory o' this Hallowed Daie." And that dear through-other Laddie Wattie dropped his in the passage as he was Going out After Dinner, and Never Soe Much as took the Trouble of Looking for it, Till Betsy found it. Truly there's a great difference in Men.'

CHAPTER XX.

'He that loveth . . . abideth in the Light.'—1 JOHN II. 10.
'He that hateth . . . is in darkness.'—1 JOHN II. 11.

CHAPTER the Nineteenth brought this chronicle down to the year 1689, a date made memorable by the accession of William and Mary to the throne of Great Britain. Consequent upon this event, divers alterations in public affairs took place in Scotland, including the fact that Popery and Presbytery exchanged positions, the downtrodden soles of the latter, so to speak, mounting where the spruce upper leathers of the former had been, and *vice versâ*.

But a brimful cup is ill to carry aright, and now that the Man of Sin was laid on the flat of his back, it is at least possible that occasionally he received more than Bible-measured payment for his past derelictions. People, albeit Covenanters, could not all at once ignore the eight-and-twenty years of 'bloodie crueltie' they had 'dree'd.'[1] But gradually things

[1] Undergone.

settled down quietly, and liberty of conscience grew once more into a recognised institution. Religious profession rose in the market, and sundry persons who had kept snug during the storm put on their silver slippers and tripped abroad delicately, now that the sun was shining again. Such an one was Laird Baigrie, although he would have been amazed had anybody told him so. As the peasant bodies about Tweedsmuir used sometimes to say, 'If the Laird was an elder afore the "Killing-Time," he is ten times an elder now,' which was true, in so far as perfunctory duty-doing was concerned. Let us glance at him and his, anno Domini 1697, that is to say, nine years after he married Katherine, and became tenant in Greendykes. As at its commencement, the household consisted of Antony and Mistress Baigrie, with the two girls, Letty and Hetty Fairlie. Except that the house-master had grown stouter and grey, and his better-half thin, and red on the bridge of her nose, they looked pretty much as of old. The lapse of time had wrought more change on the young people, as was to be expected at their age. Instead of a plump, good-humoured child of seven, Letty Gordon was now a finely-formed young woman, fair-skinned, peachy-cheeked, thoughtful, tender, and loveable. Hetty Fairlie was externally quite unlike either her mother or her late father, the Gorbals doctor, for a more magnificent girl one could rarely see. Large, dark, diamond eyes, that blazed and shimmered till you scarcely could say whether they were black or blue ; and such a complexion of lilies and roses! and such a graceful, tall, lithe figure! and, above all, such a voice! This describes their looks; what these four persons were in spirit and in truth will presently appear. Now for a few words concerning Greendykes itself.

The mansion was unaltered with regard to stone and lime, but Antony, by way of showing superiority of taste, had caused the walls to be washed with yellow ochre, or whatever was its equivalent at that time. All Marjorie's cherished plants and climbers had been rooted up, but a walled orchardy-garden stood at one end of the house, and the old tree-avenue was so well trimmed that even the most haunting of dryads behoved to move on in quest of that unpruned luxuriance wherein they are popularly supposed to delight. Inside Greendykes house, from garret to basement, the fittings and appointments were perfect in handsome heaviness, if not in pure taste. Then there were eight or ten servants, and a great caravan-looking coach that was only brought out on high days, upon which occasions four of the plough-horses officiated at the pole.

By this slight sketch you perceive that Katherine had in some measure attained her desires, and was living in style as a county-lady of the period. But not without infinite contention did she keep Greendykes up to the regulation point of fashion. Contention, I mean, with the Laird, her spouse, whose greed had expanded into a full-blown passion for hoarding, that made him grudge every plack spent in finery, albeit for his own behoof.

Having, as I said, no children of his own, he was less anxious than his wife to push into higher society than his father before him had frequented, and in these latter years to be looked up to in the district as having held fast by the Kirk in her low estate satisfied his ambition, all the more that it did not cost much. For now-a-days he was 'great upon the sin of those who had defected,' or shown a craven spirit in the fight for Christ's crown and covenant; and really, when one comes to think of it, he had not so overtly done, either one or the other, as to render his present high-flying testimony absolutely ridiculous in men's sight.

In God's estimate it might be different, but then, as you are aware, Antony Baigrie had one conscience-gauge for weekdays and another for Sabbath, so very likely he contrived to feel good for the eldership, even while ignoring the fact of having left undone sundry small duties he was bound to fulfil. Some people, knowing his stinginess, rather wondered at the lavish expenditure he permitted his wife to indulge in, the more so as the bruit ran that their domestic bliss was anything but perfect. Ah, me! little did these gratuitous censors surmise what a hideous skeleton was hidden in the highly respectable, wealthy elder's closet, or that of this chamber of horrors the wife of his bosom kept the key. Dislike her he did with all his heart, but it was not very probable he would strongly resist her wishes, when she had it in her power to disclose his fraudulent misappropriation of Letty's fortune! might any day strip off his beautiful sanctimonious cloak and exhibit him as poor and wretched and felonious. Even so far back as the days of their confabulations in the half-dark little kitchen of the wooden-fronted house, he had entertained a profound conviction that when Katherine took the bit between her teeth it was no trifle would stop her career; but since he had called her spouse this opinion had grown infinitely more decided. On one subject only had he shown fight, but the small, soft-voiced 'tartarous' woman had threatened her liege lord with instant exposure of the past, so what could he do but submit?

The point at issue was, whether Hetty should or should not be constituted inheritrix of all her stepfather's reputed wealth. Katherine willed that so it should be, while Antony (when he happened to be in his Sabbath-day's frame) was urged, by a sneaking fear of the day of judgment, to give to Angus Gordon's orphan a share at least of her own patrimony.

Poor wretch! he liked to maintain, as far as convenient, a tidy conscience; and lo! here was this woman blocking up his way back to perfect ease of mind. (But, to be sure, people were always doing that sort of thing to Antony, by his own showing.) To have brought up Letty as his heiress (seeing he had no family), would have set his old account with conscience comfortably square, and yet allowed him to enjoy the lust of wealth during life. But Katherine's ambition had centred in her daughter, whom she was determined to erect into his sole legatee; so of course there was no more to be said on the subject.

The Laird was not by nature fond of children, and had never given much heed to either of the girls; but now that they were approaching womanhood, it did grieve him a little to see how completely poor easy-tempered Letty was made to play second fiddle. Yet, with the exception of this orphan girl, the family party was pharisaical, pretentious, and unloving. Poor Letty! she knew nothing experimentally concerning the beauty of fatherhood and motherhood, but in her inmost soul felt convinced that true relational intercourse behoved to be a warmer, brighter thing than what she witnessed at Greendykes. Fain would she have lavished upon the Laird, the 'Ladie,' and even imperious Hetty, the clinging affectionateness that craved reception, but it was pouring water on a rock. Positive ill-usage would actually have caused less unhappiness to the young girl than to be left as she was, high and dry, above or beyond the reach of that loving reciprocity for which she thirsted.

In so very quiet a locality as Tweedsmuir, there was but little of the good society for an *entrée* into which Katherine had striven so hard, and therefore the arid domesticity of the family circle was seldom watered by visitors. With this selfish tit-for-tat monotony, the master, mistress, and house-daughter (as Hetty was considered), were content ; for, as the old saw has it, 'What can we expect of a pig but grumph?' But orphan Letty used to roam solitary over the muir, just as Marjorie had done before her, with an intense, albeit undefined, appreciation of life burning in her soul. 'Life, God's gift, ought to be a grand and beautiful thing! And yet, yet nobody she had ever known seemed to esteem it as such.' But, to be sure, her acquaintances were few indeed. Still, Laird Baigrie and his wife, ay, and their presumptive heiress, were looked up to by every one as serious, respectable, enviable persons. And was the daily routine of this carping, dreary existence all that life had to give?

This self-addressed query sometimes used to puzzle her—sometimes to strike through her, chill and hopelessly. At other times, the inborn necessity, so to speak, of her strong natural capacity for imbibing the fulness of that God-bestowed boon of existence, would stir her spirit as if a voice were bidding her arise out of the dark density wherein she dwelt, and come up into a purer atmosphere.

In those days, among aristocratic heads of families, it was the mode to maintain great personal state and formality, and to be addressed, even by one's own children, 'My Lady,' or 'Madam,' as the case might be. It pleased Katherine to ape this sort of thing, and to act gentility by keeping both girls at arm's-length, so that she scarcely saw even her own daughter, save at meal-times and on religious occasions. These latter, however, were frequent, for Antony's now inflated religious profession demanded that every soul within his gates should be catechised at least once, and Bible-chaptered twice or thrice per diem. Hetty, being hard and bold, always declared so much praying and preaching an intolerable nuisance. To thoughtful, gentle Letty these exercises, viewed in the light of the catechiser's daily walk and conversation, afforded endless ethical problems to be worked out, if possible, during her lonely rambles on the moor.

(At this period of the orphan's life her soul was like a dim coagulate, whereon angels, good and bad, intently gazed, wondering what the evolvement should be.)

Returning from one of these rambles one afternoon, she observed a horseman entering the tree-avenue of Greendykes. A young man (judging from his back) on a handsome roan horse, whistling and singing some snatches cheerily, as he rode up to the house. It was the landlord, our old friend Wattie Ker, now a hale, merry, good-looking man, of between six and seven-and-twenty. He had recently returned from one of his frequent foreign trips, and been despatched by Mr. Hepburn (his man-of-business) to see whether the repairs required by his tenant were absolutely needful.

'You are generally on the move somewhere or other, Walter,' he had said; 'why shouldn't you ride to Tweedsmuir and take note for yourself?' So Wattie went, and was now, as I said, riding slowly up the tree-avenue, twenty or thirty yards in front of Letty.

Before introducing him under his own roof, allow me to explain what he had been about during the nine years which have elapsed since Marjorie made the Covenanter blue knots, and he lost his in the passage, from sheer carelessness, as Betsy declared.

Madame Rougemont's, or rather Mistress Elspet's succession, added to his patrimony of Greendykes, made him, as times went, a well-off youth, albeit not a Crœsus; with funds enough to 'keep the pot boiling,' although not so wealthy as to make the choice of a profession quite a work of supererogation. But with his unliterary proclivities and boyish tastes, and no evil in him, youth slid into manhood, and still he remained the same Wattie Ker, resident in Covenant Close; bearded and broader shouldered than of old; in other particulars not one whit changed.

Marjorie, being almost dependent on her brother, naturally felt a degree of delicacy in urging him to seriously set about his studies for the bar (that being the end formerly contemplated by his mother). But the girl's hints were usually answered with an embrace and a 'By-and-by, May, dear! There's no hurry! Just let me, yet awhile, enjoy myself in my own way.'

What could she do? What could Mr. Hepburn do? He, at least, could not offer his own progress as an incentive to the youth. Had he not so dawdled away his own best years as to leave him, now that he was willing to work, but small chance of making his mark on the legal world? So his mouth was shut, and Wattie, as he had purposed, amused himself after his own devices. Thanks to his love for Marjorie, even idleness did not lead the lad off the path of virtue. Indeed, had you consulted Mr. Hepburn, he would have told you that intimacy with *her* was a safeguard to any man—a moral robe, clothed in which he might brave all the seducements of all the vintners in Edinburgh or elsewhere.

Wattie got over the clause in Madame Rougemont's will which compelled residence in the Close, by making it his home, though most of his time was spent in what, in our day, we should call excursionizing to foreign parts. Out there and back again, to be received and petted, and made as happy as a boy home for the holidays. Then off again to the ends of travellable Europe; and so on, *ad lib.* You will not therefore be astonished that Mr. Hepburn said he was always on the move, and advised him to ride as far as Greendykes, to see for himself whether the repairs, etc., Laird Baigrie insisted upon were really needed.

With the young landlord's advent a great change has come over Letty's dream of life. Oh! such an entrancing, exquisite thing mere existence seems now to be. The joy and love wherewith hers overflows impels sometimes tears to the girl's eyes and prayer to her lips. The world no longer appears the same dubious, illogical, eerie place as heretofore. No fine singing voice could Letty boast, such as Hetty's, but she had it in her heart now to sing all day long for very gladsomeness of spirit. If Laird Baigrie and the Ladie and the young Ladie (Hetty, to wit) would not have frowned upon any such sentimental demonstration, she would have felt relieved by flinging her arms round their necks and kissing them all round, just to work off a portion of the new spirit of love that was effervescing in her soul, poor child. In very truth these were halcyon days for the hungry-hearted orphan, for, albeit no logician, Wattie Ker had inadvertently answered in full her long and vainly-pondered query, how much of affection and happiness can life bring to any creature? She was sage and thoughtful, he not especially either one or the other, but he exactly fitted, so to speak, into the felt void. For the youth was naturally very affectionate, and, beside, Marjorie had learned to let his kindly feeling go forth in the guise of those little attentions whereto Letty had hitherto been utterly unaccustomed. In short, without knowing exactly what it all meant, the orphan was deeply in love.

As for Wattie, in all his travels he thought he had never seen so nice a girl as Letty, albeit the heiress was not only richer but a great deal prettier. He was made a great deal of by Laird Baigrie and his lady, and pressed not only to eat impossibly, but to remain as long as ever he pleased in his own house. So day after day slipped by, and at a fortnight's end he still was there. He had given *carte-blanche* to Mistress Baigrie anent the demanded repairs, which on nearer inspection turned out to be no repairs at all, but permission to build a coach-house for the accommodation of the saffron-coloured family chariot, which had heretofore abode at one end of the byre, in the old peel-tower. I daresay Wattie would have been amused had he been fully aware what an object of diversified interests he formed to his four sedulous entertainers. Thanks to the exaggerations of rumour, both the Laird and his wife were at one in the opinion that their guest was an eligible matrimonial party, and behoved, if possible, to be speedily captured for behoof of one or other of the young girls. But at this point the unanimity of Antony and Katherine ceased, seeing they severally prayed the youth's handkerchief might be thrown at different parties. 'The young elder,' with his usual moral obliquity of vision, saw, as he fancied, the hand of Providence providing, by means of a wealthy marriage, for Angus Gordon's orphan daughter, and thereby not only setting his own qualms on her account finally at rest, but enabling him to enjoy in peace the riches he *dared* not now return to their rightful owner, even had he wished so to do. Katherine, on the contrary, was extremely anxious that her own fifteen-years'-old daughter should win the prize for divers reasons. First, albeit she was maternally proud of the girl's beauty, that did not, unfortunately, include filial piety, and, as a rule, the two ladies lived in a normal state of *bicker*,[1] anything but agreeable to so dignified a county dame as the elder aspired to be. Secondly, it would be a boast to have got off her child thus early in life, though in those days juvenile matrimony was more common than now. Thirdly, it would be too dreadful were the orphan, whom she treated as the 'scum of creation,' to be raised to an equality with herself.

And the two candidates themselves? We have already analysed Letty's innocent virginal thoughts and feelings; so the only item to be added is that she suddenly took to brushing her hair a good deal, and larded her plump, soft cheeks nightly before going to bed. As to Hetty, with her extreme beauty, and her fine dress, and her magnificent singing, and her heiress-ship, she thought her risk of missing Wattie very small indeed; but being her mamma's own daughter in the matter of thorough-going, and devoured besides with the spirit of rivalry, she left no lure or device untried to secure her own induction into the cares and responsibilities of married life. You can easily imagine how the long summer days flew past in merry dalliance. Occasionally poor Letty would suddenly be bitten by the tooth of jealousy, and anon the pain would die down under an access of repentant grateful tenderness. And sometimes lovely, godless Hetty, waxing irate and ruthless at the low dependant for attracting so much of the swain's good graces, would patch up

[1] Small fight.

the peace with mamma, and thereafter incite her to trot out the offender's very worst points. At length the visit was over, and Wattie went back to Edinburgh, carrying away with him poor Letty's sunshine.

Extract from Marjorie Ker's Diurnall :—

'*July the 27th,* 1697.—Wattie hath returned from Greendykes, and meethinks Hee hath fallen in Love, Albeit he denies it, as is sometimes the foolish Waie of Men. Mie Dear James Was above This. But Was there Ever Such Another as Hee? Never! I imagine from What I gather that the girl of Mie Brother's Affection is none other than the poor Orphan Letty, who Formerlie Abode with Auntie's Tenant, Mistress Fairlie, and Of Whom I used to Bee so Fond Before Mie Great Sorrow Came, As was Wattie himself Likewise when he used to plaie with her as a kind of living Toy. I recollect His once asking either dear Auntie or Mee (I forget whilk) to keep her alwaies, for he likit to Make her weep, and then kiss her fat face till she laughed. It is strange how things come to pass in this world. I wonder at Wattie in regard to this Matter, and Yet I admire the Laddie for his unmercenarie Spirit ; But he has that indeed, Else would I not this Daie Bee Sitting here comfortable in his Yellow Parloir. What I admire is that he has passed Bye the other girl, who will have so Verie Large a Fortune, and is, He Sayes, as Beautiful in Face and Figure as an Angell of Paradise. Her Mother, Mistress Baigrie, is none other than Mye own Dead

Dear's Cousin Katherine. (This is a queer world.) Wattie opines Shee is ill-Willie at Mee, wherefore I Know Not, I am Sure. Wattie's present condition of feeling hath (I blush to think) raised Envy in my Breast, when I Remember the Happie, Happie Daies that Can Never Come Back! Mye Dear Hath Now These Nine Years Been An Angell in Glory, But God alone Knows How close to Mee I sometimes Feel him to Bee, More Especially when Mr. Hepburn Begins a talking, as he verie often Doeth, concerning the Terrible Killing Time, that Mie Own Beautiful Murdered Darling's Martyrdome put An End to.

'*August the Ninth*, 1697.—Mie Verie dear Friend Mistress Renwick hath of Late Been far from Strong, and Mr. Hepburn, Who toward Her and Mee is like a Second Providence, has arranged for Us to go to Broughtoun, When Wattie goes Awaie To Flanders. The Air out at Broughton is Fine and Clear, and I remember Being Much Benefited By Walking on the Muir when We went there After Mie Great Sorrow. Trulie Maie I add Mine "Amen" unto the Blessing dear Mistress Renwick invokes on Mr. Hepburn's Head, for without Him and His thoughtful Kindness what would I have done After losing Mye Best Beloved James. It is pleasant, Both to Mistress Renwick and Mee, to remember How our Dear was Fond of him, and Asked Him To stay beside us all at the last dread parting; Nay More, that He chose Him to accompanie him to the Scaffold itself. Mr. Hepburn's Kindness thus feels to Bee, as it were, a legacie from Mie lost Dear to his Mother and Mee, and is not like the Intrusion of a Stranger into our Innermost. I think he is a Verie real Christian man now, Whatever hee was formerlie, but I do not Believe ever hee was what could Bee called Bad, Albeit Hee might, being Single, and living about Taverns, take His Glass Somewhat Freelie at a time. But that was Before Wee Got acquaint with Him, and is verie possiblie onlie one of Mistress Clavers' stories. At Anie Rate a Better Man could not Bee than Hee is At this Present, or a Kinder; and last Night, when At Mistress Renwick her Request hee engaged in prayer at her Bedside with her and Mee, the Sweet, humble, cheerie way in whilk hee Spake Anent the leadings of God in Providences, Minded Mee of Mie Dead Dear's meditations concerning The "Heavenlie Vestibule."

'Wattie is to leave us on Wednesday for Flanders. I wonder what pleasure the laddie finds in for ever Running up and Down the World? Just coming Home for a Jiffie, and off Again. Mr. Hepburn Would Bee Amusing enough Companie For Anie Person, One would think. But Wattie, of Course, has the Right to Do As Hee lists, And a Kind Brother Hee is to Mee, I am Sure. Verie few Would Have Keepit Mie Lost Dear's Mother, just to please Mie Feelings, or Bring Her home Such grand Fans and Necklaces, whilk, albeit not of anie use to her, Shews his Good Heart.

'*August the* 30*th, Broughtoun.*—Wee have been Here for

Eleven Daies, and, Thank God, dear Mistress Renwick is not like the Poor Shilpit Creature she Was when Wee Quitted Covenant Close. It is uncommonlie pleasant Out here, Sitting Among the Pear and Apple Trees, And the Sunshine through the openings, Making the foliage dance Dark and Light upon the Green Grass at our Feet. But our Grand Time is When Mr. Hepburn can come from the Town to See us. Even Betsy, who is getting somewhat Stiff in the Joints, Runs as brisk as a hare to set things in order when Wee expect Him. For, as She Saies, "His Honey Words Wad Wile the Laverock Frae the Lift,[1] Albeit He's no Bonnie."

'In that last particular I think She is Wrong. Of course a Fair Haired Man is Handsomer to Look upon than a Swarthie Person, Seeing the Heavenlie Angells are Supposed to Bee Yellow-Headed, as was also Mie Dear James. But, Notwithstanding this, There is something most agreeable in Mr. Hepburn, and, Above all, Hee looks the Gentleman. Hee has Been, and Is, Such a Comfort to us, that Mistress Renwick and I Wonder Whiles to Ourselves that He does not Marrie Anie Body. I'm Sure there's Plentie Would Bee Willing to Take Him, for a Man at Fortie-Two is But in His Prime, or verie little more. That Impudent Niece of Mistress Clavers is going Fair Mad about Him, and By her Long-Tongued Auntie's Account, She will have a Good Tocher. Dear Me, How Time Runs On! I Micself Will Bee Thirtie-Two Years

[1] A lark from the sky.

old to-morrow. I have been Wondering and Wondering if in Heaven I Shall Meet My Own Dear as a Glorified Old Woman, Hee being a Glorified Young Man. Of Course every condition There Will Bee Perfect. But I cannot help feeling as if I would Bee Sorry just at the First entering if I was not quite meet for Mie Dear's Mate, even if I was an Angell.

'I do not know What Set mee Speculating about these Matters, unless it Was Some Nonsense I Overheard, No less than Mie Own James's Dear Mother Saieing to Betsy this Morning when She was out in The Byre, getting her Drink of Honey and Warm Milk, that the Doctor Ordered her. I think it Our Dutie to Keep Neat and Clean the Earthlie Tabernacle The Lord Giveth us, But since I became, as it were, a disconsolated Widow Woman, I can trulie Saie I have Not Minded about Gauds, and Aye have Worn Black raiment.

'Looking earnestlie and Just for Curiositie into the mirror in the lid of Mie Comfit-Box, on This the Eve of Mie Thirtie-Second Birth Daie, I find Mie Face, to Speak Candidlie, Not at all old looking, But the Contrarie.

'*August the Thirty-First.*—Was there Ever anie thing So Strange? Mr. Hepburn Minded this was My Birth Daie, albeit I had not mentioned it to Anie living Soul, Seeing Commemorations Do grow Painfull in This World When our Best Beloved are No More Here to Celebrate Them With us.

What does Mr. Hepburn do but Bring Mee From the Town a New Snood and the Lovliest Pearl-pink Saque and peticoat, and, of course, I behove to put them on for Dinner. But that, I must Saie, was Mistress Renwick's doing, for Shee insisted. And then When Wee (Mr. Hepburn and Mee that is) took our afternoon's Dander on the Muir, She Made mee keep on all My New Braverie, and he said, when I pulled a Daffodil for his Button-Hole, that I was like Proserpine, that Mie Dead Dear used to Saie was, in Ancient times, so fond of flowers.'

CHAPTER XXI.

'Bubble, bubble, toil and trouble!'—*Shakespeare.*

N 1699 Scotland was very different from the overdriven, misgoverned country of a dozen years before, for although still falling short of being an earthly paradise, it could at any rate boast of freedom, and tolerably settled laws.

Protestant King William was firmly seated on his throne, and, albeit a few persistent partisans of the 'outed' Stuarts might plot, and sputter, and fume, freedom and law produced their natural effects, and the country began to progress. A bank was founded in Edinburgh, where hitherto money transactions had been carried on principally through merchants, or rather booth-keepers. Numerous manufactures were established, and commercial enterprise arose. With none to make them afraid, even should they pray and sing psalms from morning till night, men's minds ran agog on money-getting, and making haste to be rich became the order of the day. Towards the close of the preceding year, through the instrumentality of an enterprising individual named Paterson, a number of Scotch people had emigrated to the Isthmus of Darien, with intent to found a colony on free-trade principles. A company was formed for carrying out the scheme, and shares subscribed for to a considerable amount.

On the 26th of July six goodly ships, carrying twelve hundred emigrants, and no end of commodities, set sail from the port of Leith, and all the beauty and fashion of Edinburgh rushed to the shore to bid them God-speed. Upon the 25th of March 1699, news came announcing the safe arrival of the intending colonists, and their first-rate prospects, whereupon there was a great illumination in the capital, and considerable smashing of windows by the mob, wherever lights failed to enter appearance. Thereafter ensued a perfect scramble for shares in the Darien Scheme. Hurrah! who would not even sell the coat off his back to purchase tickets in this wonderful lottery, where 'all prizes and no blanks' was the order of distribution. People over the length and breadth of the land were seized with an unreasoning *furore*, such as in our own day we have seen *apropos* of joint-stock banks and railroads. Every old woman who had a few bodles in her 'stocking-foot' hurried to invest them in 'the Darien,' joyously anticipative of pocketing cent. per cent. interest at the lowest figure.

Wattie Ker came home from one of his continental rambles

violently infected by the popular mania. This expedition was verily something worth going into.

'Only fancy, Marjorie,'—'brattled' the young man in his *non sequitur* way of proving that the ball of fortune had rolled to his foot, and only awaited a touch of his toe,—'Only fancy! the town is called St. Andrews, and is built on a spot that commands both the Atlantic and the Pacific Oceans.' Poor Wattie! in spite of his travels no one could be more innocent of geographical knowledge than he, and yet to hear him descanting on latitudes and longtitudes one would fancy him a second Columbus at the very least. 'Only fancy, sister mine, how splendid it must be out there, where diamonds and pearls are to be had for the taking, not to mention gold, and slaves, and oranges, and capital shooting, as much as ever you can set your face to! They tell me it's the finest climate under heaven, and flowing, as Mistress Renwick says, with milk and honey, and the olive tree, and all that sort of thing. Oh! I forgot the almonds. They're the great commodity, it seems, and won't I be my own best customer, that's all.'

It was no use trying to dismount Wattie from his hobby. Upon it he trotted continually and untiring, feeling every hour a day till the second draught of would-be millionaires, whom he was to accompany, should embark. Like everybody else, Mr. Hepburn believed in the venture, but for Marjorie's sake (and perhaps his own, in a 'hiddling' way) tried to dissuade the youth from quitting old Scotland for ever.

'Oh, it's all stuff and nonsense,' would Wattie reply, 'about dear May making up her mind to be buried beside Renwick, and cleaving to his mother till death. The old woman is very welcome, I am sure, to go with us. There's no scrimping out yonder. The more the merrier. I'll promise her half-a-hundred black slaves and white elephants for her own share, so she can ride all day long if she likes. I don't say we'll never come back to this country, but, if so, won't we cut a figure, May and I? Now, as a favour, will you promise me not to set her up again about poor Renwick's bones? You should come too. Two or three who are going are not much younger than you, I should say. Nay, my own opinion is that Evan Macpherson's grandfather is even older,' etc.

Job's comfort indeed, but in his despair Mr. Hepburn was fain to ignore the difficulty of going wherever Marjorie's brother was pleased to convey that damsel. To dwell in earth's uttermost ends, so she were there, was enough for the unsentimental-looking, black-a-vised, out-speaking 'writer' of forty-seven years old. What to him would be Edinburgh, or even life itself, were his tutelary divinity withdrawn? And then in a cold sweat he remembered that it was perfectly impossible for him to join the expedition, seeing he had not a stiver save the fag-end of his salary for the current half-year. It might be all very well for Mistress Renwick to emigrate as a poor friend, but his pride revolted from the idea of playing the hanger-on even to generous-hearted Wattie.

(As representing so much food and raiment, cash is prosaic enough, but, woe's me! there is sometimes an infinite deal of poetically tender sentiment mixed up with the entire lack of it.)

So once more Mr. Hepburn was tongue-tied by his poverty, as was Marjorie by hers, and Wattie, with the kindest of hearts, set about the preliminaries for torturing the two people he loved best in the universe, next best at least to that nice girl Letty, out yonder at Greendykes. Since his visit concerning Mistress Baigrie's new coach-house, he had made two hurried runs to Tweedsmuir, but never done what in these our slangy days would be described as 'coming to the scratch.'

For this the young fellow's chronic 'By-and-bye' was partly to blame; but over and above that, he had a sort of glimmering notion that, as the head of the family, it behoved him to see Marjorie settled in life before taking its heaviest responsibilities on his own well-poised shoulders. Perhaps in thus reasoning the wish was father to the thought; but, at all events, the result was as above stated.

Mr. Hepburn had no choice but do his devoir to his client, and hunt up the means of driving a coach and six through the body of the will he himself had drawn for Madame Rougemont. The burden of its prosy phraseology consisted, so to speak, in this refrain, 'No residence in Covenant Close, no inheritance,' etc. But, says the ancient proverb, 'Thieves are the best thief-catchers,' and, by dint of much legal burrowing, Mr

Hepburn at last *did* contrive to circumvent the late testatrix's implied design of rendering it impracticable for her successors to sell any of the property. There was nothing wrong in helping Wattie to do what he wished with his own, and he remembered thinking the clause an old woman's crotchet at the time of its insertion. But in view of the future, it was to the lawyer simply torture thus to aid in expediting, as it were, Marjorie's eventual expatriation. And yet how could he make matters different? Oh, if only he were rich, and could offer her himself and a home! But a poor wretch of a writer, who had not got on in the world, albeit he knew his talents were above the average. Again, in his humility, the man's dawdled-away youth glared at him as reproachfully as though sheer idleness were positive crime. Perhaps in truth it is. With the knell of his every-day happiness already pre-sounding in his ears, he, at least, now felt it so to be. And as a proof of the tone his character had by this time acquired, it is noteworthy that he neither blamed his faithless parents nor his scrambly immethodical upbringing, but at once placed, so to speak, the saddle on the right horse, saying, 'Lord, I have sinned.'

By-and-bye Wattie was persuaded to change his plan of taking Marjorie with him, to leave the house in Covenant Close *in statu quo* for her present behoof, and to devise the rental of Greendykes for her maintenance.

'Never mind, May,' he said, 'if you *are* rather straitened for the next month or two, the more cash I carry out to

Darien the greater will of course be the return; so, as Roderick MacDougall says, "It's absolutely a sin to leave an unnecessary penny in this country, when out yonder every copper farthing is sure to become a gold guinea."'

In this idea Wattie had many fellows, for if The Darien was considered a popular investment before the first instalment of emigrants sailed, since the grand accounts of their success had come to hand shares in the company had, so to speak, mounted sky-high. People of every degree were absolutely mad on the subject. 'Sell all that thou hast, and invest in this Transatlantic Canaan,' was the popular gospel.

Alas! the spiritual fire which had flamed so bright and warm in rough persecutional winds was like to expire utterly under the sun of prosperity. Out yonder at Greendykes domestic affection was, if possible, at a lower ebb than a couple of years previously. Plenty of cold, rigid, reciprocal duty-doing betwixt the respective family-heads, but no love, perhaps all the less because the letter of the law was so perfectly fulfilled. They felt it a weary burden which conventionality condemned them to bear, and debited one another with the pain under which they dumbly writhed.

Antony's mouth was more pinched than ever, and his reputability as an 'old Covenanter' even growing in public esteem. For a few months back he had not been feeling well; not exactly ill, but bilious and low-spirited, much to his help-mate's disgust, as she had set her heart on a trip to

Edinburgh, with a private eye to Hetty's interest in Wattie Ker. At first Antony had objected, but Katherine girt up her loins and fought it out; so he had to bid her take her own way, adding a little expletive, which, being unusual with him, must of course be attributed to the liver derangement from which he was suffering.

'Letty does not want to go to town,' suggested Mistress Baigrie, 'and will see after your comfort whilst Hetty and I are gone.'

Not want to go to Edinburgh? Why, the love-lorn young damsel, poor thing, would willingly have given half of her curls for a sight of Wattie, and Wattie was there.

Was Mistress Baigrie possessed, that she thus obtruded on Antony's unmistakable notice the small repute in which Angus Gordon's orphan was held? It roused the 'young elder's' Old Adam thus to have his buried peccadilloes called to remembrance after he had so providentially been enabled to compound with Heaven for their payment. For, be it remarked in passing, that he still clove to the hope of one day seeing Wattie Letty's husband—hoped for this consummation in spite of appearances, as a shipwrecked mariner hopes his single plank will prove good for a voyage of some thousands of miles. But meantime, while Wattie's longed-for proposal remained unspoken, the Laird's out-of-order biliary ducts imparted a lugubrious tinge to his *own* doings as regarded his ward, and of course he preferred ignoring her existence as far as possible so as to keep a 'calm sough' with conscience. And who was this wife of his that she should presume to discompose the serenity of his mind? No wonder he was annoyed (antecedents considered); or that, albeit an 'elder,' he adjured her to be gone, in speech somewhat unsavoury though pungent.

Mistress Baigrie and her daughter were going on the morrow, and, by way of getting up strength for the road, had retired early to rest. A pullet and some ale lay undigested in Antony's stomach, and a withering east wind was blowing, so, like Ahasuerus of old, he could not close his eyes in sleep. Tossing unrestfully on the couch, his thoughts flitted backwards and forwards till by a curious chance two of them met face to face. These were Angus Gordon's fortune and the final day of judgment.

'What is man at his best estate? I really feel very ill. I'm sure it's little comfort *I* have drawn from the money. After death the judgment. Inasmuch as ye did it not, etc.— If it were not for Katherine and *her* girl I'd right poor Letty now while it is called to-day. Inasmuch as ye did it not— Depart ye cursed,' etc.

Next day was so stormy the two ladies postponed their departure, and the next, and the next after that. But in the evening of this third day the sky cleared, and lo! at the front door stood a dripping man just alighted off his horse. It was Mr. Hepburn, who, in his anxiety to arrange for Marjorie's interest in the rental of Greendykes, had, seeing there was no time to lose, come in person for an interview with Wattie's tenant. What with the east wind, and what with a wordy war which had just ceased, and left the Laird, the Lady, and the putative heiress dead tired of one another's society, anything in the way of variety was welcome. So Mr. Hepburn was pressed to remain all night, and (weather permitting) eke out Mistress Baigrie's travelling retinue on the morrow. He made himself so agreeable that the Laird forgot his aches, spiritual and physical, so much as to sit up far on in the night listening in rapt astonishment to his guest's details of the grand speculation, which was indeed the primary cause of his present visit. While Mr. Hepburn spoke of the universal rush for 'Darien' shares, and the almost certainty that money so invested would multiply itself indefinitely, a great idea was taking shape in the 'young elder's' brain. It was born partly of the writer's narrative, but partly also of disgust at Mistress Baigrie's persistence in holding 'his present wealth' *in terrorem* over his head whenever he wanted to feel particularly serious, or to gainsay any of her outrageous demands. His idea was to call up those two wretched bonds that had made him so miserably wealthy, and with the proceeds go forthwith to Darien and realize money sufficient to clear off all his complicated entanglements with regard both to God and Letty. But for the prospect of personally rolling in wealth besides, I scarcely think he would have heeded so much the prickings of conscience, albeit he felt no hesitation in attributing the conjunction to a special providence, whatever that may mean, seeing all providences are in a sense particular ones.

Of a truth one never knows what a day may bring forth! Picture to yourself the amazement of Mistress Baigrie when her heretofore objective lord called her down-stairs during the night watches, and informed her that he was also going to town early in the morning, 'Wet or dry! fair day or foul! Ay, and farther than Edinburgh,' added he, chuckling in unholy delight at her startled fear lest she had in the last conjugal brawl gone so far that he was about to fulfil his threat of quitting her for good and all. 'Ay, and farther than Edinburgh, madam!'

'Where, in the name of wonder, Antony?' cried she, looking for explanation to Mr. Hepburn, who was thinking how very plain she had grown with the red bridge to her nose and her huge ruffled night-rail.

That day fortnight the second draught of emigrants embarked at Leith in presence of a most enthusiastic crowd of spectators, who cheered and wept, and cheered again in the tremendous sensational wave that seemed to have washed out everything but 'Darien' from the popular mind. Most persons were interested to some moneyed extent, for even servant lassies subscribed their 'pennie fee,' hoping shortly to be above the receipt of wages great or small. To give some idea of how the passion worked, I may state that the entire amount of cash in the country being rather under £800,000, the subscriptions reached to over £400,000. As a spectacle, it was really fine to see eight hundred persons full of health and hope covering the decks and shrouds of the three ships as they weighed anchor, slowly dropped past Leith Castle, and stood out to sea. Most of the parting tears were shed by those left behind, and so strong was the general feeling of coming prosperity that even of these there were not many.

Antony Baigrie and Wattie Ker seemed in as good case as the usual run of their fellow-passengers, albeit Wattie felt somewhat hurt when informed by Hetty that Letty 'could not be at the trouble of coming to Edinburgh to see off either him or anybody else, being taken up with a young gentleman then paying a visit to his grandmother at The Whins. He is constantly at Greendykes, and you have no conception how fond Letty is of him.' Saying which, Hetty, who was looking splendidly beautiful, did her best by 'making eyes' to console the youth for his evident disappointment.

Wattie was not so far gone in the tender passion as to fancy he behoved thereupon to lie down and die. Nay, what with the excitement of sailing, and what with his somewhat lordly way of taking people's goodwill for granted, he might, had Letty been present, have received her admiration as his due, and left the love still standing over for future evolvement. But, as it was, he felt sorer than he cared to confess, and said goodbye to Marjorie and Mr. Hepburn so pathetically that the former could scarcely quit the pier-head for weeping.

'I have it borne in on me that my dear brother will never return,' sobbed she as the lawyer led her away, consoling her with tender, Christian, cheery words that somehow reminded her of Renwick.

The small ups-and-downs of these two people's uneventful lives had resulted in a change of their relative position, so to speak. The queenly, noble-minded, poetical woman looked up for support to the poor impetuous 'writer,' who used to consider her the embodiment of all the grand virtues, as he indeed did still, only superadding thereto all the loves and graces.

CHAPTER XXII.

'Hame, hame, hame!
   Fain wad I be;
Hame, hame, hame,
   In my ain countrie.'

T the commencement of the voyage Laird Baigrie suffered a good deal from sea-sickness, but was as kindly tended by Wattie as if he had been his father. During a long passage there was ample time for talking over home affairs, and this our two friends did very frequently. All manner of subjects used to come under discussion as they paced the deck or sat smoking in the stern-sheets; but the conversation generally ended by drifting round to the girl Wattie had left behind him, to wit, Letty Gordon. Not that he openly mentioned her in preference to Hetty, but the 'young elder' guessed how the land lay, and rejoiced accordingly that, after all, Providence was (with reverence be the simile used) playing the bowls exactly to suit his wishes. But, with a spice of his national 'pawkiness,' he, on the present occasion, thought fit to join tact with his mirth; and since Wattie chose to play at admiring both

girls equally, he humoured this fancy, always, however, edging in a favourable word for his orphan ward when it was practicable. Thus by degrees Wattie learned the right version of the story wherewith sly Hetty had aroused his indignation at the unconscious Letty—'so occupied in gallivanting with a young gentleman, she would not be at the trouble to go to Edinburgh.'

'Why, my dear young friend, Hetty must have been joking when she told you any such havers.[1] The fact is, that my wife only wanted to take *one* of the girls to town, and chose her own daughter. As for the young gentleman, he is indeed young, being the baby-grandson of an old friend of ours, Mistress Adamson of The Whins.'

Wattie's bruised self-esteem was healed on the spot, and feeling within his soul that he had misjudged poor Letty, he, like the unreasoning, warm-hearted fellow he was, straightway rushed to the opposite extreme, and mentally idealized her till she would have been afraid to look up to her sublime self.

'Absence makes the heart grow fonder,' of which truism Wattie proved a case in point; albeit, in talking of the girls, he continued to fence off the Laird's quiet attempts to make him speak out undisguisedly the name of the favoured she.

One night the young man remained on deck long after Antony had retired to sleep. He paced the planks, gazed up at the stars, cogitated, stared up at the starry heavens once

[1] Nonsense.

more, and finally administered a hearty slap to his thigh, to signify his thoughts had arrived at an issue. Betimes next morning he went to tell the Laird that he had made up his mind to write and invite her to come out as his bride, by the ship that was to follow with merchandise in six weeks. But lo! Antony was laid sick in his berth; so sick that the captain suspected he was in for spotted fever, and advised Wattie to give him a wide berth. Thus Antony was made a pariah of for the time being, and tossed uneasily on his couch, uttering incoherences which, for sake of The Kirk's impeccability, it was fortunate nobody heard.

At length land hove in sight—the golden land of promise! but Antony, albeit convalescent, was still too weak to walk or be 'bothered.' Therefore, out of amiability, and nothing else, did Wattie say no word concerning the love-letter he had penned by dint of several hours' hard labour. A very so-so production it was after all, in point of caligraphy; for you remember that even James Renwick could never imbue his boy-pupil with a taste for 'pot-hooks and hangers.' The *matter*, however, if short, was to the point, being a succinct statement of his love for Letty, his brilliant prospects, and an entreaty that as soon as possible she would join him and become his wife. The epistle was duly consigned to the captain of a vessel passing homeward-bound, and then the writer drew a long breath of satisfaction, feeling he had done something to be proud of.

Land at last. Hurrah! No end of bustle and confusion and noise and curiosity. Everybody agog save bedfast Antony and the cook's boy, who had sprained his ankle. Unfortunate Antony! Within sight of the goal, yet neither aware of the fact, nor even conscious of his own identity. His fever was gone, but so, alas! was his memory. No one thing could he recollect, not even his own name, which he declared to be 'Angus Gordon, who had two coffers.' Wattie was grieved, and made preparations for carrying the smitten creature ashore.

Land! Land! Hurrah! Pinky-yellow sands, edging a great semicircular blue-green sea-bay, that seems big enough to contain all the navies of the universe. Tall palm-trees, waving their graceful, green, feathery branches, as if in welcome. A few vermilion and purple landward birds flitting out and in the rigging. A huge, ugly-nosed monster of a shark swimming close astern of the good ship, 'Pactolus,' where Antony lies so helpless. Figures on the beach moving along slowly, not hurrying with the brisk alertness one might expect of prosperous colonists, eager for news from the old country.

The anchor is dropped. The first boat, with her eager living freight, shoots away right for the shore, amid loud, cheery huzzas. Why is it that yonder on the beech no answering shout is raised? Shouts of welcome from those broken-hearted, hunger-bitten skeletons? Woe is me! Wild Indians, cruel, rapacious Spaniards, blazing forests, burned dwellings, hunger, thirst,—*these* were not cheer-inspiring experiences, and they had been those of the Scottish men and women who, with their 'all,' had settled in Darien.

With the political wheels-within-wheels among which Protestant King William had got involved, and whereby this terrible calamity was brought to pass, we have at present nothing to do, save to state that its ultimate result fell not far short of bankruptcy for Scotland. The multitude of erect, strong, earnest emigrants who in despair lay down to die is frightful to think of, albeit divers of the cadaverous-looking survivors envied those whose eyes were safely closed in death and could see no more sorrow.

As I stated, Antony was carried ashore, and by Wattie placed under a sort of half hut half awning, persistently affirming himself to be Angus Gordon, and still maintaining earnestly that he possessed *only* two coffers. And so he died! With the help of another man, Wattie buried him beneath the shade of one of those feathery palms which but an hour or two before had seemed to wave a welcome to an earthly paradise. Alas! alas!

Naturally enough, Wattie constituted himself trustee of the effects of the deceased for behoof of his friends in Scotland, and duly took possession of the same.

Time dragged on wearily, giving forth a daily bulletin of sickness and death. The colonists were literally stupefied with misfortune, becoming callous in the immensity thereof. But into this normal condition of misery there came at length a variety, for the Spaniards settled in the adjoining territory surrounded and put them to the sword. Weak and worn as were the Caledonians, their bravery was (in the circumstances) quite marvellous; and it must have been (all things considered) even sublimely pathetic to hear their battle-shout of 'Scotland for ever!' Wattie elected himself an extempore general of division, as it were, and did his duty right soldierly and well. I wonder what Marjorie and Mr. Hepburn and Mistress Renwick, sitting in the yellow parlour at Edinburgh, and 'discoursin' the dear laddie Wattie,' would have thought, could they have seen him at that very minute cleaving a ruthless Spanish Don to the brisket?

CHAPTER XXIII.

> 'If hope has flown away
> In a night or in a day,
> Is it therefore the less gone?
> ... I hold within my hand
> Grains of bright golden sand;—
> How few! Yet how they creep
> Through my fingers to the deep!
> While I weep—while I weep.
> O God! can I not grasp
> Them with a tighter clasp
> O God! can I not save
> One?'

'HERE'S a man galloping up the Tree Avenue,' cried Mistress Baigrie. 'Who can it be?'

'Shall I run and ask?' queried Letty.

Yes,' answered Katherine.

'Here's a letter the man has brought,' said Letty, coming back into the dais-room, and bearing in her hand a sheet of folded paper, large and whitey-brown, tied round with a green string, and sealed with a big splash of wax. 'It's a letter from Master Baigrie, most likely. Oh, I wish I could read write like you!'

Katherine took the missive from Letty, and felt no little

uplifted in spirit because her education included penmanship as well as reading and spinning.

Why had Wattie sent his difficult *billet-doux* under cover to Mistress Baigrie? Simply because he was aware his beloved could not, as she had just said, 'read write.'

'Letty or Hetty, which is it? Really Wattie's hieroglyphics would puzzle a conjuror.—" All this Splendour, mie Dearest Love, Shall Bee Your own, Mie Sweet—" Letty or Hetty, which is it?'

For her life Katherine could not make out that queer, twirled capital letter; but, true to her instincts, took advantage of the doubt, and turned it in favour of her daughter. What with Master Ker's actual wealth, and what with his prospective, he was surely worth stretching a moral point for, if so he might be caught and husbandized.

'What is the letter about?' asked the two girls, speaking together. 'Is it from Maister Baigrie? Is he well?' etc.

'No; this is not from my husband. It comes from no less than our young landlord, who writes to ask you in marriage, Hetty.'

Ah me! how poor Letty's heart sank, especially when she noticed the taunting glitter in Hetty's splendid diamondy black eyes.

'We must at once go to town to procure your outfit,' said Mistress Baigrie. 'The ship sails' (he writes) 'in less than three weeks from this time.' So to town they went.

'Hetty, we behove to call upon your future sister-in-law, Mistress Marjorie,' said yet again the proud little matron, whose husband, even then, had she but known it, was expiring far away in Darien, in the hut beneath the feathery palms.

'Surely this red-nosed, sharp-featured dwarf of a creature is not the cousin Katherine of my own beautiful dead dear?' thought tall, graceful Marjorie to herself. 'I was in such grief when I saw her formerly, I don't remember what she was like then.'

'I wonder such a dignified damsel could ever have *fancied* herself in love with Jamie Renwick,' soliloquized Mistress Baigrie.

'Lord, what is man?' inwardly queried poor Letty. 'I truly *did* think I could trust Master Walter Ker.'

Marjorie was very glad indeed to meet little Letty, Wattie's umquhile 'toy and tease,' and felt greatly attracted to her.

Mistress Baigrie and the two girls took up their abode with Mistress Fairlie on the Castle-Hill, and the *trousseau* was set a-going without delay, a couple of daily tailors being hired in for stitching purposes.

Satins, saies, tiffanies, beads, liripipes,[1] looking-glasses,[2] feathers, how Hetty revelled among them, and flew like a tigress at her parent when gainsaid in any of the sumptuary details.

Letty felt absolutely crushed under Wattie's rejection of her love,—for what else was it?

[1] Streamers for the head-dress.   [2] Worn at the girdle.

Marjorie wondered exceedingly at her brother's choice of a help-mate, and agreed with Mr. Hepburn that men are not always 'dependable on' in the matter of common sense when matrimony is in question. 'I wish he had selected the other girl. She would be a "gude-sister"[1] after my own heart, but God's will be done. I only trust dear Wattie may not live to rue the day he wedded Mistress Baigrie's daughter. I would fain ask Letty to stay here with me for a week or two. I wonder if they would let her come? I'm wae[2] for the lassie; she seems so broken-spirited, and so sore down-holden by Mistress Baigrie and that detestable wench who's to be Mistress Wattie. More's the pity.'

'The Delight' duly sailed from Leith, and Hetty skipped on board without even making a pretext of grief at taking leave of her mother, but very much concerned about the proper bestowal of the wedding finery.

Mistress Baigrie was happy to rid herself of Letty's presence, and *lent* her to Marjorie for as long as she chose, she herself deciding to abide for a while at Mistress Fairlie's, as it would be rather lonely all alone at Greendykes.

[1] Sister-in-law.   [2] Sorry.

CHAPTER XXIV.

'So Death has reared himself a throne,
In a strange country lying,
Far within the West,
Where the good and the bad, and the worst and the best,
Have gone to their eternal rest.'

F the twenty-eight hundred persons who had lately emigrated to Darien, a mere handful survived, so thoroughly had war, hunger, and fever done their dire work. Fain would the remaining few have sailed away home, had the means been in their power.

But the Spaniards, after setting fire to some of the ships, had taken the rest. So the cadaverous-looking remains of the erst hearty multitude had to stay where they were, chained, Prometheus-like, not to a rock, but something resembling Pandemonium. For, when satiated with blood and spoil, the enemy retired, leaving them in quiet (ah, how quiet!) possession of their ruined embryo city, instead of making the best of what could not be helped, and, as it were, 'setting a stout heart to a stey brae,' what did the foolish creatures do but fall out among themselves about this, that, and the other trifle! I suppose selfishness is more or less an attribute of our fallen nature, and 'docked human foxes' who decry their congeners' bushy tails, by no means rare in this sinful world. At any rate, it is well known that the Scotch are, as a people, somewhat of a gear-gathering disposition, and 'uppish' withal. So it was perhaps not to be expected that a few months of tribulation should entirely do away with these innate characteristics.

> ' 'Tis a curious fact as ever was known,
> In human nature, but often shown,
> Alike in castle and cottage;
> That pride, like pigs of a certain breed,
> Will manage to live, and thrive, on feed
> As poor as a pauper's pottage.'

The wreck of Darien was unmistakably a wreck, but some of the crew had been lucky enough to save a few odds and ends, having literally buried their treasure in the earth till such time as it could be safely dug up again. True, hunger and thirst were rife, and gold pieces were not edible, neither could molten silver assuage ague-thirst. But gold was gold for all that, and they who lacked it bore a grudge to those who had it. You can easily imagine the consequences. Envy, spite, sulks, severe speeches, recrimination, twaddling virtue, in the weakest Bathos of pathos. Evil passions none the less existed because their subjects were just then at a low pitch in the scale of personal comfort.

There is no rule without exception, and of course even in that great mistake called 'Darien,' there were individuals who soared in ether, while others floundered in slime. Of these was Wattie Ker. Fiery trial had expiscated the nobleness of his character, and brought into prominence sundry virtues which, but for distress, might have remained in germ only; pickled seeds, as it were, undeveloped possibilities, unsatisfactory to God and man. Prudence had led him to bury his own treasure and Antony's in the earth before the Spaniards made their onslaught, and, as a matter of course, he subsequently came in for his full share of reproach because he had foreseen the evil day, and provided for it. It was the parable of the Ten Virgins 'done' into extremely ill-tempered Scotch.

'Give us of your cash, in case we ever should get back to civilisation, and be able to use it.'

'Nay, justice is justice. My money is my own, albeit, God knows, it's of little value at present. But I am responsible both to my own heirs and Laird Baigrie's. *Ergo*,' etc.

And yet, by night and by day, was he ready to serve everybody, utterly forgetful of his own comfort, poor fellow. Verily if evil spirits and malcontents out yonder at ruined Darien did not sleep on roses, neither did their better-inclined brethren.

If anything could add to the misery of these prisoners-at-large, stationed on the fateful isthmus, it was the hot season. This came on four and a half months after Wattie's debarkation, and while he was daily expecting that the good ship 'Delight' would bring him his bride. Dear Letty! his heart bounded at the thought of once more seeing her fresh, soft, peachy-tinted cheeks; of being listened to oracle-fashion, and looked at worshipfully by her sweet, loving, trustful eyes. Amid so much sin and wretchedness he felt it almost wrong to anticipate personal happiness thus ardently; but youth is youth, and, hoping against hope, he could not help dreaming of bright days to come. He and Letty would return in the 'Delight' (unfortunately, without crowding, all the colonists might now do likewise), and spend their days at Greendykes. Ah, how happily!

Hot and hotter waxed the weather. Under the palms was the only bearable temperature, but so anxious was everybody to catch the first glimpse of the expected vessel that at the risk of a sun-stroke they kept pottering all day long on the sands. It chanced that warm weather agreed with Wattie, so instead of squabbling despondently with his poor, half-frizzled compatriots, he thought of Letty, and better thought of her, till he really felt himself one of the luckiest fellows extant, and well-nigh fancied the cool air of Tweedsmuir blowing on his sunburnt, good-looking face.

At length the 'Delight' is sighted, and the effect on the beholders is of a strikingly diversified character. Some begin to halloo, some to pray, some to weep, for is not yonder speck on the horizon the ship that is to carry them home to the Land o' Cakes?

It is full tide, and the 'Delight' lets fall her anchor close in-shore. A boat tells itself off for the beach loaded with passengers, among whom is a woman. A *young* woman, from her figure, dressed like a live tulip, in a cherry-coloured hood, yellow satin scarf, and grass-green silk saque and petticoat. The thoughts of youth are quaint, quaint thoughts sometimes, and Wattie voted himself hypercritical for the cold shiver that ran through him when he spied this approaching display of brilliant hues. Somehow, without going into the question of cause and effect, he had always associated the idea of Letty with blooming heather and mackerel clouds, and pearl-grey or lilac robes. Ah, well! he was fantastical no doubt, and, after all, clothes do not make the woman. So, with gay hope in his soul, down he rushes to meet the boat and receive dear, sweet, sensible Letty in his arms.

'What has happened? Where is she?' exclaimed Wattie, turning white to the lips, albeit they were hidden by a most patriarchal beard. 'Where is my darling? She is not dead? God help me! Say for pity's sake, Letty is not dead!'

'Letty was quite well when I left Edinburgh, and I must say I do not feel flattered by your asking about *her* before saying 'How do you do?' to me. But where is the carriage? I thought a gold one would be waiting for me, drawn by the white elephants either you or somebody else spoke about! Such an ugly fright you look, all sunburnt and red.'

He understood it all, and cursed his own stupidity. It

flashed back on his memory that at the time of writing his letter he had bungled ever so long over the formation of that *initial capital* which had sealed his fate. But more than that, before his recollective mind's eye glimmered long-forgotten occasions when, in order to pique gentle Letty into demonstrative flirtatiousness, he had shown more than requisite civility to the pretty butterfly now staring sulkily at him in the intensity of her disappointment about the expected equipage. And what if his mistake anent the letter had only backed up a previous mistake occasioned by his own silly vanity? What if he had really misled this girl into supposing it was she and not Letty who was the object of his affection? A great deal of self-abnegation may be crowded into the merest nutshell of circumstance, and what some might consider a commonplace transaction, be, in God's reckoning, an Abraham's knife raised to slay an Isaac!

'Thy will be done' is, so to speak, the testing clause in man's deed of self-dedication to God, albeit the special occasion for adhibiting individual signatures thereto generally arrives without observation by any save the interested party. Sitting at a gay banquet, with music in the air, and merriment sparkling around, the flower-wreathed young queen of the feast hears a few chance words across the table, and feels instinctively that *her* time for signing has come. 'Thy will be done. Yea, Lord, so let it be; though the bright prospects I fancied so secure are all dashed to pieces.' Without changing countenance or leaving off the lively two-handed chat in which she was engaged when the summons came, she has, in Heaven's eye, said this 'Yea,' and signed 'God's will' with anguished patience.

Standing at the water's edge, with the frothy, curling edges of the rippling wavelets wetting his feet as he helps Hetty out of the boat, Wattie undergoes some such experience. Feeling all too vividly what may and what might have been, he yet, in God's strength, resolves to do his duty uprightly, and leave the results to Providence. Think you that to espouse a young beauty and heiress was a light dispensation, not worthy to be counted among trials of faith? With his deep love for Letty and utter indifference to the other, he did not so feel it to be. And remember, moreover, albeit, as matters stood, he was not sure that the gentle girl in Scotland knew for certain how dear she was to him, he was now going to put it out of his own power ever to say the word which might make him happy.

On being told of Laird Baigrie's death and the misfortunes which had overtaken the colony, Hetty burst into just such a wild rage of tearful self-pity and reproachful indignation, as her mother had done years before on seeing Marjorie in James Renwick's cell.

She exclaimed, violently, that 'Master Ker had entrapped her to this miserable, beggarly hole for the sake of stealing the fortune which was hers, now that her stepfather was gone.'

It was an ugly scene, and Wattie, at his wits' end, began to hope that, after all, his purposed self-sacrifice might be a work of supererogation. But, unfortunately, the married couple from Galloway, in whose hut Hetty found quarters for the night, were of a hopeful temperament, and, moreover, thought highly of Wattie, who, now that they were all likely to get away from Darien, took rank again, on the strength of Greendykes, as a well-off young gentleman.

The 'Delight,' lying in the bay, trim and seaworthy, had inspired new life into the thirty or forty poor wretches still above ground, and especially into the bride's present hosts, whose geese at all times had a trick of simulating swans. So they talked and talked till the girl was persuaded it would in the end be quite a grand thing to go back to Scotland as Mistress Ker of Greendykes. 'And then there's my money,' said she. 'I can buy carriages and things with that, for it's all mine, now that my stepfather is dead.'

The 'Delight' was to sail in ten days, *i.e.*, so soon as water was laid in, and the miserable provisions procurable put on board. To thoughtful men it seemed a serious matter to put to sea with little more than half rations, albeit anything was preferable to starving where they were. And then, 'Home, sweet home!' How musical it sounded even in Gaelic, not to speak of Scotch! Even the most quarrelsome and combative began humming scraps and snatches of old ballads in a way which, considering all things, was painfully affecting.

When Wattie came to pay his respects to his bride in the morning, he was struck with her good looks, but less in love than ever.

'She's listened to reason, poor lassie!' quoth Mistress MacNab, 'and is just going to marry ye without any more ado. Trust me and my man for persuading a body to anything.'

'Well, Hetty, shall our marriage be before we set sail, or will you wait till we reach Scotland? Which do you think your mother would prefer?'

After consultation, it was arranged that the Rev. Mr. Bruce (who had just arrived by the 'Delight') should perform the ceremony the day before sailing, and straightway the forthcoming event was bruited abroad by Mistress MacNab, who considered it partly her own doing.

'No, I don't care much for him,' said Hetty to that matron, in confidential communion; 'very little indeed, now that he has no grandeur here, and is so red and ugly. I don't think I ever should have thought of him at all, had not Letty (who lives with us at home) been mad about him.'

'I am obliged to be busy all day, Hetty,' said Wattie, once and again, 'helping to get things ready for sailing'; but I do wish, when I come in the evening, you would not always have that fellow Bruce talking to you. If we are to go through life together, it seems to me it would be well to know a little more of one another before starting on our journey.'

'I do not see that is any business of yours. Mr. Bruce was very kind to me during the passage here, and is ten times better-looking than you.'

'Ne'er heed what she says, sir,' put in Mistress MacNab. 'She's but a bairn, and'll get mair sense by-and-bye. . . . He's a fine man is Mr. Bruce. His grannie[1] was a cousin o' my man's step-auntie, so we're connectit in a kind o' way.'

What to do Wattie knew not. Hetty talked to Mr. Bruce, but, with Greendykes in view, kept himself to his promise, or at least did not offer to free him from it. The fact was, ship-chaplain Bruce had, on board the 'Delight,' been charmed by Hetty's pretty face (understanding it to be bespoke for the wealthy youth whom she was on her way to espouse).

We have seen that disillusionment soon came, as regarded the riches, but, with the prospect of returning home, Mr. Bruce was not the man to marry a penniless beauty (he being of the class who creep into widows' houses, and keep a bright look-out for behoof of number one). But naturally he was often during that week at the hut of his relations, the Mac-Nabs, and heard all Hetty's personal details, her heiress-ship included.

'What became of this Laird Baigrie's effects ?' queried he, as Mr. MacNab and himself were smoking a pipe at the hut door.

'Why, of course Master Ker got everything, or, I should rather say, took possession, in trust (for this girl, I suppose).'

[1] Grandmother.

'Are you quite certain about the deceased man's cash?'

'Quite! He was one of the most moneyed persons who came out here, and a great to-do there was among some that are now lying quiet enough under the earth over yonder, when, after those bloody, rascally Spaniards took leg-bail, it was discovered that Ker had buried both his own funds and his friend Baigrie's too. Even starving folk couldna chew gold guineas; so I suppose it's to the fore, plack and farthing.'

'What is the meaning of this, Hetty?' said that young lady's purposed bridegroom next evening on being sulkily received by his *fiancée*, Mistress MacNab not being present to talk things into smoothness. 'I insist on being told what your very strange conduct means!'

'Well, then, if you must know, I have changed my mind, and mean to marry Mr. Bruce whenever we get home to Edinburgh. He has told me all about your shabby conduct in trying to steal my stepfather's money, and hiding it in the ground, and all that; and I always thought you common-looking with your blue, saucer eyes, the very colour of one of the ploughmen's at Greendykes. I'm sure Letty had little to do greeting[1] hersel' blind after you went away, because you did not ask *her* to marry you. Humph! she's welcome to my leavings. I saw plainly when I landed last Monday, and so did Mr. Bruce, that you did not care a button for me (bonnie though he says I am). It was only my fortune

[1] Weeping.

you wanted, but we'll cheat you, for as clever you think yourself.'

Oh, happy Wattie! He had acted on the principle of 'honour bright,' and now was both upright and free. He could then and there have taken pretty, godless, undisciplined Hetty in his arms and kissed her for very gratitude. The vulgarly-minded probationer had, as they say at Cambridge, 'coached' the vulgarly-minded young woman in her lesson, and she now proved herself rather an apt pupil.

So there were fresh news in circulation on the sands, in the huts, and under the feathery palms, and some people who were fond of anything *outré* were disappointed that there was to be no wedding on the ruins of the defunct colony, as it would (being quite out of the common run) have been something to speak of for the rest of their lives.

Wattie gave the engaged pair his sincerest blessing, but refused to permit the embryo reverend's interference with the estate of the lady's stepfather.

'When we get to Scotland I shall place Mr. Baigrie's boxes in the hands of his man-of-business. They have never been opened by me, and the two he seemed to value most were sealed by his own hand, as you may see if you choose to look at them.'

On the brightest of bright mornings 'The Delight' again stood out to sea, but, as I said, of the twenty-eight hundred souls who had quitted the north in that sad race for riches only thirty-two individuals (irrespective of the ship's crew) now returned. Fathers, sons, and brothers; wives, sisters, and daughters were lying yonder beneath the tall palms, and many an eye looked back from the ship's deck through bitter tears at Darien. But yet, after all, it was a great mercy to be going home, albeit not too well provided for so long a voyage. So, as night fell, and the fatal shore melted away in the horizon, first one man gave three cheers for the Land o' Cakes, and then another took up the cry, till the ship's sides (to speak poetically) rang again.

Wishing them, therefore, a safe voyage and a happy landing we shall precede them to Edinburgh.

CHAPTER XXV.

'Something sweet about my heart is clinging,
A vision and a memory.'

ETTY was so guileless that Marjorie soon drew from her the story of her disappointment and innocent romance.

'You have no idea, dear Mistress Marjorie,' said the girl, 'how much good he did me. Till he came to Greendykes I used to wonder if God, who was so kind, who spotted the fields with clover, and made the apple blossom, never, never gave us our fill of joy till eternity. I used to think it such a pity to see the evening clouds and the red roses, and the honey-suckle, and no earthly love to correspond with these in beauty and sweetness. But when your brother came, I felt how nearly earth and heaven may meet, running as it were into one another. I have through him learned that, and can never forget it any more. Not till—

'The sun grows cold,
And the stars are old,
And the leaves of the Judgment Book unfold.'

How Marjorie doated on the simple, peach-cheeked lassie! Why! oh why! had Wattie fallen a prey to black shimmering eyes, which, after all, often looked neither black nor blue, but only sparkles of brightness.

As for Mr. Hepburn, he quite delighted in Letty, so much so that at sundry times and on divers occasions Marjorie hated herself for the distress this gave her. Ah me! as if at forty-seven one is likely to change the love of one's whole loving hitherto. As if one's innermost holy place could ever become common ground.

They were a very happy little party in Covenant Close, Mistress Renwick not the least so, in her own quiet way, albeit now and again her James's cruel death would feel as fresh a sorrow as if it had taken place but yesterday.

On such occasions Mr. Hepburn and Marjorie would speak of the past, and the 'Vestibule,' till time and a blessed eternity seemed to meet, and the severest earthly griefs appeared fleeting indeed.

Now-a-days it was 'Mr. Hepburn and Marjorie' even with Betsy, albeit she had unwillingly at length given up the expectation that by-and-bye she should see him wedded to her young mistress, who, however, in point of fact, was no longer so young as she had been, although Betsy, with her sixty-three years, considered thirty-four mere chickenhood.

Mistress Baigrie came sometimes, but not very often, to the Close. She entertained a grudge at poor Marjorie for robbing her (so she thought) of all the beauty that *might* have been, in her past life. In her now so arid, loveless existence, she felt sometimes that for her it would be as rain on parched ground even to remember she had once been purely, deeply, unselfishly loved. And but for Marjorie Ker, she fancied this might have been her lot, and hated her accordingly.

It was midsummer, and glorious weather. The days so long, and the nights so infinitesimally short, that people in Edinburgh had taken their horn lanterns off the hooks projecting from first storeys, and left nature to do the street-lighting.

In the market, women in short petticoats were selling quantities of dulse and tangle, which, as being good for the blood, were readily bought and eaten on the spot. Dwellers in high 'lands'[1] could, by stretching their necks out of window, catch a glimpse of the distant Bass Rock, and the cool, clear, blue sea. Shopkeepers, looking hot and perspiring, leant over their half-doors, and wished for a breath of air. The wooden fronts of the sunny side of the High Street, to wit, the north one, felt as hot as hot could be.

Passing along the Luckenbooths, with his hand full of law-papers, Mr. Hepburn stopped to purchase a posy of violets and thyme.

'Grand weather for the country, sir,' said the woman, counting some coppers into the lawyer's hand.

[1] Tenements.

'Fine dulse and tangle, fresh from the sea!' cried another street-seller. 'Come, buy my fine dulse.'

Anything for coolness and freshness! So he invested in a great handful of the shining, moist, salt weed. Thus loaded, away he hied to the Close, and delighted the three women there with what Marjorie called the marine poetry of hot weather. He was for ever going there, on such self-made errands, making these visits the point around which his days revolved.

Marjorie, so to speak, reckoned her time by them too, and would have felt 'in the dark' without the brightness they shed on her daily life. Sometimes (but, to do her justice, not very often) she would be seized with a panic of startled dismay when Mr. Hepburn spoke *very* kindly to Letty, feeling the solid earth crumble away, as it were, from beneath her very feet.

'Yet wherefore?' would she ask herself. 'Wherefore? Our friendship will never change. I feel sure of that. It ought to make me happy. We are quite old folks now.'

But somehow this day, when Mr. Hepburn came in, with his posy and dulse, so cheery, and kind, and masterful, a streak of sunshine falling a-down the Close, and through the window, showed plainly the grey in his hair, and the wrinkles gathering round his eyes; and thereupon tears sprang to hers.

'Why, May, what's the matter?' said the lawyer. 'Come, put this posy in your girdle, and let us see how it looks.'

For years upon years he had been doing similar kindnesses, till they had become, as it were, an institutional necessity to queenly Marjorie; but somehow to-day that disclosive sun-streak stirred her strangely—roused intense longing pity for him, that with all his wealth of feeling and his loving capabilities life was far spent, and he passing hence without having ever consciously received, in kind, the deep, strong affection he gave so freely to others. It did seem such a pity that he should grow old, and fancy life no dearer a boon than his own experience showed it to be.

'Come, May, let's see how the violet posy looks fastened in your girdle.'

'*I* have lived and loved,' thought she (harping mentally on this new string, while pinning the flowers in her waist-belt). 'He, poor fellow! ah! for his sake, I think I should feel glad to see him truly cared for by any one he valued.'

'I've got to be very busy in the Court to-day,' said Mr. Hepburn, rising to take leave, 'but I shall perhaps look back again in the evening.'

What had come over Marjorie that she, who for nine long years had daily received the writer's friendly calls, should now get into a nervous, anxious flutter lest any chance should prevent him returning on that particular evening? Was not there to-morrow, and to-morrow, and a score of to-morrows, all likely to contain his visits in their bill of fare? That sun-gleam which brought out the curved lines around his eyes and the almond-flourish on his head was to blame for it all. In its revelation she had, as it were, been suddenly driven to take note of time's flight, and to feel (absurd though it seemed) as if Mr. Hepburn, honest man, must also know the necessity there was to make haste, if so be he would, even at this eleventh hour, pluck the fruitage of reciprocal affection. It appeared to her fancy that possibly, seeing there was so little time to spare, he might, even before she saw him again, fall in with what she made believe she was hoping for for him, and then adieu to their cherished friendship, as it *had been*, at least. That afternoon Mr. Hepburn did not make his appearance till so long past his usual hour that Marjorie, when his tirl was heard, could scarcely refrain from running to the door, just as she might have done more than a dozen years ago. That nervous sense of urgency was still on her, and she actually felt the writer's return as an escape her friendship had made from sudden dissolution in the deeps of somebody else's love for Mr. Hepburn.

'I've got news to tell you about myself which will take you by surprise,' said he, addressing her.

(Queenly Marjorie, noble-hearted, Christian Marjorie, dead Renwick's bride, Mr. Hepburn's sincere friend, and an hour ago so sorry that his life should be passing away without some experience of the pleasure she remembered life could hold,—what a bound and fall your heart gave just then!)

Had her morning's undefinable presentiment of approaching change come true after all? Had he met his fate in the interval between the two visits of that day? She had never thought of herself otherwise than as the martyr's widow, but this speech of Mr. Hepburn's sent her cold and hot by turns. He looked agitated and not like his usual self. 'Yes, yes! he has seen somebody to love,' thought she, and therewith a great gulf seemed to open between her own nine-years' old friendship for the writer and somebody else's elderly grey-haired swain. It all passed in a moment, her passage, so to speak, from warm nearness to the cold distance, where his friendly offices would be different in kind from what they had hitherto been. Perhaps, too, this mythical young lady, who it was presumed had so suddenly captivated Mr. Hepburn, was quite young, and thereupon poor Marjorie (sitting at the supper table in her sweet majesty, which the writer was thinking more exquisite than ever) bethought herself almost in tears that she was four-and-thirty. Anon she tried to feel that all was as it should be, and that she really rejoiced that her wishes for Mr. Hepburn's happiness were likely to be fulfilled. But next minute, over her like two rolling waves, came, firstly, pettish annoyance because he did not understand she would fain be told the worst at once, and then, wave the second, to wit, a sense of great blank desolation, which, so to speak, knocked her down entirely. As I said already, these diverse feelings and sentiments, which take long to describe, passed in a minute, and on looking at Mr.

Hepburn again she observed he was still agitated. But never a word said he. So Mistress Renwick (who had in her the making of a first-class matron) said 'she was going to fetch her knitting,' and left the room. Presently however, before quite closing the door, she turned back, and said with a kindly smile to Letty, 'Come here for a moment, my dear, and hold the pirn for me, will you?' for all the world as if she were a manœuvring mother of the nineteenth century. But, in sooth, a touch of nature makes the whole world kin, and I imagine she considered it quite natural that the two people she liked best should say their say without the presence of two other persons whom they could not very well ask to quit the parlour. I verily believe the dear old woman partly guessed what was in the wind, and sat that long half hour in her stuffy, dim bedcloset praying with might and main for a benediction on her dead James's bride.

Letty, innocent as she was, had also a glimmering idea that an elderly romance was afloat, and sent up *her* earnest little petition, that it might speed better than her own youthful one had done, poor child!

At length, after waiting and waiting ever so long, they heard Mr. Hepburn go away, saying, in his pleasant, breezy, masterful manner, 'Yes, dear; tell them I'll be here the first thing to-morrow morning.'

In rushed Letty to the parlour, and found Marjorie on one of the four high-backed chairs, crying as if her heart would burst. Flinging herself on her neck, the girl wept (just for company), wondering, in her simple soul, whether, as the psalm says, 'All men were perfidious,' and made a point of deceiving females in general?

While the two were performing this lachrymose duet, in came Mistress Renwick in a state of consternation, and presently waxed very indignant that her dear James's only love should be 'lightlied' by any plain-looking, rough old man in the country; albeit she must own he had ever been most kind and consolatory to herself.

(Again I must state that this long explanation did not take three seconds to act out.)

'Can you pardon me,' sobbed Marjorie, 'not for forgetting my dear (that I can never do), but for marrying at all?'

'My daughter! my dear daughter! I only pray you may be as blessed as I wish you to be. My boy himself, could he speak from heaven, where he is, would say, "Bless you and him." I have often thought (for he always considered others before himself) he had some notion that, in God's providence, such a day as this might come to pass, and so gave you, almost with his dying breath, to each other's friendship. My poor murdered, noble, dear boy!' She warmly embraced Marjorie, and ended, as she uttered the last sentence, in a burst of tears.

'My mistress to be Lady Hepburn?' cried Betsy, when informed that, after all, her patient expectation of yet seeing

Mr. Hepburn married to her young mistress was to be rewarded. 'Lady Hepburn, and Sir George Hepburn! It dings a'! I'm real sorry Mistress Clavers didna live a month langer; it would ha'e garred her turn blew wi' spite. The auld limmer![1] to gang and get me into sich a fasherie about that ill-deedy hypocrite, John Bold! Hepburn Castle, did ye sae it is called, My Lady? Losh! I maun rin ben and tell the Swanston's lassie. I'll no be a minute, My Leddy.'

It was a very old baronetcy to which Mr. Hepburn had succeeded by the death of a distant relative of his mother's, whom he had never seen. The estates were valuable and situated in a well-cultivated part of the country; so when Marjorie deigned to accept him and them, he considered he had nothing left to wish for.

Deigned to accept! Oh, if he could only have read her sentiment thermometer! But she wasn't obliged to tell tales against her own dignity, and in those days neither mediums nor spirit-rappings were known. So the new baronet rested quite satisfied in the belief that his lady-love had done a deed of infinite condescension in permitting him to endue her with his title and worldly goods, not to speak of his heart.

[1] Wretch.

CHAPTER XXVI.

'Ah! you 've been good to me, in fair and cloudy weather,
  Our Father has been good to us, when we 've been sorely tried;
I pray to Him, when we must die, that we may die together,
  And slumber softly underneath the clover, side by side.'

VENTS generally come in bunches. The very day after Sir George Hepburn proposed to Marjorie, the 'Delight' anchored in Leith Harbour.

'Shall we go to the port, and learn if there 's any news from Wattie and Laird Baigrie?' said the *ci-devant* writer to his bride-elect. 'We can ask Mistress Baigrie to ride with us. She must be anxious about her husband.'

Marjorie expressed her pleasure at the proposal, and horses being speedily procured, the whole party proceeded to Leith. In arranging this little excursion, Sir George's chief reason was to let Marjorie enjoy a whiff of fresh sea-air; and, albeit hopeful to hear news of their three absent friends, he had no expectation that any of them was on board the 'Delight,' which had been sent to Darien as a private speculation by some half-dozen merchants.

Under the lee of Leith Castle, the 'Delight' lets fall her anchor, and anon the passengers come ashore. Since quitting Darien, five are dead and buried at sea; but the remainder seem fat and fair. Marjorie and her party are seated on a projecting rock, close by the castle, and commanding a full view of the pier, along which all persons going ashore from the vessel behove to pass.

'I should say that fellow has had tolerable rations,' exclaimed Sir George Hepburn, as Master MacNab passed along. 'Capital rations, and not put them into an ill skin either. But in the name of wonder who is this that's so like our own Wattie? It's surely his ghost. Good gracious! it surely is the laddie himsel'! and that limmer[1] hanging on his arm,' added he, oblivious that Mistress Baigrie was close to his elbow.

Imagine Letty's state of mind as she beheld Wattie, *her* Wattie once, Hetty's now, leading up the pier that flirtatious and very handsome individual. For the mercenary probationer had been half-dead of sea-sickness, and was still utterly unfit to walk ashore, far less escort his intended. During the voyage, he and Hetty had had half-a-dozen skirmishes, but, as a rule, kissed and made it up again. The young man had been no little annoyed by Wattie's persistent guardianship of the late Mr. Baigrie's effects, and his refusal to permit the young heiress's purposed husband to intermeddle therewith.

[1] Spicy young woman.

'No, no,' replied he, to the joint entreaties of Hetty and her friend; 'wait till we get ashore, and then I'll make the boxes over, intact, to the Laird's own man-of-business.'

Mistress Baigrie gave a shrill shriek, and Letty a soft low murmur of pained astonishment, when Hetty, leaning on Wattie's arm, proceeded up the pier.

'God help me to behave kindly to them,' was the honest young girl's prayer. 'I cannot do it without Thy aid, O Lord, my God.'

Wattie glanced up at the rock and blushed. Letty looked down thence and sighed.

'O Lord, *do* help me to bear patiently and kindly the sight of him and her as man and wife,' she inly prayed again.

But everything was soon explained. Poor Antony's death, Wattie's mistake, and Hetty's engagement to marry Mr. Bruce.

Widow Baigrie tried hard to squeeze a tear or two from her eyes, but failed. To be sure, she was practised in widowhood; and even while her loss was being announced, was privately regretting that Sir George Hepburn had already proposed to that odious Marjorie, who seemed born to trip her up.

Dear, gentle Letty, imagine, if you can, her exquisite delight on discovering that Wattie was hers for the taking. She had done what she could to act Christianly, and God, who lets none of us be tempted overmuch, rewarded her openly and amply.

But the best part of this chronicle, at least in regard to merely material things, is yet to come, as follows :—

Wattie made over the late Antony Baigrie's boxes, as he had promised, to Sir George Hepburn, albeit that baronet had ceased practising as an advocate's clerk or servitor. On looking over the enclosed papers he came upon a curious document, written and signed by the late Laird, to the effect that in case of his demise it should be understood every bodle he possessed, except certain specified items, etc., etc., belonged of right to Laetitia Gordon, his ward, etc., etc.

When after some necessary legal steps to prove Letty's rights, etc., the final issue was announced, it was something terrible to see the despairing rage of Katherine Baigrie and her daughter. The former especially felt ready, as it were, to curse God and die. At any rate, she, in her first access of jealous disappointment, uttered maledictions against 'the young elder,' deceased, enough to make him turn in his far-away grave. And then her daughter and self fell to blaming each other and everybody else. Altogether the exhibition was so painful that we had best say no more about it.

Letty was very glad not to go home a penniless bride to Wattie, but earnestly entreated that half of her fortune might be given to Hetty. However, Sir George and young Ker very rationally argued that the fact of Angus Gordon having left his only child a large fortune, was no earthly reason why the daughter of a Glasgow doctor should be made an heiress of.

However, the matter ended by the assignment of a small dower to the embryo reverend's bride, which, I may mention, was received with indifferent grace.

The weddings of Marjorie and Letty took place in the High Kirk on the same day, and each bridegroom considered his special bride perfect.

They both wore dresses of a new material, recently come into vogue, and termed silver-satin, being a shiny white silken fabric, dashed over, as it were, with minute silver rays.

Sir George was in pinky-salmon colour, which, you may recollect, suited him remarkably well; and Wattie being fair (nay, at the then present time, ruddy and tanned), had on a pale-blue velvet coat, and canary-coloured 'small clothes,' as knee-breeches were called.

I don't believe that four better or happier people ever joined hands before a minister. It may seem a strange assertion, but were I asked upon soul and conscience to testify which of the two couples entered most intensely into the full depths of joy, I should (in spite of their age) say, Sir George and Lady Hepburn. Yet Wattie and *his* better-half were as happy as possibly they had it in them to be. There is a manifest difference in people's natural capacity for imbibing pleasure, and a dish, be it pewter or wooden, can but hold its fill.

The Kers went to reside at Greendykes, and the Hepburns took up their abode at Hepburn Castle, but once every year they visited each other.

(Can't you imagine to yourself Marjorie walking over her old haunts—on the muir, out on the roof, etc., and telling Sir George—who generally went with her—how she used to feel.)

(One of his queer quaint pleasures was this diving, so to speak, into the depths of his spouse's 'lived life,' and thus he kept clear of the shallowness wherein some people get stranded when their great fact of matrimony is accomplished.)

Mistress Baigrie, *née* Renwick, continued to reside in Edinburgh, and was, in her latter days, said to be addicted overmuch to the use of strong liquors. Beyond the increased redness of her nose, however, there seems to have been no foundation for this charge, and, as you know, her nose was red on the bridge thereof long ere this rumour got afloat.

The Reverend Mr. Bruce lived a cat-and-dog life with his beautiful, bright-eyed Hetty till such time as, seeing it needful to take the domestic reins into his own hand, he one day gave her a sound thrashing, after which she became easier to get on with.

I forgot to mention in its proper place that 'the Martyr's' mother resided till her death at Hepburn Castle, where she was so much honoured and beloved, that strangers used to suppose her the real grandmother of the little Hepburns.

Jamie Renwick, the eldest boy, was her chief favourite, and of a summer's afternoon it was sometimes a touching sight to see the little, gentle, blue-eyed fellow lead grannie to her seat below the big pear-tree, and set her a-telling him how his dear uncle James lived and died.

'*I* shall be a martyr too, grannie,' he once exclaimed after one of these narrations.

'God in heaven forbid, my jewel!' said the old lady; 'and yet why should I say so? To win up yonder is,' as *he* used to say, 'the grand matter, mind that, my own dear wee laddie.'

(An old legend of the House of Hepburn tells how this very James Renwick became a blessed martyr, albeit not in the same way as the other James, but that story does not form part of this chronicle.)

Take, I pray you, a parting view of Sir George and Lady Hepburn five years after their marriage.

It is a lovely autumn day, and the two have just returned from a long ride on horseback, an exercise of which both are very fond. It is 'James Renwick's' lesson-time, for Marjorie always hears him say his A B C before the nursery-dinner is carried in.

'Goodbye for half-an-hour,' says she gaily to her husband, as with an embrace they part in the porch, after the horses have been led away.

'Don't be longer than you can help, May,' he answered. 'I really begin to grudge that little chap so much of my wife's company. I'll take a turn in the grounds till you are ready.'

(As you may infer from what has been told, those two elderly people were not the sort to weary of life, even had they remained lone folks, but as things were, their companionship was a still-beginning, never-ending delight. In one sense no true union ever does end, does it? Begun here, it is adjourned up yonder.)

But to return to Sir George going out for a turn in the grounds till Marjorie can rejoin him.

> 'He passed through the door, . . .
> And a light wind blew from the gates of the sun,
> And the waves of shadow went over the wheat;
> And he sat him down in a lonely place,
> And chaunted a melody wild and sweet,
> Which made the wild swan pause on her cloud,
> And the lark drop down at his feet.'

www.ingramcontent.com/pod-product-compliance
Lightning Source LLC
Chambersburg PA
CBHW020741020526
44115CB00030B/734